UNDERSTANDING CHANGE IN EDUCATION

RURAL AND REMOTE REGIONS OF CANADA

Earle Newton and Doug Knight (Eds.)

Detselig Enterprises Ltd.

Calgary, Alberta, Canada

Earle Newton
Doug Knight

Canadian Cataloguing in Publication Data
    Main entry under title:
    Understanding Change in Education

    Includes bibliographical references.
    ISBN 1-55059-059-6
  1. Education, Rural—Canada. 2. Rural schools—Canada.
3. Educational Change—Canada. I. Newton, Earle E.
II. Knight, Douglas George, 1950-
    LC5148.C3U52 1993   370.19'346'0971   C93-091694-8

©1993 Detselig Enterprises Ltd.

210-1220 Kensington Rd. NW

Calgary, Alberta, Canada

T2N 3P5

    Printed in Canada   SAN 115-0324   ISBN 1-55059-059-6

Table of Contents

Contributors

Lynn Bosetti is an Assistant Professor in the Department of Educational Policy and Administration, University of Calgary. She teaches graduate and undergraduate courses in post positivistic research, future studies, and school administration.

Kenneth Cameron is a recently retired professor in Educational Administration, Faculty of Education, University of New Brunswick. He was a teacher and principal in public schools in the province for twenty years before joining faculty at U.N.B.

Rod Campbell is the Executive Director of the New Brunswick Centre for Educational Administration, Faculty of Education, U.N.B. Before accepting his current position, he was a teacher and a professional staff officer with the New Brunswick Teachers' Association.

Don Downer is Associate Professor and Coordinator of Education at Sir Wilfred Grenfell College in Corner Brook, Newfoundland. His career includes being a science department head and publishing a book in 1991 called *Uprooted People* – a social history of the people of the Indian Islands off the northeast coast of Newfoundland where Don was raised.

Wynanne Downer is doing graduate work from Saint Francis Xavier University. Her twenty years of teaching and her early years in a small town on the west coast of Newfoundland led her to feel strongly about potential benefits of distance education for improved school-community interaction.

Parnell Garland has been a junior high school teacher, vice-principal, principal, and consultant. For ten years he was Chief Executive Officer for Regional School Unit 3 in Prince Edward Island. At the present time he is Director of Educational Services for the P.E.I. Department of Education.

Tom Gee is Director, Appeals and Student Attendance Secretariat, Alberta Education. Earlier in his career, he was Director of the Distance Learning in Small Schools Project, of the Initiation into Teaching (Internship) Project, and of the Grande Prairie Regional Office of Education.

Bill Gulka recently completed a doctoral dissertation in which he investigated the management of multiple innovations in rural contexts from the perspective of directors of education. He is currently an elementary school principal in a mixed farming area of Saskatchewan.

G. B. Isherwood is a Professor in the Department of Administration and Policy Studies in Education, Faculty of Education, McGill University. He has worked with aboriginal people across Canada in the development of educational governance systems and in the hope of increasing native self-determination.

Cecil King is a member of the Manitoulin Island First Nations. He was the first Director of the Indian Teacher Education Program at the University of Saskatchewan. He is now Director of Aboriginal Teacher Education, Faculty of Education, Queen's University.

Doug Knight began his career as a teacher, principal, and superintendent in rural New Brunswick. Since moving to Alberta, he completed doctoral studies. At this time, he is a Superintendent of Schools in a rural school system and a sessional lecturer in school administration at the University of Alberta.

Bryce Knudson has devoted his career to educational leadership in northern areas of Manitoba and in the N.W.T. He is presently Assistant Director of Education for the Dehcho Division Board, N.W.T. His special interest is the involvement of parents and community in schooling.

David Marshall is President of Nipissing University located in North Bay Ontario. He has held a number of positions in education at the school system and ministry levels. He has worked in the Baffin region in the N.W.T. and was Director of Curriculum for the island of St. Lucia in the Caribbean.

Peter Murphy has been involved for years in providing professional development opportunities for rural educators. From his present position as Associate Professor in Educational Administration at the University of Victoria, he is coordinating a special distance education Master's program.

Earle Newton is Education Coordinator for the Confederation of Tribal Nations in northwestern Saskatchewan. During 1991-1992, his final year as a faculty member in educational administration, University of Saskatchewan, he was Director of the provincial Educational Leadership Unit.

Murray Sandell is Principal of Hants West High School, a large, comprehensive school in rural Nova Scotia. His research centers on the supervision of teachers and stages of professional development.

Bob Sharp has drawn upon his background in both regional planning and education to fill many positions over twenty-five years in the Yukon. He was a principal of small, rural schools for seven years and is now Coordinator of Curriculum Development, Department of Education.

K. B. Sorensen is a retired senior school system executive and currently an educational consultant working with native and non-native educators across Canada in the development of school governance systems.

Keith Sullivan is a Professor and Director of the School of Education at Dalhousie University in Halifax, Nova Scotia. His research interests focus on the administration of educational institutions both nationally and internationally.

Bruce Wiebe is the Principal of McBride Centennial Elementary School near Prince George, British Columbia. Recently he has been very active as a member of an accreditation team, an advisory committee on adult education, and a group reviewing assessment techniques for rural schools.

Financial support for Detselig Enterprises Ltd. 1993 publishing program is provided by the Department of Communications, Canada Council, and The Alberta Foundation for the Arts, a beneficiary of the Lottery Fund of the Government of Alberta.

1

INTRODUCTION

Earle Newton

With authors from each province, the Northwest Territories, and the Yukon, *Understanding Change in Education: Rural and Remote Regions of Canada* is a book of shared successes, insight, and optimism for schooling in rural and remote regions across Canada. For parents, community, trustees, superintendents, principals, teachers, ministry officials, and scholars alike, the developments reported in each chapter reveal how political, technical, and cultural factors "trigger" and shape change processes in each unique setting. Newton and Knight pull together what can be learned from each of the cases described and challenge leaders at all levels to further capitalize on the special advantages of small communities to provide quality schooling for learners of all ages.

Contributions

While there may be some advantages to having education as a provincial responsibility, Newton and Knight believe that education in this country is suffering increasingly from the lack of national perspectives. Shortly after Confederation, Sir John A. Macdonald wondered if it had been wise to make provinces responsible for education when schooling could do so much to determine national character and national destiny. Former Prime Minister Brian Mulroney linked the quality of schooling with Canada's performance in the international market. *Understanding Change in Education* offers the reader a national perspective on promising developments in schooling in rural and remote regions of the country.

The many "ups and downs" of the fishing, mining, lumbering, and agricultural industries receive much attention in the media but the special challenges related to schooling in isolated areas is neglected in Canada. This is not so in many other countries. The National Rural Education Association in the United States had its 83rd annual meeting last fall. The Federal (Commonwealth) Government in Australia recently adopted a strategy for rural education and training called "A Fair Go." It has also initiated a Country Areas Program which in 1989 gave 12.6 million dollars to schools for educational excursions, cultural enrichment, consultancy services, professional development, regional newspapers, and teleconferences. This book meets a need in Canada by providing for the sharing of ideas, information, and insights about schooling in isolated areas.

Much has been learned in the last decade about change processes in education. Michael Fullan's book, *The New Meaning of Educational Change* (1991), provides vital background information on the adoption, implementation, and institutionalization (continuation) phases of change processes and the many dynamic, interacting factors which affect each phase. It is now realized that we cannot understand, nor effectively bring about, changes in schooling without giving much attention to broader, societal factors (the "big picture") as well as to local community and organizational aspects. A third contribution of Newton and Knight's work is that they have used this expanded knowledge base about change in education to analyze developments across the country and to draw implications for the further improvement of schooling.

A Framework for Thought

A framework for this book has been drawn from Tichy (1980) and from Corbett and Rossman (1989). Tichy had identified the following on-going dilemmas which he claims are faced by all organizations:

1. technical design problems – producing the desired product,

2. political allocation problems – distribution of power and resources, and

3. ideological and cultural mix problems – values and beliefs held by organizational members (p. 165).

He emphasizes the dynamic nature of organizations and states that each dilemma or problem area goes in cycles. At a peak in the cycle a change will be "triggered" that will eventually interact with the other two cycles. The later, related work by Corbett and Rossman is based upon a study of change processes in 17 schools. They concluded that it is important to view change processes simultaneously from all three perspectives – technical, political, and cultural.

In a rural Canadian context, Gulka (1992) found that exemplary superintendents first address political considerations (support of the board and key players), then technical aspects (support for teachers and principals), and eventually cultural aspects (symbolic leadership, values, beliefs, norms) become central. Readers are invited as they read the chapters in this book to identify and reflect upon the factors which affect the change processes described at various stages.

Many voices can be heard in the developments shared in this book. Together they provide a national perspective concerning schooling in isolated areas. The reports are rich in description and the analysis enables us to build our knowledge about the many interacting factors which affect change processes. Throughout, there are challenges to our thoughts and to our practice.

Challenges

One major challenge in relation to schooling in rural and remote areas is to emphasize the positive – to realize, for example, that many important developments in schooling such as individualized instruction and multi-age grouping have their origin in small schools. This is a challenge because if population drops and the economy falls there is a tendency to also lose spirit – for people in small communities to feel relegated to second rate status compared to city life and city schools.

Some important urban-rural differences have been adapted from work by Nachtigal in his book *Rural Education: In Search of a Better Way* (1982). Most readers could likely add to the list of differences shown in Table 1.1. The rural context is why schools in those settings typically have certain advantages and some disadvantages. These have been illustrated by Hathaway in Table 1.2. The point we wish to stress is that there are many real or potential advantages of schools in small communities. Leaders must avoid the tendency to model city schools. The challenge is to realize the advantages to be found in every situation – to capitalize on context.

Table 1.1 Rural-Urban Differences

Rural	Urban
Personal/tightly linked	Impersonal/loose
Generalists	Specialists
Homogeneous	Heterogeneous
Nonbureaucratic	Bureaucratic
Verbal communication	Written communication
Who said it	What was said
Time measured by seasons	Time by the clock/calendar
Traditional values	Liberal values
Entrepreneur	Corporate persons

Rural	Urban
"Make do" response to environment	Rational planning to control environment
Self-sufficiency	Leave problem solving to experts
Less disposable income	More disposable income
Less formal education	More formal education
Smaller	Larger
Low population density	Higher population density
Acquaintances – fewer, diverse in age/culture	Acquaintances – many, similar to self
School – to preserve local cultural/community	School – to get ahead in the world
Teachers – central to community	Teachers – separate from community
Students – known by everyone	Students – known by teachers and friends

Adapted from Paul Nachtigal, *Rural Education: In Search of a Better Way*, (1982), page 270.

Table 1.2

Advantages and Disadvantages of Small Rural Schools

Factor	Advantages	Disadvantages
Financial Administration	–Less bureaucracy and red tape. –Flatter organization. –Principal knows students	–Higher than average costs. –Principal has few peers with whom to interact. –Lack of administrative assistance makes it necessary for principal to engage in administrative details.
Teachers	–Lower pupil/teacher ratio. –Teacher knows students. –Teacher closer to overall administration of school and more aware of administrative concerns. Better able to integrate curriculum concepts across multiple subjects	–Must prepare and provide more courses. –Teachers have few peers with whom to interact

Advantages and Disadvantages of Small Rural Schools

Factor	Advantages	Disadvantages
Students	–More involvement in extra-curricular activities. –More leadership opportunities. –Achievement is equivalent to achievement in larger urban schools.	–Students experience modest culture shock when moving out of the community for further education or employment.
Community	–School is center of community. –High levels of community support for school.	–Small schools may resist change. –Lack of cultural diversity limits opportunities for broad socialization.
Guidance	–Teachers able to offer personal guidance and counselling.	–School may be unduly influenced by community values.
Atmosphere	–More humane and productive. –More involvement of students, teachers, and community in cooperative ventures means better attitudes and higher expectations.	–Smallness and remoteness may lead to feelings of inferiority.
Program	–Results on achievement tests are often as good as results in larger schools and in some cases better (science may be an exception). –Good achievement potential in the affective domain.	–Limited program choice. –Limited resources. –Little up-to-date technology. –Lack of specialists capable of demonstrating excellence in areas of curriculum (e.g. fine arts, athletics, academics).
Other	–Greater community awareness and acceptance of school policy	

Source: Warren Hathaway, "Rural education: Challenges and Opportunities," *Prairie Forum on Rural Education*, Brandon, Manitoba, November, 1990.

A second, related challenge is more general. Our studies in more than 30 rural school systems indicate that a large majority of students, particularly in lower grades, are happy with their teachers. We have found, too, that most parents rate teachers, principals, bus drivers, and support staff highly. In our experience most people view learning, teaching, and general school operations quite positively. Problems arise in the planning component of school operations. Students say no one outside of the classroom listens to them; staff relations are often strained; school-community communication is frequently inadequate; superintendents are seen to appear only when there is a problem; very few partners are aware of what the school board does or how they do it. Our findings reveal that in many situations a major potential advantage of small school-communities is missed – that is a high level of participation by all partners. The simple step of listening to the voices of all concerned is neglected. This topic is explored in some detail in *Voices, Vision and Vitality* (1992) by Earle and Patti Newton. Another perspective is offered by Carkhuff in his book, *The Age of the New Capitalism* (1988). In addition to emphasis on human capital (good people who are getting better) and on information capital (organizations with current relevant information move ahead), he identifies three levels of operation within organizations:

- ✔ thinking individually,
- ✔ relating in groups, and
- ✔ planning at the organizational level.

Our work in rural and northern schools has convinced us that they are strong at the level of individual thinking. Difficulties arise in linking the individual efforts to action in groups and to planning at the school or system level. Herein is a second challenge that is central if remote schools are to realize their many advantages – if they are to capitalize on context.

There are, of course, many challenges associated with schooling in remote areas of our vast country. The importance of capitalizing on context, including the effective linking of individual, group, and organizational endeavors, has been selected for special attention in this book.

This Book

This book is based upon the rural or northern background of both editors and many contributors. They have genuine respect for people in isolated communities and a deep appreciation of the fascinating complexity of every setting. It was thought at the outset that there were many promising developments in schooling in isolated areas across Canada and that much could be gained by a compilation of those experiences. An invitation was extended to colleagues in each province and territory and we now have the results.

The twelve cases from the provinces and territories reflect the diversity of issues and changes in rural and remote regions of Canada. Chapters vary in content and language just as people in different parts of the country differ in perception, interests, and expression. The book begins with an introduction by Earle Newton which elaborates upon the theme of capitalizing on context – the positive view that "You Can Do That Here!" The last contribution, by Doug Knight, is a synthesis of what can be learned from this book about political, technical, and cultural factors which initiate and affect change processes in the schools of rural and remote regions. The intervening chapters are organized into four sections.

Section One, "Continuity and Change: An Aboriginal Perspective," is a rich and special contribution from Cecil King, one of only a few native people in Canada to have a Ph.D. degree. We feel confident that readers will agree that it is appropriate to consider first the views of some first people (Chapter 2). Cultural considerations are prominent.

The focus of **Section Two** is connecting with partners in education, specifically school boards and parents. Isherwood and Sorensen (Chapter 3) provide a connection with the first section by sharing views of the development of divisional boards of education in the Northwest Territories. Chapter 4 by Marshall outlines how boards in a remote region of northern Ontario have reorganized to provide shared services. In contrast to creating and recreating school organizations in isolated, northern areas, Chapter 5 shows us how a school organization can "come apart" in an isolated province. The section concludes with Chapter 6 and 7 which highlight the participation of parents in British Columbia and Manitoba contexts. A common thread in Section Two is emphasis upon political factors.

Attention turns to more technical considerations and to students in **Section Three**. Distance education initiatives in Alberta and Newfoundland (Chapters 8 and 9) raise the question of equality of opportunity for students in rural and remote regions. Engaging students through experiential programs in the Yukon (Chapter 10) and the implementation of whole language in two schools in the Northwest Territories (Chapter 11) leave us with a focus on students.

It has been found that factors which provide impetus for change are not necessarily the ones which will sustain improvements. Two major intervening variables, teacher supply and administration, (including leadership development, professional development, and school improvement) in Nova Scotia and New Brunswick settings respectively constitute **Section Four** (Chapters 12 and 13). The availability of these human resources is affected by cultural, technical and political considerations.

This book is meant to inform and to inspire partners for schooling in rural and remote regions of Canada. The ideas contained in this book enable readers to develop and extend personal visions of "how things could be better" and to gain insight into effective change processes for schooling in small communities.

References

Carkhuff, R. (1988). *The age of the new capitalism.* Amherst, MA: Human Resource Development Press, Inc.

Corbett, H. D. & Rossman, G. B. (1989). Three paths to implementing change. *Curriculum Inquiry, 19*(2), 163-190.

Fullan, M. & Stiegelbauer, S. (1991). *The new meaning of educational change.* Toronto: The Ontario Institute for Studies in Education.

Gulka, W. A. (1992). *Managing multiple changes in rural school division: The director's role.* Unpublished doctoral dissertation, University of Saskatchewan, Saskatoon.

Hathaway, W. (1990). *Rural education: Challenges and opportunities.* Paper presented to the Prairie Forum on Rural Education, Brandon, Manitoba, November.

Nachtigal, P. (1982). *Rural education: In search of a better way.* Boulder, CA: Westview Press.

Newton, E. & Newton, P. (1992). *Voices, vision and vitality: Redesigning small schools.* Calgary, Alberta: Detselig Enterprises Limited.

Tichy, N. M. (1980). Problem cycles in organizations and the management of change. In T. Kimberly, & R. Miles (Eds.), *The organizational life cycle* (pp. 164-183). San Francisco: Jossey-Bass.

Section One

Continuity and Change

An Aboriginal Perspective

2

OMACHEWA-ISPIMEWIN

EDUCATION AND COMMUNITY IN A NORTHERN SASKATCHEWAN CREE VILLAGE

Cecil King

Introduction

This is Omachewa-ispimewin's story. It is the story of how Omachewa-ispimewin's people tell of the forces of continuity and change that have shaped them – and how they in turn shape those forces. It is a story of how "their" school, Keethanow, is the meeting place of these forces and the prevailing traditions. It is the crossing place of the Aboriginal and the non-Aboriginal cultures, the coming together place of north and south and the interface for the Aboriginal and Metis children of the village. The village is more than a collection of dwellings and roads, as Omachewa-ispimewin's heart pulses the cycles of winter and summer, spring and fall, of a living soul and punctuates the physical components that make a village. Omachewa-ispimewin to Stanley Mission is that story.

This is an ethnographic study of a village that is made up of more than a collection of dwellings and roads – it is a study of a village's soul.

Omachewa-ispimewin's Earth

"Omachewa-ispimewin" means "the upshooting place" when literally translated from the Cree language. Long ago, before the Strangers came, in the days of hunting with bows and arrows, whenever the people of what came to be known as Stanley Mission set out on their hunting trips, they would paddle by on the waterway in front of a tall rock precipice. As they passed, each hunter would shoot an arrow upward to the top of the cliff. As long as the arrow did not return, it signified good fortune for the trip.[1] Within the dominance of this traditional rock, the village came to be. Whether because of the spiritual significance of the rock or the countless ages of hunters who depended on the rock's oracle-like prophecy, the dwellers at Omachewa-ispimewin have nestled within its shadow a long time.

The rock rises steeply out of the water of the Michinippi, making it the highest place along the waterway. Huge moss-covered boulders adorn its feet at the water's edge, while plants have rooted themselves, taking over the aged rock face. Today, viewing the rock from the water, it is almost completely dominated by trees. The lithic strength of Omachewa-ispimewin was no match for the invasion of Earth's trees. Yet the rock predominates. The mighty waterway, the Michinippi, holds the secret of the age of the rock.

The rock and the water are Earth's make-up kit. Combining the two ingredients she can redo her countenance to suit her whims. It is in one such whim that Earth presented a cove on her waterway in which to nestle a gathering place for a people. Protected from the prevailing west winds or the harsher north winds coming through the pass holding the Michinippi, the village faces eastward. In facing eastward, each sunrise elevates the soul of the village and excites the hearts of the dwellers. The sun in its stewardship punctuates time in its perpetual reawakening of the village, to its day, the same day over again, season to season, winter after winter. As each day happens again, the pulse of the village continues nurtured by the benevolent Earth.

Earth's whims are many. With rock and water, she creates collages of rugged beauty. She accentuates her curving shorelines with rocks, boulders, and periodic pebbly beaches. She varies her green color with subtle tones to create deceptive islands, deep bays, and intrusive capes. The water course to the village threads through a maze of named and unnamed lakes. Rivers are numberless, as they festoon Earth's great waterway. Ever going by, its sameness is altered near the village, where Earth gave it Nistoyiak, a panorama of white cataracts and roaring falls branching the waterway into three directions which regroup to become one again in the flat lands of the trees.

Besides creating the lithic borders that mark where the water ends and the plants begin, Earth brings water and plants together in another kind of alliance, to be a haven for all her natural creatures and yet to serve as a barrier to impede intruders. This alliance is conserved by the deceptive muskeg. Whether it be in its steamy luxuriance of summer, its frozen expanses of barbed interlocking thickets of winter, or its alluring innocence of bird songs, insect tumult, and mirror-like pools, it awaits to impede man's attempts to penetrate it. Yet it teems and vibrates with Earth's creatures.

The water and the rock are always there, and watchful of their roles in keeping the village, guarding the front side. More ominous are the pressing trees. Earth programmed her trees to take land where man has stripped it of trees. Any open area, if man is not watchful, the trees will reclaim. The militant trees stand as the watchful sentinels of the south, west, and north sides of the village. As Earth undulates, vegetation-covered moraines evidences ancient glacial activity

The Earth that hosts the village might be described as moderately hilly, somewhat rocky, with a gravel-clay overburden. In the village, seas of sticky mud go hand in-hand with the regular cycles of the seasons. The plant life around the village is abundant, moderately luxuriant, exuding stability. Pine, spruce, jackpine, poplar, birch, and alder fringe the village while beneath, Earth spreads the fertile blanket of smaller plants. The mosses, lichens, wild flowers, shrubs, and berry bushes bear tribute to Earth's prudent nurturing. To maintain this nurturing, Earth left lessons for the dwellers to understand the delicate balance between her plants, creatures, and man.

To maintain her pristine state, Earth was armed with just enough of her own weapons to impede any concerted man-made intrusion, up until this time. The muskeg, the viscous clay, the marching plants, reinforced with rock, water, and weather, served her faithfully until the intruders' technology ultimately vanquished her spirit. Earth first succumbed to the clearing of trees and plants to bare a space which was then kneaded flat so that man's air machines might land safely. As traumatic as this may have been, it was as nothing compared to the construction of an artery gouged through the plants, rocks, and muskeg. In the cataclysmic aftermath, a road was left. Earth relentlessly resists the road. The road prevails at the whim of Earth and until such time as man's technology advances to the point where it appeases Earth, the road will continue to exist as the tenuous intrusive invention of man's technology.

Earth has succumbed to the intruder's technology and has permitted the imposition of the air strip and the road upon her domain. The waterway still awaits the technology of the intruder. Even as the road was under construction, the intruders were lusting for the mighty Michinippi. To harness her potential, the intruders proposed a mammoth dam for her Wentigo Rapids. The dwellers of the village protested with a moral appeal to attempt to quell the intruders dreams. "Building a dam will flood the domain of the trees, destroy the natural homes of Earth's creatures, and threaten our way of life as a people," the dwellers contended. For the time being they have been heard.

Omachewa-ispimewin's Cree People

The story of Omachewa-ispimewin and its Cree people is begun from the stories of the Kataayuk (the Old Ones). Oral accounting is a tradition of the Cree people and their link with the past. They have sustained a vision of the past and the explanations of what makes the world as it is through an oral tradition that reaches back into ancient tribal memories. The past stretches by word of mouth from the creation myths to the events of the present in an intricate interweaving of what would be called by western man as "legend" and "historical fact."

There is no doubt in the minds of the Cree that they have always been here. The idea of their great ancestors migrating from the other side of the Earth just does not exist. Ernest Tootoosis, a Cree elder of the area, simply states:

> Our people were put here by the Maker. We did not come from some place else. The world was started here. Moose and buffalo do not live on the other side. They are special animals put here by the Maker for us to use. Our language is not found on the other side, nor are our food and medicine plants. Our people have always lived here and our Maker taught our ancestors how to use the things he put here for us.[2]

The Cree Story – The World Began

A first world existed before our present world. The Kataayuk say this world was destroyed by a flood (literally, the world filled up with water). As a result, Wesakechak was the only one to have known the different worlds. Wesakechak had great powers. In restoring our present world, the Maker involved Wesakechak with all the orders and the people who inhabit it. Wesakechak lived at the time when our animal brothers and inanimate things had the gift of speech. All understood.

The beginning of the story takes place in the first world. Nothing existed, except the view of the world from "the back of a turtle." The sky was there, the sun, the moon and the stars. It is in this original world, in the company of giant animals, beings strangely resembling men lived. Wesakechak told of these first people. For while the Maker oversaw all this, it was here that the knowledge of a spirit of evil began. The originals received gifts from both the Maker and the Spirit of Evil by which to live together. But the gifts were paradoxes – the knowledge of good and evil resulted in man rising up against man.

Rivers, lakes, streams, even the sea, did not exist in this first world. It did not rain and the days were warm, heated by Sun, while the nights were cool and looked after by Moon. Giant trees found a way to grow, but there was no fruit, grass, copse, or shrubs. All animals, even the buffaloes and the first horses, ate meat. There were no high stone mountains and fire was the sacred secret of one single human being.

Lost in this world, man lived in his waskuhikun (house). Gifted with many powers and secrets, man's conflict with the gifts of evil grew. Man had great strength to survive but Evil taunted him increasingly. Man finally lashed out, resulting in the destruction of Man and the first world. There were four eras of destruction. The first was by fire; it failed. Plants intertwined themselves to immobilize the Spirit of Evil; this too failed. Then rocks rose up to the sky, but they too failed. In a fourth and final era, the roaring river flooded earth. Only then did the rivalry stop. The boiling sea claimed the Spirit of Evil to itself by transforming it forever into the most voracious of all fish, the sturgeon (Misinamew).[3]

Finally one day, the rain stopped and the great canoe rocked gently once more as the winds began to stop blowing. Wesakechak realized to his horror that he had forgotten to bring along a piece of the earth with which to re-create the new world. The only way to obtain it was to dive to the bottom of the ocean; therefore, he tied a vine to kitchi-amik, a giant beaver, and told him to dive into the depths for some clay. After some time had passed Wesakechak pulled up the limp body of kitchi-amik into the boat. To his disappointment, there was no clay. Next he told Nin-gig, the otter. The otter . . . drowned. In a last attempt Wesakechak sent Wa-jusk, the muskrat . . . Wa-jusk drowned but in his tiny paws was a piece of clay. With the clay Wesakechak reformed the land.[4]

It is said that Wesakechak watered the new world with the tears of his sorrows. He peopled the earth with the Indigenous people and brought back all the other living things. And they talked to him. Only the water and earth could speak. Wesakechak travelled everywhere because he had no home.

Throughout their woodlands, the Cree will point to objects which they associate with him. There is Wesakechak's seat in a split rock on the banks of a small winding creek called Owawakim Newewim (Wesakechak's windings). There is Wesakechak's spoon, a great spoon-shaped rock on the upper Severn River. There is a row of hills about Beaver Hill Lake where Wesakechak danced with his eyes shut. There is Island Lake which Wesakechak made when he broke a beaver dam,[5] and there is Omachewa-ispimewin (the Upshooting Place) – Stanley.

The Academic Story of Omachewa-ispimewin's Land

The account of the peopling of Saskatchewan is recorded by Dr. Zenon Pohorecky, an authority on Saskatchewan's Aboriginal heritage, who states that the story probably began about 40 000 years ago.[6] He states:

The peopling of Saskatchewan began during the last ice age (before 20 000 B.C.) when much of the water in the world was locked in vast sheets of ice which covered the land . . . . The earliest tracked giant through the great plains which stretch from the Arctic coast to the Caribbean. They followed an ice-free inland corridor along the Mackenzie Valley, passed Lake Athabasca, into Saskatchewan, hundreds of centuries ago. . . . Mammoths ranged around Saskatoon over 20 000 years ago and man was there long before the ice sheets finally melted.[7]

Dr. Pohorecky goes on to say that 10 000 years ago the Agassiz Channel cut Saskatchewan in half, reaching from Clearwater River in Alberta to Porcupine Hills in Manitoba. As the ice and water retreated, new lands in the province were opened for plants, animals, and man.[8] During this period mammoths, mastadons, and ancient species of bison were hunted throughout the area by the early people.

Dr. Pohorecky dates the emergence of a distinctly forest people in Saskatchewan at over 8000 years ago.[9] These people lived in the forests of central Saskatchewan and north of the Great Plain. Their tools consisted of "big woodworking tools" which had been pecked, ground, and polished in stone, and stemmed and notched spear points. They are part of the "Boreal Archaic" culture.[10] About 1 A.D. the more northerly people from the forested region of Saskatchewan had tool kits which resembled those of the "Middle Woodland" cultures of the Upper Great Lakes region.[11]

The designation of what became Northern Saskatchewan as "Woodland" did not occur until approximately 8000 years ago. However, by that date the "Big Game" had disappeared and the rabbits, elk, caribou, moose, and bear inhabited the area.[12]

Tangible traces of these early woodland people are entered in Earth's log-book, the rock faces along the waterways. Over a very long time that people travelled these waterways, an ongoing account was entered in pictograph signs representing the inner thoughts of the people. These symbols are respected as having souls. Offerings are made to them. Wherever a pictograph lives, the ground was considered sacred, and when visited it was as entering Earth's sanctuary. The waterway of the Michinippi (the Churchill) is cradled in the lithic canal of the Cambrian Shield. Travellers in their canoes would pause in their journey to enter a sign in Earth's log-book, the vertical rock faces of the river. Since certain symbols contain modern images such as a hunter with a gun, contemporary entries are juxtaposed beside ancient records of the past. All along the Churchill the evidence of the past life of the northern Woodland people unfolds on those rock pages of Earth's history book. Time, of course, has erased many of the pages.

The Old Way of Omachewa-ispimewin's Past

The following description of the life of the Woodland Cree was told by a Cree elder in the traditional way.

We always knew that Earth was our mother and that all which is seen and unseen around us had been made by the Creator and that He alone owned all things. We, last in the Order of Things, were His beings and given life by him, and allowed to live here on His spouse, Earth. We were to give honor and thanksgiving to Him each day as we walked on earth. These things we knew and all Earth was our Church.

We understood that to honor the Creator, we had to regard His plants as sacred, both those which were used as medicines and those like tobacco, sweetgrass, cedar, and sage which were used when praying to him.

We saw that the animalkind who we referred to as brothers had a life like our own and that life was sacred and precious to them. We knew that when we took the life of one of them for food, we must give thanks to the Creator, to mother Earth, and to the spirit of the animal. Our prayer acknowledged the animal's right to its life, expressing our need was greater. We walked on this Earth in a sacred way.

We saw the harmony of all things and we saw that everything in the universe – the sun, the moon and stars, the water and the wind, the night and the day, the four seasons, spring, summer, autumn, and winter – each did its work as the Creator determined it and governed our lives and ways in sacred harmony. We saw our Creator had provided for all our needs and we trusted Him.

It was the Creator who gave us the sacred pipe to pray with and honor special times. It was the Creator who taught us the sacred purifying of the sweat lodge. It was He who taught us the sacred songs so that we could have good fortune, health, and long lives. He heard us when we prayed in that way. It was He who taught about the Four Orders, the Worldview, and the Four hills of life, Infancy, Youth, Adult, and Old Age, and how Earth is divided in four quarters, each with its special work, and its special season. He taught us. His voice we heard in the wind. In our Grandfathers, the thunder we saw the strength of his great power. When in the cold of winter the frost exploded Earth's trees in the silent night, we knew He was near. The beauty of the northern lights made us think of Him and peace would warm our hearts.

Last in the Order of Things we gave honor and thanks to Mother Earth. We apologized to a tree before taking its life support for our own, prayed before a hunt, fishing, or trapping. We prayed to the plants before pulling them from the ground for food or medicine. We did not kill what was not needed because we believed that the life of each plant or animal was sacred, that is why sacred tobacco was offered to its spirit by burying it in Earth. We believed that in honoring all things we were honoring Him who made them. We believed that in using our minds and bodies to the highest level possible, we were following in the way of the flowers and plants who were giving their greatest honor to the Creator by blossoming to the highest level of perfection.

Christianity was not known, but we had our spiritual way that governed everything about our lives and we believed that the Creator was father to all. Knowing we were last in the

Order of Things, our prayers were humble. We would say, "Father, have pity on us, have pity on us." We knew we were not perfect. We looked towards death as "returning home." We honored our dead. We honored the Kataayuk and the children. We honored each other. We followed pure ways of our minds and bodies and harbored no ill will to anyone. The Creator, in the harmony of His works, His spirit world, set the religion that is our way of life.[13]

The Cycle of Life in Omachewa-ispimewin's Meanings

The elder, on the cycle of life, went on to say:

We lived in harmony with the seasons. In the severity of winter, we moved closer to Mother Earth by withdrawing with our family deep into the sheltered recesses of the woodlands. There, safe from winter's rigor, fuel was available, food near, and Mother Earth supplied building material for our waskihigan. We were close to the animals in these times. We each understood. There was communication. We shared each other's food. In the long winter, the Old Ones would tell the sagas of the past. The young ears would hear instructions on how to live good lives. We would tell the lessons of Wesakechak.

With the first trickle of spring and the first honking of the Great Geese returning to their nesting grounds, our people grew restless. The animals left to busy themselves with their urge to prepare the receiving places for the coming family. We ventured from our peaceful winter haven to return to the "gathering place." Here new stories were traded. We feasted not only to honor Earth's bounty but to bring all our people together after winter's separation. The feast was a living testament to our ancestors. To have a feast was to pray together and in one mind in the warmth of fellowship, eat the food prepared communally for the occasion. Our people would sit in a circle on Earth, to be near her. Servers would know who they are, and food would be served in a clock-wise direction to those in the circle. Starting from the Elders, everyone in their order, to the last child, all would be fed.

Many things we did during those times, things that were always done. It was our tradition to have ceremonies when a wife would be picked for a young man, or to have marriages, sweat lodge ceremonies, walking out rituals, and the name giving ceremonies. Mostly, it was the men that did these, because it was their place to carry on the proper customs and traditions. Besides this, the men had to provide the food, a need which was not changed by seasons or ceremonies.

We tanned hides, sewed clothes, repaired boats and nets, picked roots and medicine plants, and harvested tobacco for offering to the Maker. Medicines were prepared by the traditional inheritors of the gift. No moment of summer could be unused. The women, strong and committed to duty, lived their tasks from sun-up to sun-down. They raised the children, cooked, helped the aged, the feeble, and the ill. The white birch tree released its bark for our peoples to use. The ripened berries were picked and the fish smoked as summer waned. We would travel to other communities up the river highways. Setting up and taking down portable dwellings, making fires, and manning our crafts were pleasant changes from the hectic pace of our summer village. These last-days-of-summer treks were good in other ways. We would refresh our knowledge of the area, rediscover places we had forgotten, honor sacred ground, and remember where our brothers lay, having returned to Mother Earth. Summer after summer, travel on the river would take our people to new places and old ones would be remembered. It was on these travels that the custom of "Omachewa-ispimewin" was followed to ensure good luck.

The slanting of the sun more and more into the west and the days becoming shorter, we would watch for the first sighting of the Great Geese beginning their journey to the warm lands of the south. Now our village would slow down, the noise of summer would be gone and once again our people would get ready to move to the winter trapline, outside of the village. For as long as there have been people living here this custom has happened without change. Our people grew in knowledge and wisdom of the ways of Earth, her seasons, and her cycles which made our lives strong. Mother Earth was a wise teacher and we knew that without her we could not live long. And this is how we lived, for as long as the Old Ones have said we have.[14]

The Newcomers Arrive – An Elder's Prophecy

Many years ago, in the time of the Great Mother, Chief Almighty Voice of the Wood Crees decided to talk to Ah-we-kaw, the Great Spirit of the Forest. One night he asked

Ah-we-kaw if the white man would ever conquer the Land of the Trees. The Great Spirit answered:

The white man will come. He will cut many trees. His fire will destroy the trees. He will kill many animals. He will try to drive the People of the Forest from their teepees. He will do a woman's work; he will put seeds in the ground. He will make the waters disappear; many fish will die. All this, and many other things he will do. Much will be changed. But the land of the Trees he will never conquer.[15]

The Creator gave us many prophecies like that. Our ancestors knew long before it happened of the coming of the Strangers to our land. Our ancestors told that these Strangers would not be good for us and there would be much sickness, much hunger, and despair. Everybody would suffer and many would die. My grandfather would tell of the time of the great sickness when they believed that everyone's life had come to the end, but there was a special prophecy that told them about the great purification that was about to begin. It was this prophecy that made their minds strong in wanting to live on. Our ancestors said there would be a return to the sacred-pipe and our people would come back in numbers and rise up again as nations.[16]

Researching Omachewa-ispimewin

In ten years of my acquaintanceship, the face of Omachewa-ispimewin has changed. The all-weather landing strip has eliminated the total isolation of spring break-up and fall freeze-up. A landing strip, though still at the mercy of the weather, has given an air link with the outside. The water route remained unchanged; still the traditional connection with the outside. The building of the all-weather road has opened the community to the outside. The school, as a system, has moved from provincial to federal and Band control. Dial telephones now replace the unpredictable old radio transmitters, while high voltage transmission lines are now connected to the community, beginning an era of satellite receiving very much evidenced by "the dish" beside the council hall. But to what extent have these obvious trappings of modernity affected the soul of Omachewa-ispimewin?

The name, "Omachewa-ispimewin," for the village is still used by villagers of Stanley today. One hundred and thirty-two years ago the name of Stanley Mission was given by a British clergyman. Today the name has shortened to "Stanley."

Ethnography is a suitable strategy for studying Stanley and its school. The community's systems can be seen as part of a cultural transmission process, yet those systems which establish a persistence against this transmission within the community can also be studied. The Stanley people are understood within the context of their cultural world, which provides them with the milieu against which change and persistence take place. The people present to the observers a complexity of who they are. Both those who are changed and those who are not are seen as individuals who live within that community. The functioning of both is seen as tied to ethnic backgrounds and is of critical importance. In the context of Stanley in the past, the school has shown to have not transmitted the same culture nor to be teaching the same values as the other teachers[17] in the community. With Aboriginal control, the school is supposed to reflect the community reality. To study the school itself in isolation of the community would reveal very little about the relationship of the school and community. Thus, the school must be studied together with the background of the students, the families, the community, and its heritage.

Researching Stanley Mission

The precise location of Stanley Mission is 104° 33'W by 55° 25'N. The village is around fifty miles northeast of La Ronge, on the south bank of the Michinippi (Churchill) River. The village, perched on the edge of the Precambrian Shield, is ensconced in vegetation of the Southern Boreal Forest area. This is the land of the Michinippi Cree, who are variously known as the Woodland Indians or Swampy Cree.

The village has always been accessible by water, recently by air, and now by land. Following provincial highway No. 102 (a road that seems to be perpetually under construction) about thirty miles northeastward from La Ronge, a little road sign indicates, "To Stanley Mission." Turning to the right, one travels southeastward for almost twenty miles to the village. This precarious, newly built road has become the main land link with the "outside." In summer, the road surface ranges from hard clay, to loose gravel, to soft sand. Extremely dusty when dry, it becomes soft and slippery when wet. Whether travelling through the billowing clouds of road dust or skidding on the slick clay surface, one cannot help but be threatened by the high jagged rock embankments characteristic of a road constructed through rock and muskeg. In winter, the surface freezes solid. With insufficient shoulders, the snow creates deceptive edges to the road, making the meeting of on-coming traffic risky. Seasoned drivers from the village speed over this road, oblivious to the road conditions. To the novice, it is a harrowing experience.

Stanley Mission, the village proper, is part reserve and part crown land. The total area is no more than 100 acres. Aboriginal reserve No. 157 of the La Ronge Band on which part of Stanley Mission rests is approximately 624 acres in total, while the crown land that includes the other part consists of about 40 acres. Since the village is situated on a curve of shoreline, its depth varies from very narrow to perhaps a quarter of a mile. Its width, which follows the double curve reaches two kilometres. The village is hemmed in by the trees on three sides and by water on its main side. Along the shore are the tie-up places for the dwellers boats, as well as two docks, one in front of the Bay, the other on the "Metis side" where water planes tie up. Foot paths and roads crisscross the village awkwardly converging at the school. One main road appears to be graded occasionally. With the completion of the road to the village, the single foot paths had to adapt to road vehicle traffic. The main road has access to the water's edge in two places where boats on trailers may be launched. With access from highway No. 102 to the Michinippi, road traffic through the village has increased. In summer, tourists, mostly Americans, shorten a long water journey from La Ronge, entering the river at Stanley Mission to head northward.

Stanley Mission is a large village, as far as villages in northern Saskatchewan go. In 1980, the population comprised 974 treaty Indians and 208 Metis,[18] making a resident population of 1182. However, the number of children and adults of both the Treaty and Metis present in the village at any given time is subject to considerable variance. The trapping cycles affect population numbers, as does the road to the "outside" which draws an ever increasing number of the working adults away for periods of time. Furthermore, while family and village ties are strong, they do not preclude a fairly easy movement of children and young adults among households in the village and between villages as Stanley Mission extends outward to such villages as Brabant, Grandmother's Bay, Little Red, Sucker River, La Ronge, and others. "All the people at Brabant are from here (Stanley)" one Elder explained, "as it is at Grandmother's Bay, too."[19] The trapper people travel at least 125 miles north of the village to the farthest trapline. Utilizing this as one distance and allowing an east-west distance of sixty miles establishes the recorded outward reaches of the village – an area of over two and a quarter million acres harvested by the trapper people. Boundaries, therefore, are relative and all that can be said is that the village extends as far as there is a person from Stanley Mission. According to Bill Roberts, a local resident employed by Canada Wide Mines Limited to determine the demographic characteristics of the community in 1981, there were 129 occupied residences[20] on both the Treaty and Metis side of the reserve. However, this number fluctuates depending on the seasons or the personal circumstances of residents. The inhabitants arrive and leave, boarding up or unboarding their residences accordingly. A few residences stand with gaping window holes and doors left wide open. However a question remains as to whether these dwellings are indeed unoccupied. For at any time a family could claim them as their own.

Stanley Mission's link with the "outside" is La Ronge. It is a larger, organized town of about 5000 people serving as the regional centre of northern Saskatchewan. It is the gathering place for both the Aboriginal and non Aboriginal people. La Ronge typifies a frontier town. Its resident population is primarily concerned with mining, fishing, trapping, and the services that these primary enterprises require. In addition to its resident population, it attracts the tourist, transient, and private entrepreneur.

For the villagers of Stanley Mission, La Ronge is where they go for a meal, to trade furs, drink beer, play bingo, or "shoot pool." Chinese cafes, pizza parlors and a Kentucky Fried Chicken restaurant, and beer parlors show the southern intrusion into the northern frontier. The town has two banks, a credit union, a Liquor Board store, Sears Order Office, and a collection of insurance and legal offices, as well as a variety of small stores, a pharmacy, bakery, and a laundromat. It also has the grocery store chains of IGA, Co-op, and the Bay (now the Northern). For the tourist, hunter, and fisherman, most stores have a line of sport and outdoor equipment. One used car lot and three garages thrive on vehicle demands brought on by rough roads and supply the extra fuel needed for the long trips. La Ronge is the northern metropolis and the government centre for "northerners." It is also the centre for the northern resource development. To house the hordes of civil servants, an ultra-modern edifice rises on a rock knoll and is referred to by the locals as the "Taj Mahal." Two hotels and four motels are usually taxed to capacity and provide the only accommodation for the many travellers. The highway, both summer and winter, is a river of campers who "overnight" on the streets of La Ronge, virtually filling every inch of the one main street, by sundown. With the uranium development, the pace of La Ronge as a boomtown has quickened with speculators, developers, and private entrepreneurs. The influx of transients doubles the resident population. Three major oil companies operate fueling stations for marine and air travel besides the land traffic. Large and regular air traffic is served at the airport, while three air marinas service the sea planes of local air travel companies. A Co-op fish plant maintains a sporadic production. The community hospital has resident doctors and fifty beds. There are three churches with both resident and visiting ministers. The film fare is in keeping with the antiquity of the building that serves as the theatre. La Ronge has six high rise apartment blocks scattered in the area, a result of the uranium development farther north. The numerous modern houses in suburbia, built by the late Department of Northern Saskatchewan (D.N.S.) are rented as subsidized housing to relocating public servants from the south.

The west side of La Ronge abuts the La Ronge reserve. The La Ronge reserve is "just another Indian village"[21] with its scattering of Indian Affairs houses, garbage stands, privies, and abandoned cars. The reserve, like La Ronge, bustles with the coming and going of the Aboriginal people, walking on the road or helping to maintain the local taxi enterprises with frequent trips to or from La Ronge. Taxi vehicles are mostly suburban vans, with a passenger capacity of ten and a brisk trade is carried on both night and day with the reserve. A newly completed modern multi-grade school, "Kitsaki," unique in design, is under local control of the La Ronge Band and provides the education for the student population of the status Aboriginals. Qualified Aboriginal teachers comprise the majority of this school staff. The reserve serves as the official centre for the La Ronge Band office. A new administrative building houses the Band administrative staff. Since administrative services are provided for four other reserves that compose the La Ronge Band, there is a constant "going to La Ronge" by Aboriginal people either to the La Ronge Band office on the reserve or into the town of La Ronge for its services. Then there are the Aboriginal visitors, all who have relatives or acquaintances either on the reserve or in town, but crowd the bars for a weekend of socializing. In La Ronge both Aboriginal and non Aboriginal live side-by-side, associate in business contacts yet, administratively and socially, appear to live in separate worlds. A superficial mixing happens in the beer parlors, restaurants, and business establishments as well as in the evident attempts of non-Aboriginal employers to employ Aboriginal employees. Beyond this, each lives within his own groups. As with any town, social strata prevail, and in this case, the lower class appears to be composed primarily of the Aboriginal people. Being more visible, the Aboriginal people present to the non-Aboriginal society the usual image of the social outcast or the negative stereotype of poverty, idleness, and drunkenness. Some Aboriginal peoples, however, have risen out of this stratum to roles ranging from waiters to government employees. Still the minority, these workers are significant in their presence amid the non Aboriginal society and stand as models for Aboriginal people in the employment market.

Smaller Aboriginal and non-Aboriginal settlements, though at a distance, surround La Ronge. Constant travel and interaction with these settlements happens from La Ronge. Furthermore, its location on the north shore of Lac La Ronge allows water travel to other Aboriginal villages, like Stanley Mission, and is the access to numerous inland waterways. La Ronge Lake is large and supports a commercial fish industry. Very few Aboriginal people are involved in this enterprise and none from Stanley Mission. Forest fires in the summer cycle are a traditional event attracting Aboriginal people from all the area reserves for firefighting. Aboriginal people with their families will leave their reserve homes to camp a few weeks each summer on the fire lines which are coordinated and monitored from La Ronge.

Generally travel for the people of Stanley Mission is undertaken only insofar as it does not sever the Aboriginal people from their way of life. All travel outward is viewed in relation to how one will return. Travel to La Ronge is now daily and trips to Prince Albert are increasing. It can be said that the permanent residents of Stanley Mission have travelled more in the last two years than perhaps they did in the remainder of their lifetimes. Stanley residents have journeyed to pick sugar beets in Alberta, to visit in Manitoba via the Michinippi, and to tour the Maritimes by car. In the last three years students have been taken, through school projects, to see the mountains, the Pacific, and the southwestern United States. The people of Stanley Mission have become a well-travelled people. However, the travel is only to visit and to see but rarely with the prospect of remaining away from Stanley Mission. Few Stanley residents have ever left the community and stayed away.

The increasing awareness of life on the "outside" is making the people of Stanley Mission critical of what they understand of it. They see the social problems of urban life and the anguish of a world they view as completely amoral. What appeal could there be to travel to such places, they wonder? "I was born here, my father was born here, my grandfather was born here, why should I want to leave here?"[22] sums up a growing conviction among the younger adults of today. To them, Stanley Mission is the best place to be and it still is Omachewa-ispimewin.

Schooling Arrives at Stanley

Schooling for Stanley goes back 132 years. Over that time a succession of western ideologists shaped the attitudes and experiences of a people who, today, say "We want control of our own schooling." The people of Stanley have all attended school, all believe their children must attend, and all believe schooling is paramount to live the good life.

The first formal schooling was offered by Mrs. R. Hunt to the children of Omachewa-ispimewin at Stanley Mission beginning in 1852.[23] Mrs. Hunt was the wife of the Reverend Hunt, builder of the Holy Trinity Church. In 1853, a year later, a fire at La Ronge mission destroyed the school and resulted in the transfer of the Stanley children from La Ronge to Stanley.[24] The La Ronge school had taken in orphans and destitute children or children who came to the mission under "tragic circumstances." These children were fed, boarded, and clothed, as well as educated.[25] This tradition of boarding children was continued by Reverend Hunt who took in not only the destitute but also children of Hudson's Bay Company officials.[26]

Hunt sought to teach the children and adults to read and write English. He saw the value of the syllabic system of writing in allowing for quick recognition of sounds and words. Reverend Hunt requested and received a press from the Church Missionary Society which allowed him to lithograph Cree syllabics and "print short passages of the Scriptures in Cree and on cards so the people of Omachewa-ispimewin may learn to read during their visits at Stanley and take with them when they were hunting."[27]

Reverend T. Thistlewaite Smith succeeded the Hunts in 1862. Supply lists show that Reverend Smith had the Lesson Books of the Irish Council of Education, alphabetic books, and copy books sent to him in 1864.[28] Reverend Smith attempted to teach this curriculum for two years before he too moved on.

Reverend John Alexander MacKay, a Metis clergyman, replaced Reverend Smith and followed the methods established by Reverend Hunt. Reverend MacKay's journals show attendance at school was sporadic depending on the hunting and trapping cycles.

The attendance fluctuated from as low as 10 children to as many as 60 children between 1871 and 1872.[29] Reverend MacKay accepted this situation and attempted to facilitate the continuous learning by reinstituting Reverend Hunt's "homework" philosophy. In 1866 Reverend MacKay ordered a small printing press, "large enough to print two octavo pages at a time with print sufficient for four pages together with syllabic type."[30] Reverend MacKay believed in the important contribution of the syllabic system to teach the Aboriginals to read.

In the summer of 1871, Reverend MacKay travelled to Red River and returned with J. Sinclair, a Stanley Aboriginal who had fallen ill while studying and was forced to end his schooling and return to Stanley.[31] In 1871, Red River had an established school. Sinclair was placed there by his Metis parents for a basic education but did not finish due to illness. In September, Mr. Sinclair became the school teacher in his home community. Reverend MacKay recorded in his diary on February 10, 1872 that he occasionally taught in the school as the teacher and "was competent only for Indians."[32]

The quality of the education offered at the Stanley school was questioned again after the departure of Reverend MacKay in 1880. J. Sinclair continued between 1880 and 1889 though his abilities had been considered minimal by Reverend MacKay.

Amos Charles, Chief of the Crees of Omachewa-ispimewin from 1878 onwards at Stanley, was a strong supporter of education for his people. Both Amos Charles and Reverend MacKay were aware of the commitments made by the federal government to the education of Aboriginal children. Reverend MacKay had been an interpreter at the Treaty signing at Fort Carlton and Amos Charles a signator of the adhesion to Treaty Six at Montreal Lake in 1889. Even after Reverend MacKay left Stanley, he attempted to get government grants for the school there.

The decades of the 1870s and '80s were fraught with upheaval and change. With the signing of the Treaties, the officials of the federal government responsible for Aboriginal affairs wrestled with the difficulties involved in settling Aboriginals on reserves. The policies of the federal government were based on the assumption that a short period of transition would be followed by the inevitable assimilation of the Aboriginal people. The federal government, however, was sold on its assumption that the missionaries were proper agents for delivering education to the Aboriginal people.[33]

The aims of the missionary teachers and the government were in concert. In Chalmers' words:

Since Christianizing the natives or at least elimination of unacceptable pagan practices was a primary objective of the government, both principles and expediency suggested that the churches continue in the educational role.[34]

With the boarding school at the La Ronge mission established again, the government and church officials of the day felt that the educational needs of Stanley were settled. However, Chief Amos Charles and his Band wanted their own school at Stanley and refused to send their children out to the mission school at La Ronge. In 1910, they requested a school from the federal government.[35] The government refused on the grounds that the cost of a teacher's salary would be too much.[36] But conditions were changing. The demands on the church were, as Bishop J. A. Newnham reported to the Synod, that "the complexion of the Diocese had largely changed from red to white, the work which had been almost entirely among Indians now being very largely among English-speaking fellow churchmen."[37] Bishop Newnham, however, did ask the government that a school be established at Stanley, as the Aboriginals were "a nice set of people."[38] At the end of the year of 1913 the government did agree to pay $250 towards the construction of a school, with the church covering the remainder of the cost.[39] In 1914 temporary quarters were made allowing a school to operate during the summer when the Band was on the reserve. The government also agreed to provide a mid-day meal to the children of the hunting families.[40] However, as it happened, the opening of the school was delayed for two more years. The hunting parents were expected to leave their children in the community and provide supplies for their keep. However, since fishing and hunting had been so poor, they were unable to provide supplies; they consequently just took their children with them to the traplines.[41]

In the summer of 1916 a school was constructed, and the government provided someone to prepare the mid-day meal, as long as attendance justified it. This mid-day meal provision did keep the children attending during the summer months.[42] However, such was not to last and the school remained closed during the winter of 1919. In 1920 the parents, anxious for the school to succeed, requested an increase in rations from the government in order that the children who remained on the reserve during the winter might be properly cared for.[43] The government refused, saying that if the parents wanted their children in school, then it was their responsibility to provide for them.[44]

For the winter of 1921, the school remained closed. It was, however, hoped that when the new school at La Ronge opened it would take some of the Stanley children.[45] It is unclear whether there was schooling from 1921 to 1924 when, again, the government was to have given approval for the opening of a "summer school" at Stanley.[46] That same summer Chief Amos Charles again asked the government for a full-time school with a teacher. He promised that his people would look after the "trapper kids" and provide fish and moose meat for the teacher, if the government would pay the salary.[47] Again the government refused on the grounds that it would be too expensive.[48]

The pattern was to continue. The church, which was moving more into ministerial work, having greater visions for its white parishioners, decided not to dedicate any further time toward the education of Stanley children. Further, it was now clear to the church officials that the education of Aboriginal children was the government's responsibility. Although acknowledging its "Treaty Ten" obligations of maintaining a year-round school at Stanley, the government felt that it was just not worth it, while the children continued to be available for only three months of a school year. The people of Stanley, having experienced a conventional type of school since the 1850s, had seen that the church seemed capable of carrying out its ministry as well as teaching the children. They, then, found it difficult to understand the government's inability and refusal to provide the required education at this point in time. The people of Stanley, in their cyclic way of life, faced the dilemma of continuing to take their children with them on the trapline, thereby disrupting the possibility of schooling, or of leaving their children in the village, without someone to care for them. Chief Amos Charles, an advocate for year-round schooling of the children submitted proposal after proposal, but was never able to convince the federal government officials.

A "year-round" school was not started at Stanley until 1952. This development was the result of concerted pressure on the federal government and the provincial Aboriginal association. The initial provincial foray into this northern hinterland was in 1939. In a two-day survey of school facilities in five northern communities, Mr. N. L. Reid, then Director of School District Organizations reported the appalling conditions that he saw to the provincial Liberal government of the day – and it too did nothing. However, the Cooperative Commonwealth Federation (C.C.F.) government elected in 1944 was committed to equal education for all people of Saskatchewan – Aboriginals for whom federal government was responsible included. From 1945 this government dedicated itself to improving northern education for the citizens under its jurisdiction and applied pressure on the "Indian Affairs Branch" which at that time was under the federal Department of Mines and Resources. The provincial government amassed data on the number of Treaty Indians in the north who were without schooling. A report in 1948 by M. F. Norris showed that of the 67 Treaty children of school age in Stanley, 12 were attending school at Prince Albert, and the other 55 children were receiving no schooling.[49]

In a provincial report on Indian Affairs in northern Saskatchewan, the following had become evident:

With the advent of the fur traders in northern Saskatchewan, the Indians were soon reduced to a state of subordination and dependence, a pitiful spectacle and example of constant reproach to the Dominion Government and the Department of Indian Affairs.[50]

Norris noted that the population residing at Stanley were mainly Treaty Indians, stating that while Treaty Indians are constitutionally the responsibility of the federal government and the Department of Indian Affairs, they are also citizens domiciled with the Province of Saskatchewan. Norris further observed that the government of Saskatchewan had fulfilled its obligations toward providing educational facilities in the northern settlements of Saskatchewan for Metis and other franchised citizens. This was in keeping with their mandate, which maintained:

So long as any person or group of people in this province is underprivileged, the social and economic democracy to which the government is pledged cannot be realized.[51]

In the case of Stanley, the responsibility is primarily one for Ottawa and the Department of Indian Affairs. The C.C.F. Government of Saskatchewan had appointed C.H. Piercy, a former Superintendent of Schools, to survey the educational facilities of northern Saskatchewan. His report reiterated the now forgotten Reid report, and recommended the need for schools in the settlements in northern Saskatchewan where populations were predominantly Treaty Aboriginals. Piercy recommended construction of schools with grants provided by federal and provincial governments on proportional bases.[52]

The Union of Saskatchewan Indians, representing all Treaty Indians of the province, asserted the need for a progressive program of education for their people in every part of the province. In 1947 they had outlined their educational needs and again in 1948, at their annual convention in Saskatoon, reaffirmed their request for educational facilities.

A day school was finally built for all. Resident accommodation was provided for the orphans and others without permanent homes, and a staff was hired, all paid for by the federal government and Department of Indian Affairs. In 1952-53 Stanley school showed an enrolment of 18 – all in grade one. The dream of Chief Amos Charles was a reality. Though he was not to see the fulfillment of his dreams, schooling was established at Stanley, and has continued since. Although a very thin educational strand stretched from the 1850s through the cooperation of the church and federal government and with the Saskatchewan government's efforts to provide "equal educational opportunity," all agencies were largely indifferent to any real consideration of the parental aspirations or community input in the school. It was clear by the end of the decade of the school opening that the Department of Indian Affairs policy was to amalgamate the Aboriginals into the larger society. Commenting on Canada's Aboriginal administration in 1945, Harper of the federal government summarized the government's policy as follows:

> Thus the purpose is to have the Indian abandon their cultural differences and to be biologically amalgamated with the white race. In other words the extinction of Indian *as Indians* is the ultimate end.[53]

It followed that in order to acquire contemporary non-Aboriginal schooling privileges, the Aboriginal would have to become white. While church and government had set the precedent for education, and now that the people of Stanley were aware of their Treaty right to an education, they felt justified in expecting an educational reality for themselves.

However, the fact that the government had ruled "that the education of the Indians shall be carried on without cost to them"[54] likewise meant that the Aboriginals had no right to comment on its efficiency or direct its outcome. To strengthen its intent, the federal government moved to revise the Indian Act "to prepare Indian children to take their places as citizens." To do this, the use of the provincial school as the transforming vehicle was becoming considered for "whenever and wherever possible Indian children should be educated in association with other children."[55] That the parents of Omachewa-ispimewin would have any say in their children's education was not thought of, let alone the possibility of Aboriginal people perhaps managing their own schools.

Throughout the 1950s and 1960s the federal government seemed preoccupied with attempting to divest itself of direct responsibility of the education of Aboriginal people. It had authorized the Minister of the Department of Indian Affairs to enter into agreements with public and separate provincial school boards for the education of Aboriginal children. Aboriginal pupils were to be removed from religious institutions to provincial schools where they were to be "integrated."

To the people of Omachewa-ispimewin it probably mattered little which reason the government settled on. A full-time school was in place in the community, stopping the federal government's aim of integrating or assimilating these children in respect of the parents wish to keep their children in the community. The people of Stanley's staunch belief in the Treaty right of the school in their own community was what mattered.

By the end of the 1960s the time had arrived when the federal government must change its policy "to make possible the full participation and partnership of Aboriginal people in all decisions and activities connected with the education of Indian children."[56]

The questions facing the people of Omachewa-ispimewin on the education of their children were revealed to the Canadian people in a Report to the House of Commons, June 22, 1971 which had been prepared by the House Standing Committee on Indian Affairs. For two years the Committee had heard testimony from Aboriginal leaders and others documenting the failure of the school system to provide Aboriginal children with a suitable education. A testimony in 1967, labelled the "Hawthorn Report"[57] by the federal government, had been the first official study of the concerns of Aboriginal parents for the schooling of their children.

At the same time, Aboriginal organizations across Canada established education as their top priority. In 1972, the National Indian Brotherhood, in conjunction with all provincial Aboriginal organizations, launched a national policy paper on Aboriginal education. The resulting document of "Indian Control of Indian Education" stated the philosophy, goals, principles, and directions as compiled from the Aboriginal statements on education. The central themes to rise were "local control" and "parental responsibility."

In February, 1973 the federal government conceded that its long-held strategy of integration (or assimilation) would have to yield to other schooling arrangements. The paper, "Indian Control of Indian Education," served as the comprehensive statement of what they expected schooling to do for their children.

The Aboriginal people of Omachewa-ispimewin spoke with one voice to the government in claiming their right to have a say in the kind of education which would teach their children "all they need to know in order to live a good life." Across Canada, from one reserve to another, these words of the policy were heard again and again: "As our Fathers had a clear idea of what made a good man and – a good life in their society, so we modern Indians want our children to learn that happiness and satisfaction come from: pride in one's self, understanding one's fellow man, and living in harmony with nature."[58]

The Story of "Indian Control"

To conceptualize Aboriginal control of Aboriginal education is a complex exercise. While on the outside one might tend to view it as strictly a political process, it goes far beyond the political realm of the Aboriginal people. For Aboriginal control of Aboriginal education must contain those principles that govern and give meaning to their entire lives. Although Aboriginal control of Aboriginal education involves the contemporary issues of setting up advisory bodies funded by the federal government, assessing school programs, creating curricula, and the myriad of other details that constitute a school system, an essential process involves instituting cultural definitions of the situation, and evolving Aboriginal educational structures based on Aboriginal cultural values. Aboriginal control of schools is seen by the Aboriginal people as the key to the development of human resources and institutions. Gerald Clifford, an Oglala Sioux, has argued that the underlying cause for the movement is that "Indian community control of education leads to the development and survival of the total Indian community."[59]

With the National Indian Brotherhood policy paper, the Aboriginal leaders acknowledged the conflict of values which Aboriginal people had experienced in the past. They attributed the withdrawal and failure of Aboriginal children in formal schooling to this conflict of values. The school system brought by the Hudson's Bay Company, the missionaries and later the federal government employed teachers who represented a value system foreign to the

Aboriginal child. Furthermore the nature of what was taught was determined by the educational agency's conception of the Aboriginal – his mental capacity, his aptitudes, and his cultural environment. Education for Aboriginal people was not a reflection of their expectations but the consequence of factors contained in the economic aims of the Hudson's Bay Company, the missionary objectives, and the dreams of non-Aboriginal politicians.

Local Control Comes to Stanley

Under the aegis of "local control," the era began in the 1970s for Stanley. The term "Indian Control" as posited, meant the creation of an educational authority by the Band which would control monies and be empowered as a decision-making body. It would mean the total transferring of funds allotted for Aboriginal education by the federal government to the Band itself. The Chief and Council of the Band would establish the relationship between their Education Authority and itself, determining its own philosophy of education and the policies to administer them. The Federation of Saskatchewan Indians (F.S.I.), the political body of all the Chiefs of the province, took an active part in the establishing of the N.I.B. policy paper, "Indian Control of Indian Education." During this period the F.S.I., having launched a province-wide evaluation survey of the education provided on each of its reserves, handed down its report. The F.S.I.'s findings were as expected and verified what the Chiefs already knew – that the education provided for their children was no longer working, if it ever had. Many recommendations were submitted with the report and among the stronger was that the Bands take over total administration of their education programs. One of the strongest advocates for the takeover was the Chief of the La Ronge Band, Myles Venne.

The assumption of "local control" became a conscious act by the people of Stanley. Under the leadership of Chief Myles Venne and his councillors, the people sought to utilize the school which they recognized as an agent of change for cultural retention. They attempted to create an institution for Stanley which would meld the forces of tradition and the forces of change to prepare their children to face the future securely grounded in their past, proud of their people's accomplishments of today, and capable in the future, with the knowledge and skills of the mainstream culture. In addressing the young graduates of Stanley in 1982, Chief Myles Venne summed up the picture as he saw it in these words:

> The goal of life and therefore education is the development of the complete person, . . . a vision that sees the Indian living

not "between" two cultures as in the past, but "in" the best of two cultures in the future. Be proud of your accomplishments, see pride in what has been accomplished by those who came before you.[60]

The people of Stanley appear to view the school as instrumental in the realization of their aspirations in the education of their children. Though schooling is still that force from the "outside," the local people, having taken it over, feel they are directing it. Under the name "Keethanow," "ours," the people feel their school incorporates their input. Community involvement is evident. Community academic expertise is in a state of evolving; and the melding of both has begun.

In 1974, La Ronge Band officially assumed local control. Maintaining that the Band Council was the government of the Band, the Chief and Council negotiated on a new level with the federal government's Department of Indian Affairs officials who, by Treaty obligations, were responsible for the provision of all elements of education for the people of Stanley. This Treaty obligation applied to the status people only. The existing school, begun as a parochial type, later was sustained by the provincial government under the jurisdiction of the Northern School Board of Saskatchewan. The status people outnumbered the non-status and Metis people.

A new Education Committee, under the new regime, set to work to formulate the Stanley community school system. The Band authorities had adopted "local control" with the objective of using it to build an education system which would reflect their traditional values.

The outcome of these meetings, completed in 1978, reflected the means desired by the people of Stanley for achieving each of the four objectives through their education program. The following very specific set of expectations was devised and served as the foundation of the school program.

Objective I

THE SCHOOL PROGRAM WILL INSTILL PRIDE IN THE INDIAN CHILD

- ✔ the school program will include sports;
- ✔ the school program will include local history;
- ✔ the school program will include Indian Studies;

✔ the school program will include the Cree language;

✔ the school program will integrate the Cree language, Indian Studies, and local history into other subjects;

✔ the school program will include a history of great Chiefs;

✔ the school program will include a history of explorers led by Indian guides.

Keethanow, "ours" in Cree, became the name of the Stanley school. As "ours," one informant explained the vision he had of his school in these words:

> The school would promote the trapper way of life. It would allow the trapper people to take their children with them on the trapline. For parents who could not take their children with them, the group home would be available for them. The goal of Keethanow is to allow our people to live off the land as they always have and at the same time to give the children a choice to go to school and to learn how to live off the land.[61]

The people of Stanley presented what they viewed as an appropriate school program for their children. They then turned the responsibility for implementation of the program over to the professional educators.

Omachewa-ispimewin Teachers of Keethanow

In 1977, La Ronge Band authorities hired the entire staff for Keethanow School, officially commencing the era of local Band control. The Band authorities had adopted "local control" with the objective of using it to build an education system which would reflect their traditional values. One informant expressed it this way:

> We want the children to be comfortable and happy at school. This is first. English will come, but first we need the primary things, the building blocks, and after that other things will follow.[62]

Keethanow's Programs

To develop and implement the "Bilingual/Bicultural program," as the program for Stanley school was now defined, a Curriculum Developer was hired. Likewise a qualified librarian was contracted to set up the new school library. Construction of the new addition to Stanley school had commenced, and in 1978 opened as "Keethanow School."

With Department of Indian and Northern Development funding, a Bilingual Teacher Training Program began in Keethanow School. The objective of this program was to train local candidates as qualified teachers. Known as Nihithow T.E.C.H., "teachers of every child," one informant explained it this way:

> We were brought up in the Cree language, we were born in it, so we are different. We have been through a lot, we have lived – we have been in the woodland and know the sounds – like the buzz of a bee or fly when it is warning of something, our senses are attuned to everything in nature. Whites would have to learn this first, we don't have to in teacher training. So much teacher training is knowledge oriented – so much of the content is not what we need. To train our own teachers, they work with students here and they learn together, this is an asset in our teacher training program.[63]

The emphasis in the teacher education program was the teacher's interdependence with the community. Wherever the training took place, in the community or at campus, the trainees were acutely aware of their responsibility. The entire progress of "Indian Control of Indian Education" depends on its teachers. To quote Kaltsonis,

> These Indian teachers will be able to stand up for the rights of the Indian parents. They will be able to persuade more Indian children to stay in school and through education lead more of them to power. These Indian teachers will be able to stand up for the rights of Indian parents and achieve closer cooperation between school and community. They will know Indian history and culture and will be able not only to include it in the curriculum guides but teach it with respect and purpose.[64]

Bilingual-Bicultural Education

The Lac La Ronge Band is developing school programs to reflect each child's background – culturally and linguistically. To assure success for their children the Band is emphasizing a bilingual-bicultural program based on the Cree language and culture. This program begins when the child enters school life and is greeted by a kindergarten teacher who is Aboriginal and speaks Cree. This teacher attempts to make the child feel secure and confident in what he knows. Sometime during the year the Cree child will learn the Cree sound system and learn to recognize Cree symbols.

The mastering of these symbols is deemed crucial to the Cree language as well as being a traditional skill. It is claimed by the Aboriginal teachers that the symbols are very easy to learn, "a child can learn them in half a day." The Elders maintain that when once learned, the symbols are never forgotten. Referred to locally as the "Cree Syllabary System," it is a form of writing invented by the Methodist Minister James Evans in 1882 at Norway House, a place farther up the Michinippi River from Stanley. Remembered by the Elders who use it as a standard form of writing, it is they who wish to continue the tradition as it is viewed as an integral part of the culture today. Further, the hymnals, missals, and bibles used in the liturgy at Stanley are all written in the Cree syllabary.

The two kindergarten groups have instruction entirely in their Cree language. The readiness group which is an interim group of kindergartners and grade ones receive their instruction in Cree but the transition to instruction in English begins here. After grade one, instruction in English is increased with each grade until grade four when it is totally in English. Other than Cree being the language of instruction in the initial years, requiring the modification and development of pertinent curriculum materials, Stanley children receive the same curriculum as prescribed by the Saskatchewan Department of Education for other students in the province. Language Arts, Reading, and Social Studies vary little. Art, Physical Education, Home Economics, and Shop indicate some modification in order to make the subject matter more relevant, as well as to utilize the expertise of a particular teacher. The secondary level, that is division four, grades ten to twelve, in order to be accredited for provincial certification, are handled through the Department of Education's correspondence program which is monitored in the school. Students in these grades are tutored and instructed more or less individually by a teacher designated the responsibility. These students attend regular sessions at Keethanow where they can be tutored and their lessons monitored.

The aim of the bilingual-bicultural program is to bring the child to a point at which he can function equally well in English as in Cree and will understand the white man's culture as well as the Aboriginal culture. "He will be literate in both cultures and understand the value systems of both cultures. He will face success in both worlds."[65]

The Education Committee of Keethanow

Based on the community survey of 1977 by Stobbe, the following are the functions submitted by the people to the Education Committee: all school matters; interviews; hiring and firing of teachers; looking after school funds; planning meetings; handling bicultural money; to make sure the school is open during the year; they are the ones who say yes or no on decisions; choose new teachers; permission for class trips; to keep school clean, provide lunches, hold meetings; inform the community of what's happening in the school; set school rules; to know about student problems; deciding what will be taught in school; decide on matters of the teacher training program; help children that have problems; should have Elders teach culture; deal with problems in school; program development.

The duties of the Education Committee on specific matters in the community are comprehensive and specific, as understood by the people of Omachewa-ispimewin. Responsible to the Chief and Council of the La Ronge Band, they are mandated to carry the education portfolio for Omachewa-ispimewin, for Keethanow . . . for Stanley.

Inside Keethanow – Omachewa-ispimewin

✎ *The Setting*

The anatomy of Stanley is such that the school building becomes the central organ of the village. The pulse of the village is very much regulated by the school. The village day is punctuated by the morning bell that commences the school day. Then, there is the mid-morning recess bell which is followed by the noon dismissal bell. In the afternoon, the process is repeated until school terminates for the day. The villagers entire day becomes structured by the school into segments which, in turn, affect the comings and goings from the homes. The school rests where all the roads converge, making it accessible to people walking by in any direction. The location of the school, according to one informant, was with the intent of making it the focal point of the village. Villagers could enter and visit freely as they passed by the school. This was in keeping with the new era in which the school was to be viewed as "the school," "our school" as the name implies. Keethanow means "Ours" in Cree, therefore Keethanow School is understood by the people of Stanley to belong to them.

✎ The School

The Stanley school is a new building, though on closer observation an older section is evident. The older section is the typical rectangular, flat, shoe-box structure, a favored design for the Department of Indian Affairs and Northern Development schools in the era past. The older section has a worn-out look, not so much from its long history but more as a testament to its over simplistic design and over-economic construction material. The old section is a frame building, sheeted with plywood and covered with paint of dubious quality and color. The building, constructed on top of piles, rests suspended off of the earth. The skirt of plywood between the earth and the floor sills only contributes to its overall look of "time beingness." The building looks awkward, unlevel and unsure. Yet this structure was the first multiple classroom school operated at Stanley.

Connected to the old structure by a corridor is the new school. This new building is completely different in design. Its construction, like the older structure, is of wood, but its woodiness is accentuated. The trees that are part of the framework are emphasized in their natural state. Log beams, varnished lumber and wood-colored carpeting all contribute to a harmonious blending of the building with its environment. Instead of the rectangular shoe-box form with classrooms all under one flat roof, the new part is constructed of five separate units with conical roofs. These units are locally referred to as "pods." Each pod is connected to a central, carpeted corridor that slants with the grade of earth. The sensation of hills and hollows is built into its design. The hills actually lead either up or down to each separate pod. The hollow itself is the central rotunda where plants grow and where the people of the village can come together.

The pods are eight-sided. The octagonal construction tends to make them seem round. Radiating inwards from each of the corners are eight larger trees angling upwards and converging in the centre around a clear sky-light. The sky is visible anywhere inside the pod. The large open areas in each pod become the teaching and learning places. Carpeted and with a free feeling of space, the pod contrasts with the rigid, bare-floored, square "desks-in-rows" older section. In character, each pod is different. The distinction is established by the use. There is the "shop pod," the "home ec" and "science lab" pod, the library pod, the gymnasium pod, and the open area classroom termed the "learning places" pod.

According to Chief Myles Venne, "it is based on the premise that schools are for community use. The labor was provided by local people and local materials utilized." However, its distinctive architectural design is to heighten the feeling in the hearts of the people of Stanley that this is their school and, as such, stands out from the typical western-design schools of the area.

On entering Keethanow School from the main entrance of the new section, one is somewhat taken aback by the carpeted hall floor slanting gradually upward and disappearing around the bend. On the wall, straight ahead, hangs a weather-beaten, aged, wooden object. Rectangular, about the size of a basement window, its surface, hand carved ages ago, reveals not immediately the face of the original sun dial created by a local carver as Stanley began its first school. The hall is in soft wood colors with a lot of natural wood visible.

To the left of the entrance is the door to the science lab. Comprised of half of a pod, it is a long room equipped with stools, desks, and an array of glassware, apparatus, white smocks, and charts. Its walls are lined with cupboards containing the mysterious chemicals, completing a very typical science lab. Next to the science lab is the "home ec" room utilizing the remaining half of the pod. The "home ec" room contrasts the modern and traditional. Beside the electric range is a wood-burning cook stove. With the modern electric washer and spin dryer is a wash tub and scrub board. Sewing machines are electric and manual along with particular sewing equipment indigenous to the area. The materials used range from tanned moose hide and glass beads to store-bought prints. Foods from beaver meat, bannock, and preserves to angel food cake mixes and pizza enrich a "home ec" program which attempts to reflect the conflicting aspirations of today's Stanley parents. The program allows for local input. Different women of the community can come in to instruct the girls in the skills of moccasin sewing, scraping hides, traditional cooking, or even the bathing of an infant, while the qualified teacher of the south teaches the necessities of modern living and that good life "out there."

Up the sloping ramp and around the bend to the left is the shop. The typical manual training room, largely for woodworking and carpentry, is also tooled for small engine repairs. Again, as with the "home ec" room, the shop allows for local input. Local craftsmen can instruct the more adept boys in such skills as paddle making, snowshoe making, boat repairing, or wood carving. The

La Ronge Band, at one time, made canoes, an art that the local academics would like to promote. The setting of traps, the skinning and drying of furs are taught which means the school has its own trap line. The shop is also equipped with a darkroom and equipment for picture developing.

Across from the shop, slightly down the slanting hall and around the bend to the left, up a short flight of stairs are the double doors leading into the gym, a high ceilinged, regular, basketball type. The gym's main wall leaps out with a huge Aboriginal motif, created by the hands of a series of art students who collectively assembled it and somehow pasted it on the open wall. A small stage is at one end. A balcony for spectator seating faces it at the other end. The gym's gleaming hardwood floor is marked for basketball, badminton and volleyball.

Sport and recreational facilities provide a range of athletic experiences. The athletic program for Keethanow is typical of athletic programs found in schools anywhere in the province but also includes the Aboriginal skills of skiing, snowshoeing, and canoeing.

At the right of the main entrance is the principal's office. It is complete with a receptionist's desk, filing cabinets, and the usual classroom monitoring equipment. On the same side, the next door opens into a spacious, bright library. Its resources, though, having a very new look about them, reflecting a regular library that is as new as the building and therefore evolving.

The windowed corridor veers to the right, connecting the new section to the old. The soft natural wood tones are contrasted with the monotonous greenish colors of the hall and classroom walls of the old building. Years of repeated coats of paint no longer brighten the pronounced drabness. The bare tiled floors, worn looking, add to the dingy atmosphere of the long halls. In spite of the faithful daily efforts of the janitorial staff, the floor always looks unclean and in a constant state of clutter. For some reason, debris is always visible, spilling out of the classrooms and washrooms. Green and orange garbage bags, bulging with the production of discarded paper, evidences the amount of newsprint used each day in the classrooms. In spring and fall, the floor becomes covered with tracked-in mud, captured on a kind of rubber carpet placed there for that purpose.

The classrooms are numbered one to ten, with two portable-like units attached to the far end of the building, house the nursery and kindergarten. Well furnished with the usual equipment denotes a typical nursery or kindergarten room. Classrooms are typical classrooms. Old desks, tattered textbooks, green chalkboards and clothes racks accentuate the used look of each room. At the front is obviously the teacher's desk, while at the back are built-in cupboards which either gape empty or are cluttered in a disarray of construction paper, jars of slopped over tempra paint and dried paint brushes. Some classrooms exhibit a globe, others mathematical equipment for the chalkboard and, usually, one classroom has either the movie projector or the video playback unit which are trundled from room to room. The dreariness of the classrooms is countered by festooning the walls with students' work, which contributes to cheerier atmospheres.

Keethanow School's new section, for the Aboriginal people of Stanley, conveys in its design the oldest symbols which give meaning to Aboriginal culture. The circle of the eight-sided rooms, the conical shapes, the open classrooms are elements that are as timeless as earth upon which the structure rests. It is in touch with the environment and acknowledges earth of hills and hollows. The log rafters angling upward, converging, have been the standard design for Aboriginal structures from ancient times and embody the meaning of relationships, and the unity of family. The central area, the rotunda of Keethanow, a place where the people come together, follows the traditional custom of gathering inside the "tipi." That the structure is located where people converge in their routine living is consistent with custom. Smith Atimoyoo, a Cree Elder and coordinator for the Elders in Saskatchewan, uses the tipi as the model to teach Indian values following the ancient custom. The architectural design is a holistic exemplification of all elements common to the Cree people of the woodlands. To incorporate them into their institution of learning was to regenerate the pride exhibited by the ancestors of these people and make today's people of Stanley draw closer together through a structure that reflects themselves.

The old section of Keethanow School conveys in its design the contemporary symbols of western culture. The flat, shoe-box rooms, desks in rows are the necessary elements of the modern society dedicated to efficiency, economy, and bureaucracy. That the structure is suspended on stilts in order not to touch earth, alone conveys its separation from earth and the natural surroundings. Its linear straight and rigid symmetry represent the character of western society's worldview resulting in the creation of a cold impersonal structure. It is a structure dedicated to regimentation, submission to authority, and the imposition of western values.

Competitiveness, aggressiveness, and independence become the natural offshoots of this kind of learning environment.

✎ *The Demography*

In 1980-81, the enrollment at Keethanow was 259 children from kindergarten to grade twelve. The students are more or less evenly distributed through grades, with a decreasing number in the four upper grades. This total of 259 students includes both the status and the Metis children.

The Omachewa-ispimewin Child Goes to School

In Keethanow, the Stanley child enters at the first level, termed "kindergarten." It is consistent in appearance with most kindergarten rooms found anywhere in the province. Here is where the Omachewa-ispimewin child meets his first teacher.

The kindergarten teachers of Stanley are both Aboriginal women. They both have children of their own, they live in the community, are totally fluent in Cree, and both know the children and the community. The concept of "mother" is easily conveyed by the two teachers. Their image and presence helps the Stanley child relate easily to his own home experience. By the manner in which they operated their classrooms, the kindergarten teachers appear to be responding to the children's world. The children, dominant in the Cree language or speaking a composition of English-Cree, can communicate and be understood as if at home. In the classroom, the children are free to roam, to explore, to touch, and to talk to each other. They may sit, stand, or lie down where they want and move on when they feel the sit, stand, or lie down is over. Only they know this, and they do not need teachers to tell them.

The atmosphere in the classroom is gentle, maybe slow on first impression, but one can see a motion of purposive activity as each child is importantly involved in his or her own task. The teachers move around the room, rarely interrupting an activity, yet if a child looks up or transmits some other kind of non-verbal message, the teacher sees the message, "the child wants help." It was observed that through all that goes on in the kindergarten classroom, the teachers responded to changes created by the children. Rarely did they order the change, outside of the usual school dictated changes. However, in this regard, one kindergarten teacher explained that the children learned better from one another. She therefore felt that she could respond in ways that did not interfere with this natural process of learning.

In a formal lesson in the kindergarten class, the teachers would give very brief directions, then allow the children privately to try the task. This way of teaching is consistent with the traditional forms of learning of Aboriginal people. After the child would have mastered the skill on his own, then he would exhibit it to his group. The child would never be in a position to demonstrate a partially mastered skill, and suffer the recriminations of the group. In the kindergarten class of Keethanow, the children are observed individually slaving over a chosen task. The teachers circulate and, when the child needs them, they are there.

The teachers appear to have control. Yet there is no continual verbal monitoring of the children's behavior. No child was singled out either for a compliment or a reprimand. When one youngster, after an heroic effort, had managed to hold the door open for the whole class, the teacher complimented the entire class in the statement, "It is so good to have such good helpers." In another incident where one of the youngsters had been particularly bad, the teacher said, "I know one little boy who has been very bad today." The two kindergarten teachers accommodated the children's rate of completing work and judged when the children were ready for things to change; in this way control over the child happened. Yet, it appeared as if the child felt he was in control.

The children were not kept busy, yet they kept themselves busy. The pace of the classroom, though relaxed, was smooth and unobtrusive. The children talked, yet it was quiet talking. As the child would have acted under the control of parents, his behavior at school was not required to be different. As he was able to communicate at home and he understood, so too would his teachers of the kindergarten communicate and understand him. The children were relaxed, happy, and seemed at home in their new world of school. For the child of Omachewa-ispimewin, at least in the kindergarten class, there appears to be no observable discontinuity between his home and his school.

The world of the white teachers and the world of the Aboriginal teachers co-existing as they do, likewise carry over into the Aboriginal child's world. An Aboriginal child is socialized in his own environment in kindergarten and has learned to do things one way. When he enters the world of the white teacher, he is expected to do things a different way, and by implication learns the one right way is the white way. The kindergarten classes, at the end of the school year, have a full-fledged graduation exercise complete with gowns and mortarboards. That this exercise is done is to the credit of the Aboriginal kindergarten teachers who, in their creativeness, stage from their miniature world an important senior exercise that happens in white schools. However, it becomes treated as a very special day. Everybody is proud of the youngsters. They are marched down to the central gathering place, lined up on stage, photographed and awarded make-believe certificates, and the parents attend. The principal, dressed in a three-piece suit, solely for the occasion, addressed the tiny scholars with ". . . now you are ready to enter the real world of school . . . be good students . . ." Implicit in the exercise is that it is important, it is right, and is of the white world. King, in describing an Aboriginal school run by white teachers, perceived it this way:

> Two distinct domains of social interaction exist independently: White man society and Indian society . . . . The white man maintains his social order according to his own perceptions of reality. The Indian bears the burden of adaptation to a social order that he may perceive more realistically – and surely he perceives it with a different ordering of reality – than does the white man.[66]

In the contrasting of cultures, or two worlds, no matter how familiar one may be with the other, one always gives deference to the other. The object of "local control" at this point appears to be one of swinging from one form of control completely over to another form, while utilizing the same system to do it. Substituting brown faces for white and then giving deference to the white results in a system that is the same as the one that they started with in the first place. This is reinforced by King in his statement:

> From his perceptions, the Indian finds it impossible to accept the social order and, at the same time, impossible to reject it completely. He therefore creates an artificial self to cope with the unique interactive situations.[67]

The practical implications of this in the world of Keethanow are many and whether they are just becoming realized by the Aboriginal education authorities of Stanley, much has yet to be realized. As Berry points out:

> While no small amount of research has been done on the content of the Indian cultural heritage and on the extent to which this has survived into the present, relatively little seems to have been done on the problem of how this impinges upon the school situation, and on the question of how the problems might be resolved.[68]

The teacher as a white adult accepts the child as in a state of becoming a full person. In the community, the child is always accepted as a full person and a part of the community. The child is included in all that happens in the home and is never excluded or isolated because of being a "child." White adults usually set the standard of what is considered a "good child." In this way the child learns what is expected of him. The white teacher sets the standard of the "good child" in the classroom. This does not always correspond with the community standard which the child already understands. There are occasions when the children are on their own, at which times they set what is expected or meaningful to them. Conflicts exist in the expectation of proper behavior. While in the community, children are free to roam, to run, talk, and laugh, to eat and drink what they please or not to eat, if that's their choice. They can smoke, chew snuff, or stay up all night if that is their inclination. Children can tag along with the adults anywhere. They don't have to do homework, can be late for school, need not wash or change their clothes. All are perceived from the Aboriginal child's world.

In the classroom, the Aboriginal child is grounded to a desk, can't run in the halls, must be silent, is told to "shut up," must eat nutritious food, and for the first time encounters an authority figure who verbally recites all that he must do, as well as declaring things he had done as being wrong, bad, or even sinful. The training of children to be responsible in school becomes one of being told what and how to do it. No autonomy or relatively little is granted to the child's own initiative for he must be treated as a "child." The white teacher derives this authority to set what is expected from sources considered right and which support that world. When the white teacher asks the Aboriginal child a question, and if the child is silent, the teacher concludes no answer and so, in some instances, asks the question again – maybe reworded. The Aboriginal teachers may have an advantage here, for they too use questioning, but they can reword their question in Cree which results in spontaneous replying. The white teacher's inference in any case is that the child cannot answer the question. The teacher defined the amount of time to allow without considering that perhaps the Aboriginal child requires time to think before responding or that the child's silence itself indicates a form of answer in his own world.

Under "local control" the white teacher and the Aboriginal child are moving toward a more equal base from which to accept each other. A mutual acceptance or understanding requires the teacher to develop some comprehension of the world of the Aboriginal child. By virtue of the teachers position as authorities of the classroom and as definers of what must be meaningful, the "Aboriginalness" of the children needs to be evident and, therefore, everything the teacher does must have relevance in that context. That such is or is not happening can be viewed from both the white and Aboriginal worlds. The evolving philosophy, as determined by the Education Committee with the community input is there, however its actual implementation is still subject to interpretation from the world of the teacher.

Omachewa-ispimewin – The Community

The people of Stanley refer to themselves as the "Cree People," the "Trapper People," or even "Omacha-ispimewiniuk." They take their identity from the past and from their culture. For them, their "Ihtowin" is more than a collection of houses. The "Ihtowin" is "what makes the place tick."[69] The "Ihtowin" is the community of people who, belonging together, living in close proximity, share a set of commonalties so comprehensive as to include their lives. Further, to the Crees, Stanley Mission is also an "atenowehns," that is a collection of modern dwellings, Holy Trinity church, Keethanow school, the stores, and all the elements of western life, including a satellite dish. From Omachewa-ispimewin to Stanley Mission there is an "Ihtowin" spanning two worldviews brought together over time and forcing the community people to literally stand in two worlds. The worldview of Omachewa-ispimewin is continuity and persistence; the worldview of Stanley Mission is change and modernity.

The persistence of Omachewa-ispimewin is present in the language itself which embodies the worldview which, in turn, reflects not only the tribal memories but the relationship of each individual with the environment, the Creator, fellow men, and creatures. The informal community standards, passed from generation to generation, set the observable behavior. The visible culture includes the round of life – of smoking fish, tanning hides, and skinning rats. Stanley is also beaver tail, blueberry picking, hot bannock with lard, cooked moose nose, fried deer meat, moose steaks, and stewed muskrats. Life is to fear the Weetigo, the hideous giant who eats children and represents absolute evil and they caution at the mysterious barking of the dogs or sight of the "balls of fire."

Aspects of modernity are also evident in the village: high powered aluminum boats, taxi service, the Band-owned satellite dish.

Yet remove these or the store, the church, the school, and the town of Stanley would not change, since it is what maintains continuity; life would continue with little adjustments. The people would go on being the people of Omachewa-ispimewin. For Stanley, the behavior of the dogs, children wending their way to school, old ones visiting, men leaving for work, housewives, a poker game, the bingo, and the people "boozing it up" at some house, all present what Malinowsky, in his day, termed the "imponderabilia" of what he as an outsider observed.[70] The "imponderabilia" of the round of life is the ihtowin of Stanley.

References

1. In conversation with Tommy MacKenzie, a Stanley Historian and Informant, Spring, 1981, Stanley Mission, Saskatchewan.

2. In conversation with Ernest Tootoosis, a Cree Elder, Spring, 1979, Saskatoon, Saskatchewan.

3. Kuska, Patchees. *Swamp Cree Legends*. Toronto: The MacMillan Company of Canada, 1938, pp. 7-24.

4. Carl Ray and James R. Stevens, *Sacred Legend of the Sandy Lake Cree*. Toronto: McClelland and Stewart, 1971, pp. 23-24.

5. Patchees, op. cit.

6. Zenon Pohorecky, *Saskatchewan Indian Heritage*. Saskatoon: University of Saskatchewan, 1970, p. 8.

7. Ibid.

8. Ibid., p. 14.

9. Ibid., p. 17.

10. Ibid.

11. Ibid., p. 18.

12. Ibid., p. 17.

13. In conversation with Smith Atimoyoo, a Cree Elder, at the Saskatchewan Indian Cultural College, Fall, 1979, Saskatoon, Saskatchewan.

14. Ibid.

15. Legend of the Wood Crees told by Chief Red Cloud (Joseph Bruneau at Red Earth Indian Reserve, Saskatchewan).

16. Atimooyo, op. cit.

17. Kenneth Pike, *Language in Relation to a Unified Theory of the Structure of Human Behavior*, Vol. 1. California Summer Institute of Linguistics, 1954, p. 8.

18. Local Advisory Council, Stanley Mission, L.A.C. Stanley Mission census, April 10, 1980.

19. In conversation with Amelia MacLeod, a Cree Elder, Stanley Mission, Summer, 1981.

20. Bill Roberts, Survey of Stanley Mission of Canada Wide Mines Ltd., January, 1981, Saskatoon, Saskatchewan.

21. Terminology used in H. F. Wolcott, *A Kwakuitl Village and School*. New York: Holt, Rinehart and Winston, 1967, p. 2.

22. MacLeod, op. cit.

23. L. Marshall, "The Development of Education in Northern Saskatchewan." Unpublished M.Ed. thesis, University of Saskatchewan, Saskatoon, 1975, p.112.

24. Ibid.

25. Ibid., p. 110.

26. Ibid.

27. Quoted in Marshall, op. cit., p. 111.

28. Marshall, op. cit., p. 113.

29. John H. Archer, *Saskatchewan: A History*. Saskatoon: Western Producers Prairie Books, pp , 95-113.

30. Quoted in Marshall, op. cit., p. 115.

31. Quoted in Marshall, op. cit., p. 115.

32. Quoted in Marshall, op. cit., p. 109.

33. Tony Loos, Professor of History, University of Saskatchewan. Paper delivered at Native Law Seminar, February 17, 1979.

34. J. W. Chalmers, "Education Behind the Buckskin Curtain" (unpublished n.d.), pp. 159-160.

35. Federation of Saskatchewan Indians, *Documents Relating to Indian Education in Saskatchewan*, 1870-1950, p. 257.

36. Ibid.

37. W. F. Payton, *An Historical Sketch of the Diocese of Saskatchewan of the Anglican Church of Canada*. Prince Albert, 1973, p. 84.

38. Federation of Saskatchewan Indians, op. cit., p. 257.

39. McLean to Chisholm, November 3, 1913. Quoted in Federation of Saskatchewan Indians, op. cit., p. 258.

40. Ibid., Chisholm to Secretary, March 5, 1914.

41. Ibid., Paying Officer, Treaty 10, MacKay to Scott, October 18, 1915.

42. Ibid., Assistant Secretary Steward to Inspector Crombie, November 2, 1916.

43. Ibid., Reverend Norris to Indian Commissioner, October 4, 1920.

44. Ibid., Assistant Deputy Williams to Graham, November 30, 1920.

45. Ibid., Reverend MacKay to Secretary, September 14, 1921.

46. Ibid., McLean to Graham, June 2, 1924, p. 260.

47. Ibid., Chief Amos Charles to Graham, August 10, 1924.

48. Ibid., Graham to Secretary, September 9, 1924.

49. M. F. Norris, "Brief Outline of Educational Requirements, Treaty Indians, Northern Saskatchewan," November 12, 1948, p. 5. (T. C. Douglas, files of T. K. Shoyama, I Numerical Series 291A - Indians, Saskatchewan, Regina, Saskatchewan, Archives Board.)

50. Report of Indian Affairs, Northern Saskatchewan, n.d., n.a., m.p. (T. C. Douglas, files of T. K. Shoyama, I Numerical Series 291A - Indians, Saskatchewan, Regina, Saskatchewan, Archives Board, p.1.)

51. Norris, op. cit., p. 3.

52. C. H. Piercy, "Survey of Educational Facilities in Northern Saskatchewan." Regina: Department of Education, 1944. Saskatchewan Archives Board, Regina, Government Publication ED6.

53. A. G. Harper, "Canada's Indian Administration: Basic Concepts and Objectives (SIC)," *American Indigena, Vol. V, No. 2,* April, 1945, p. 127.

54. Annual Report of the Department of Indian Affairs. Ottawa: King's Printer, March 3, 1928.

55. *Annual Report of the Department of Mines and Resources, Indian Affairs Branch*, 1948-1949, p. 199.

56. National Indian Brotherhood, *Indian Control of Indian Education*. Ottawa: National Indian Brotherhood, 1972, p. 1.

57. H. B. Hawthorn. *A Survey of the Contemporary Indians of Canada*. Ottawa: Queen's Printer, 1967.

58. National Indian Brotherhood, op. cit., p. 27.

59. American Indian Resource Associates, *Indian Education Confronts the Seventies, Vol. II.* Tsaile, Arizona: Navajo Community College, 1975, p. 5.

60. Myles Venne, Chief of the La Ronge Band, at Stanley graduation, 1982.

61. In conversation with Tom MacKenzie, Councillor for Stanley, Stanley Mission, Saskatchewan, April, 1983.

62. Ibid.

63. Ibid.

64. Theodore Kaltsonis, "The Need to Indianize Indian Schools," *Phi Delta Kappa, Vol. I, No. iii,* January, 1972, p. 292.

65. La Ronge Band Education Branch, *Information Kit*, Orientation, Fall, 1981, B.6.1.

66. A. Richard King, *The School at Mopass: A Problem of Identity.* New York: Holt, Rinehart and Winston, 1967, p. 87.

68. Bewton Berry, *The Education of American Indians*. Washington, D.C.: Office of Education, Bureau of Research, 1968.

69. In conversation with Smith Atmoyoo, Saskatoon, Saskatchewan, Summer, 1981.

70. B. Malinowsky, *Argonaunts of the Western Pacific*. New York: Dutton Paperbacks, 1961; quoted in Frederick Erikson, "Some Approaches to Inquiry in School-Community Ethnography," *Anthropology and Education Quarterly, Vol. VII*, May, 1977, p. 61.

Section Two

Connections

Partners in Education

3

Educational Development in the NWT

Creating Divisional Boards of Education

Geoffrey B. Isherwood and Knute B. Sorensen

Introduction

This study is about decolonization and social integration, the decolonization of the educational system of the Northwest Territories (NWT) of Canada and the integration of aboriginal people into the Canadian cultural mosaic. By decolonization we mean the transfer of powers from the Department of Education to regional educational authorities across the NWT, and the consequences of that transfer. We recognize that decentralization is more than a shift of powers. It includes the emergence of new people in the power structure. More fundamentally, the transfer of powers to aboriginal people can be viewed as another step in the long-term process of building a new province in Canada's far northern lands.

This chapter constitutes a brief review of educational development in the NWT, a review of selected theory and research related to decentralization, and an analysis of development in the 1980-1990 period. The chapter ends with a discussion and conclusions.

Background

In the 1980s, the Department of Education of the Northwest Territories of Canada became committed to educational reform through the decentralization of their school system. Decentralization was viewed by the political elite to be a prime vehicle for making northern schools vital institutions more closely reflecting the aboriginal culture while contributing to the development of the entire north. Decentralization would "contribute to the development of more responsive government . . . and to the positive advancement of the people of the Territories" (Graham, p. 267). In sum, the wealth of the north was in its youth and their knowledge, knowledge needed in a society in cultural transition.

Self-determination in education is more than just an administrative or political issue. O'Neil (1990, p. 159), in the health context, has pointed out, "The quality of the relationship between providers and clients . . . can have profound implications on . . .

(one's education). The fundamental premise of the contemporary approach to (education) is that individuals must have confidence in their ability to influence their life circumstances . . . ."

Prior to this time, schooling was directed from Yellowknife, the Territorial capital, by a centrist Department of Education. The purpose of schooling had been to provide youngsters with an opportunity to succeed equal to that of youngsters in schools in southern Canada. Northern schools were organized along southern Canadian lines; they used southern programs of instruction and tables of organization. They were largely staffed by non-aboriginal people. Little value was placed in school programs supporting a northern lifestyle. The language of instruction was English. Teachers discouraged the use of aboriginal tongues in school. It was left to parents to see that youngsters learned their native tongue and culture.

As well, schools were dispersed across the vast expanse of northern Canada from the Eastern Arctic to Inuvik in the west — over 3000 kilometers as the crow flies. Heretofore, this great distance made it difficult to virtually impossible for the Department of Education to provide extensive support for local curriculum development. Department specialists could not spend extended periods in a community.

There was little local parental involvement in education into the 1980s (Isherwood, Sorensen, and Colbourne, 1986). At community Local Education Authority (LEA) meetings and at regional Education Society (ES) meetings administrators sought advice from parents, but clearly the administrators (the department of education representatives) were in control of educational decisions. Parents were encouraged to report their "concerns" at these meetings. If the LEA or ES saw fit, concerns were forwarded for consideration to the Department of Education. The process of isolating and forwarding concerns indicated how little actual control aboriginal people had over education. It took a crisis for parents to get quick action. In one case, it took the publication of an immoral act to create enough of an impetus for immediate Department action.

The commitment to decentralization of educational decision making was part of a greater commitment to power sharing with aboriginal people. Control would become local and aboriginal people would make educational decisions as opposed to just expressing concerns. Politicians came to believe that schools would be more effective, more relevant to students if they were governed by aboriginal people. While few aboriginal people had experience in LEAs and ESs, they were to be trained and quickly installed as members of newly created community educational councils (CECs) and divisional boards of education (DBE). These two agencies were to insure that aboriginal rights were not infringed upon across the Territories. Fiscal, personnel, and curriculum support would be provided by the Department of Education.

As the political will for decentralization was growing in the 1970s, major problems existed in northern schools. Student attendance was poor. Few students completed an elementary school education. Fewer finished high school. The language of instruction was primarily English, thereby threatening the maintenance and development of aboriginal language skills in communities that valued their retention. As well, few aboriginal teachers existed – the schools were organized and taught by "foreigners" to the northern way of life. As well, a high turnover of the non-aboriginal teaching staff each year created instability.

Perhaps, more importantly, aboriginal leaders had been divided on the value of formal education. They have questioned the form and content of schooling which subtracted from their culture and language. They have supported schooling which reflected and reinforced their culture and language. In the 1970s, aboriginal leaders emerged with a new vision of northern schooling – and their voice was being heard. The Government of the Northwest Territories (a unicameral legislature) was becoming more sympathetic to the emerging will of the aboriginal people. The government view had been that the aboriginal people were "not ready" to take charge of their affairs; the emerging view among government leaders was that they had to take charge. If mistakes were made, if problems were encountered, the aboriginal leaders would learn and develop governance skills. The Territorial Government was taking the position that aboriginal people are responsible for their destiny – or at least, aboriginal people should have a major say in their destiny.

This "new view" of the role of aboriginal people in their destiny was not limited to education. It was having an impact on local government, health care, and wildlife management (Dacks, 1990).

In March, 1982, the final report of the Special Committee on Education, *Learning: Tradition and Change*, was tabled by its co-chairmen Bruce McLaughlin, MLA (Pine Point), and Tagak Curley, MLA (Keewatin South). The report, growing from a series of consultative meetings in 34 communities that included aboriginal parents, aboriginal LEA members, and school staffs, outlined a series of recommendations relating to schooling. The report recommended:

☆ A new structure for the education system

☆ The creation of Divisional Boards of Education (DBE)

☆ An administrative structure for the system

☆ Curriculum recommendations related to school program and language of instruction

☆ Changes regarding the teaching staff, adult education, and special services

Political will had solidified as reflected in this document. The recommendations were first realized in April 1985, when the Baffin Divisional Board of Education came into existence, the first of many northern divisional boards. The Baffin DBE published its mission, goals, and priorities in the booklet, *The Future is Now*. As a first child, its parents, the Department of Education, would have to grow with the child, and would have to work out a viable division of powers and responsibilities growing from commission recommendations and current practice.

The creation of a DBE was in keeping with practice all over North America in the 20th century. Houle (1990, p. 1) pointed out, "In government, in business, and in the countless organizations and associations by which people seek to achieve common purposes, councils of citizens acting together exercise guidance and direction."

According to Lippett and Schmidt (1967), organizations are created and mature going through three stages. At birth, concerns center on survival as an organization and the development of legitimacy in the eyes of their partners. In the youth stage, efforts focus on establishing and maintaining organizational effectiveness, building a positive reputation, and hiring solid personnel. Finally, in the mature stage, the focus is on organizational uniqueness and large contributions to society. This process may not be linear – regression and fluctuations among stages can occur. We found DBEs seemed to go through another stage – incubation – prior to birth.

Regions and hamlets had established Education Societies and Local Education Authorities during the 1970s that, while officially powerless, had the effect of socializing aboriginal people to ways of governance prior to actual empowerment. As well, training activities were set in place in the mid-1980s to support LEAs and ESs before empowering them as CECs and the DBE. In the Baffin case, 30 days spread over 1985 and 1986 were devoted to studying "board" operation. The focus was on bylaws, establishing a mission and goal statement, analyzing the role of board members both at board meetings and back in their communities. Particular emphasis was placed upon policy making. Through policy, the board would exert its beliefs and perspectives (Carver). Visits were made to other boards, both aboriginal and non-aboriginal. It seems fair to say that educational development, particularly board member development, was an incremental process. Years were devoted to the anticipatory socialization of aboriginal people. As well, training time was devoted to senior administrators as their responsibility shifted from the Department to the DBE.

At birth, communities elected representatives to CECs who, in turn, appointed members to the DBE. Aboriginal leaders took their place as chairpeople. By-laws were set into place. Mission statements and goals were defined. Policy-making procedures were defined. Superintendents became the employee of and reported to the DBE instead of to the Department of Education. Members of boards embraced their new roles. As the beginning years went by, problems of a technical, political, and cultural nature emerged. The resolution of these led to a refined board, committee, and administrative policy and practice.

Later, as other divisional boards in the Kitikmeot, Keewatin, and the western Arctic came along between 1986 and 1989, like second and third children, they differed in some respects from the Baffin Board – in their origins and in their community needs. Yet they shared common origins as former units of the Department of Education.

Board members and school administrators across the Arctic found themselves still working with Department of Education staff. In fact, many new Department of Education staff members had been administrative leaders in the "new thinking" about aboriginal governance. The old guard in the Department was being replaced by activists of the new guard who had worked within divisional boards. Certainly, decentralization did not mean divorce. Between 1986 and the present, The Department of Education has had to raise many "children," many new divisional boards.

The purpose of this study is to analyze the emergence of DBE as they grew toward full-fledged organizational status. First, the theoretical framework of Tichy will be stated as it is most relevant to the investigation. Second, there will be a brief review of research on decentralization at the state level in a few other jurisdictions. Then, we will discuss the emergence of DBEs from our unique and somewhat biased point of view.

We had the opportunity to work with and train both aboriginal people and senior administrators as DBEs came on line between 1984 and 1990. During this period, we spent over 30 weeks in contact with aboriginal leaders and senior administrators in communities across the Arctic. We are not aboriginal people; we are not northern administrators. We are two educators with varied backgrounds in the practice and theory of educational administration and in educational development or reform. We have many friends in the north, and we have a bias toward cooperative development. We are less concerned with "master plans" and more concerned about bringing along people who will develop plans and policy. We are more concerned with the process of development than the facts of development. In sum, we have no rigorous study to report but rather some detailed observations on decentralization and governance in education in the NWT.

We are concerned about the ethical side of our presentation. We will avoid using names, times, and places that would link specific people to specific events. We trust that our readers will understand.

The Tichy Framework and Selected Research

For Tichy (1983), organizations are confronted with three dilemmas: a technical design problem; a political allocation problem; and, an ideological and cultural mix problem. These problems are never "solved" permanently, rather they recur over time as the social dynamics within an organization shift and as environmental factors impinge upon the organization in changing ways. Specifically, the technical design problem has to do with arranging both social and technical resources to maximize output. The political design problem refers to how powers are allocated within the organization. The ideological and cultural mix problem is concerned with which values, beliefs, and norms will serve to integrate organization members and insure a fit with the values of the community. Once again, these problems are never fully resolved, except in a very traditional setting where social dynamics are firmly established. But even in traditional societies environmental shifts will bring out the dilemmas.

We found that there is limited research on a national or provincial level devoted to educational decentralization as a means to development in Canada. Elsewhere, the works of Hanson (1988), Rondinelli (1983), and Grindle (1980) are notable as studies of decentralization. Hanson has devoted years to these concerns, but not in the Canadian context. He points out that the major problems associated with centralized educational agencies seem to be: (1) inefficiency stemming from a high level of bureaucratization; (2) system rigidity originating in elaborate procedures for task accomplishment and centrist values of bureaucrats; and, (3) a lack of participation by those affected by decisions made centrally. And because of these problems, (4) the centralized agency becomes incapable of internal adaptation. An external body becomes involved in change typically through political action.

Decentralization, the process of shifting powers and/or duties from one core agency to another can take on three main forms. Hanson (1988) notes, decentralization "can be examined in terms of degree and territorial space. The degree of decentralization can be viewed along a continuum involving the transfer of decision-making authority" to lower units.

1. *Deconcentration.* The transfer of tasks and work to subordinate units without the transfer of decision-making authority. The superior authority is "decongested" but little power is shifted. This is a very low degree of decentralization.

2. *Delegation.* The transfer of decision-making authority to subordinate units. However, the superior unit sets a policy framework within which the subordinate units function. Ultimate authority remains with the superior unit. This is a medium degree of decentralization.

3. *Devolution.* The transfer of authority to a relatively autonomous subordinate unit that can act virtually independently of its (possibly former) superior unit. This is a very high degree of decentralization (Rondinelli, 1981; Conyers, 1984).

Of course the outcomes of decentralization can be affected by many factors. For example, "a wide range of intractable interests, inadequate planning, ingrained centrist attitudes, differences of opinion between politicians, reformers and bureaucrats" can influence the best of intentions (Rondinelli, Nellis, and Cheema, 1984).

As well, whatever mix of decentralization occurs does not guarantee success in terms of organizational goals. The rearranging of powers can be like rearranging deck chairs on the Titanic. Decentralization still requires meeting ongoing problems as Tichy (1983) suggests.

In a study of decentralization that spanned a decade, in the Ministries of Education of Venezuela, Columbia, and Spain, Hanson (1988) found eight factors associated with the goals of decentralization (the three countries followed different paths to decentralization and had different degrees of success with decentralization):

1. *Collaboration.* The extent to which political actors involved in decentralization policy were able to work together after decentralization began. Hanson found that higher levels of collaboration seemed to enhance decentralization. These political actors clearly would include not only elected and appointed officials but also the administrators that work with them.

2. *Political party politics.* The extent to which party politics affected educational policy, programs, and personnel appointments. He found that political decisions seemed to hinder decentralization.

3. *Incremental approaches.* The extent to which decentralization was accomplished in stages. He found that slower decentralization seemed to work better.

4. *Continuity.* The extent to which administrative personnel remained in place over the span of decentralization. He reported that high levels of staff turnover seemed to hinder decentralization.

5. *Costs.* The extent to which the costs associated with decentralization were met. Hanson noted that insufficient development funds hindered decentralization.

6. *Budget control.* The extent to which control over personnel appointments and financial expenditures were given to local units. Hanson found that continued centralized budget control seemed to hinder development.

7. *Regional boundaries.* The extent to which school system boundaries reflected the social reality of the communities they served. Hanson noted that enclosing communities within boundaries that did not reflect common community wishes seemed to hinder development.

8. *Formalization.* The extent to which the superior unit produced policy that was in tune with subordinate unit needs and that

helped subordinate units. Hanson found that such policy seemed to facilitate local initiatives.

Organizations, as well, tend to be "loosely coupled." That is, different organizational levels – often influenced by proximity or lack thereof – function somewhat autonomously. In the case of the NWT educational system, one might expect the Department of Education, the Divisional Boards, and the local schools – far apart, and with somewhat different daily concerns – to have different views on the effects of decentralization.

If we view Hanson's research findings in terms of the Tichy framework (see Figure below) we estimate that four problems fall predominantly into the technical category, three into the political category, and two into the ideological and cultural category. We can see that decentralization will likely invoke an abundance of problems.

TICHY FRAMEWORK

Hanson's Findings	Technical Problems	Political Problems	Ideological & Cultural Problems
1. Collaboration	XX	XXX	XX
2. Party Politics	X	XXX	XX
3. Incrementalism	XXX	X	XXX
4. Continuity	XXX	X	X
5. Costs	XXX	X	X
6. Budget Control	X	XXX	X
7. Boundaries	X	XX	XXX
8. Formalization	XXX	X	X
XXX = Strong Connection; XX = Moderate Connection; X = Weak Connection			

Having briefly reviewed the Tichy framework and associated research on decentralization, we now turn to the case of the school board development in the NWT.

Educational Development in the NWT: 1980-1990

The development of Divisional Boards of Education (DBE) took years. Political leaders adopted a "process" approach as opposed to a "blueprint" approach. "Advocates of blueprint or programmed implementation see detailed policy design as the engine which drives execution. In contrast, the process approach conceives of policy as necessarily being in a continuous state of evolution"

(Graham). The process approach would bring more and more people on board. Furthermore, this evolution took time because aboriginal and non-aboriginal leaders evolved together as decentralization progressed. This is the Tichy perspective in action.

Aboriginal groups viewed each other differentially. Some groups did not want to be lumped with other groups within DBE because they were different people. Some groups thought their schools were better than other groups' schools and did not want to be put in an inferior position (voting-wise) within a DBE. They sought independent board status. There were status concerns among aboriginal leaders, and these concerns, real or imaginary, shaped DBE boundaries and policies.

The transition to power for DBE was marked at times by clashes between former and emerging values. For instance, when one new board held an election for its chairperson two names were brought forward. One of a wise, old, respected community elder, a unilingual aboriginal person. The other of a young, active, bilingual person; his "southern" education and current position in a wage earning job gave him a good command of English. Board members were divided on the candidates. The young person, himself, was torn. While he thought the chairperson should be competent in English as well as his native tongue in order to conduct the board's business and to represent the people to higher powers, he respected the role of the elder. The young person won by a narrow margin; the elder became vice-chairman by unanimous vote.

The history of aboriginal development is marked by people who have been able to "bridge" two cultures. With Indian bands, this dates back to the first contacts between European traders and natives. The person who has been able to provide a successful bridge from both aboriginal and non-aboriginal perspectives has altered aboriginal culture. Some would say to its betterment, others would question this, a question of what is valued.

Of course having the power of a chairperson may go to one's head. One beginning chairperson lost his job, removed from the chair by board vote, because he acted unilaterally in transferring a teacher from one school to the school in his community because his community needed her specialty.

Aboriginal chairpeople need to maintain their credibility among their own people. They need to be seen to be in charge of non-aboriginal leaders. In many instances, aboriginal leaders have publicly chastised senior administrators and then, minutes later, in private (or sometimes publicly) been seen to calm the waters. People with feet in two camps, two cultures, must attend to both constituencies – they need both.

This leads to a most important point. There is no question that a few charismatic people existed in the educational system as decentralization took place. These few people embodied reform values. They believed aboriginal leaders had to take charge; they had to be free to grow and to make mistakes in governance. One such leader was loved and feared. "He would not back off!" Challenges to his views were met with "Bullshit!" Over the years, he and others have risen in the administrative hierarchy. An administrative oligarchy has emerged that strongly supports aboriginal development. As Heymann has pointed out, "The best (senior leaders) can do is to make clear to those who manage . . . the broad themes and specific proposals of (their) administration . . ." Senior leaders can determine who is in charge, but they cannot take charge. They and their views become touchstones for others. It is these leaders that daily engage with courage and conviction the technical, political, and cultural problems facing the NWT. These new, largely non-aboriginal Turks appeared on the scene at just the right time. Or, the times were ready for them. Take your pick.

As mentioned earlier, Education Societies (in regions) and Local Education Associations (in hamlets) had been in place for a number of years before DBEs came on line. These "committees" of parents served two functions. They provided advice to educational administrators, local input to decision making, and they socialized aboriginal leaders to committee ways of acting. But, they socialized them to "advisory ways." The focus was on local "concerns;" on the needs and wants of specific communities. The focus was not on them assuming control of the decision-making process. The societies and LEAs did not help most aboriginal people learn the corporate viewpoint, the viewpoint that DBE served all communities at once as opposed to each community individually. If a community school needed repair, it needed repair. It was hard to see that schools in six communities needed repair and that priorities would have to be established. It was hard for DBE members to return to their communities after a board meeting only to say that their school's repairs were two years away. Aboriginal board members were confronted with the classic dilemma of being a representative of their community on the DBE, and at the same time, being a delegate to the board where they had to act in the best interest of all board schools and students.

Yet a few board members where capable of embracing the larger picture of board operation. These people invariably emerged as chairpeople or as very influential individuals on the DBE. Other individuals who emerged as informal leaders were people who espoused strong interests in preserving aboriginal culture and language. For example, a debate emerged among future board members as to whether the DBE office should be established in a largely non-aboriginal community even though that community was the only one with office facilities and a bank. "Shouldn't the board be located in an aboriginal community?" argued aboriginal activists. The board was established in the non-aboriginal community, but the decision was to be reviewed in a year.

Technical concerns could not easily dominate cultural ones without a strong debate. It was more important to hire an aboriginal secretary – who could serve the people – than to hire a person with exceptional typing and word-processing skills. Jobs were needed by aboriginal people, too.

The training of school board members, which varied across the NWT from a few weeks to a few months, seemed to be more functional in discussing and defining DBE by-laws, mission statements, goals, policy-making procedures, and powers of the board and its committees than in developing insight into the role of the board member. Perhaps there are some things you have to live to understand and appreciate. Future training might be more effective in the role area as board members bring personal experience to the training.

DBE supported principal training, too. They spent funds on the development of largely non-aboriginal leaders to manage their schools. Principal training seemed to be more effective when it supported educators in bringing community members into schools and into understanding schooling than when it focused more narrowly on administrative problem solving or in-school issues solely. The school principal in an aboriginal community had the opportunity and the mandate from superiors to have an impact on the entire community and its growth and development.

As new boards functioned across the NWT insights into their decision-making processes emerged. There is a view that traditional aboriginal decision making is by consensus. Action is not taken until all agree. If there is disagreement, the group waits for further developments. Observations of DBE members across the NWT revealed something else. Yet it is hard to tell if we can project current observations back in time. Whatever their origins, aboriginal board members exhibited shrewd political skills when division emerged on agenda items.

First of all, when division existed among board members during formal meetings, divisive agenda items would typically be referred to a later time in the meetings. DBE meetings would last days but were infrequent because of travel costs in the NWT. During coffee breaks, lunches, and into the evening, board members could be observed discussing their differences at length. Lobbying took place among interested stakeholders. Arms were twisted. Trades were made. In short, consensus among aboriginal leaders seemed to evolve as it does in other Canadian jurisdictions. Consensus was the product of intense informal interaction.

Secondly, chairpeople consistently ran their meetings with dignity and decorum. Rarely were verbal outbursts in evidence. There was a shared concern to value all members' input, to get that input on the floor, and to recognize each other as equals. Yet there was concern for the importance of the newly formed DBE. For example, at one board meeting it became evident that a member was in town, but not at the meeting. The DBE moved to an in camera session. (We were permitted to observe.) Discussion proceeded about what to do about his absence. It was calmly decided to reprimand the offender by not paying the honorarium for the time away. When the culprit returned the next day it was apparent he knew what was in store. He asked for a moment and apologized for his actions. He was sorry, it would not happen again. Everyone knew where he had been and what he had done, but no mention was made of this. The DBE disciplined its own in a quiet, dignified way. As one board member said commenting on their chairperson, "She doesn't ever get mad. Who could be that good?" This revealed, we think, aboriginal reverence for being calm and collected when faced with adversity.

It became evident that DBE members thought modeling was an important part of their role. There were things that DBE members did and did not do. They believed they had to be role models and a source of inspiration, not degradation, to the larger population.

Third, decisions seemed to have a very personal impact on board members. When a board confronted issues related to drug and alcohol abuse among students and staff, DBE members exhibited genuine feelings of concern. They seemed to experience sorrow and fear. The aboriginal culture seemed a decent "concerned" culture.

Compromise and consensus development seemed a part of the aboriginal cultural fabric. This was not something that had to be learned; mechanisms were in place culturally and emerged in DBE meetings.

Discussion

Decentralization in education in the NWT can best be described as delegation. Clearly, the locus of decision making is moving away from the Department of Education toward DBEs. Yet Territory-wide concerns remain and act to keep fiscal, curriculum, and personnel decision making with central input as well as local input. That is to say, DBEs have considerable operational autonomy within an emerging policy framework established by the Department of Education. Deconcentration, the transfer of tasks without authority is not the norm. Nor is devolution, the transfer of authority to a virtually autonomous sub-unit. Devolution is a tainted concept in the NWT. Devolution implies abandoning the DBEs, and that is not acceptable to the political leaders or the Department administrators. Some may think the Department holds on to power a little too much, while others may think the DBEs want too much power. What is at issue and remains a part of daily endeavor is the balancing of powers between the levels.

The Tichy framework for understanding organizational development highlights the process of governance. It points out that shifts have technical, political, and cultural dimensions. On a particular issue, one or another dimension may dominate. Yet the framework is not heuristic in providing insight into the interactions among the three dimensions.

Hanson's research findings on administrative reform were supported in the present study. Collaboration among political, aboriginal, and administrative stakeholders was continually observed. It was related to the successful establishment of DBE. In addition, it was observed that the emergence of a few charismatic non-aboriginal administrators enhanced collaboration, they insisted upon it, and they modeled it. Their tenacious, courageous leadership moved the process along.

Incrementalism was evident. Depending on which DBE we are referring to, a span of four to eight years lapsed between the publication of *Learning: Tradition and Change* (1982) which called for divisional boards and the establishment of boards. One cannot underestimate the value of the glacial movement toward DBEs for regions. Some would say the process was too slow, while others thought it appropriate. Few would say it was not successful. The slow process enabled leaders, aboriginal and administrative, to come forth, to become chairpeople of boards, to rise in the administrative hierarchy. It provided time for new leaders to emerge without undercutting traditional leaders. It provided time for training. It provided time for the development of mission statements and goals of education by boards. It enabled the development of a consensus. Perhaps most fundamentally, incrementalism let schooling emanate as a most valued endeavor across the NWT.

While there were changes in administrative postings, continuity was enhanced with the promotion of administrative leaders who shared the new vision of aboriginal governance. New people who shared this vision ascended to administrative posts. In addition, aboriginal leaders emerged and acted as "bridges" between the old culture and the emerging one. A few people retired or sought employment elsewhere facilitating decentralization.

The cost of decentralization was well supported from Department of Education coffers. A substantial Donner Foundation grant aided in the development of aboriginal lay leaders and senior administrators (Isherwood, Sorensen, and Colbourne, 1986).

While there were some bureaucratic difficulties in handling budgets and personnel matters, increasingly DBE concerns were resolved. Aboriginal leaders had been active in staff recruitment for years and this practice continued. As well DBE members had increased control over operating and capital budgets.

DBE in the NWT continue to struggle with the growth of schools, curriculum issues, and high student absenteeism. Traditional aboriginal culture and ways of decision making uniquely fit demands of DBE operation. Concerned thought, concern for due process and giving voice to all, informal discussion when division occurs on issues, and personal respect for each other set aboriginal leaders ahead as DBE members.

Difficulty in adopting the "corporate view" as a DBE member remains for some. Local concerns still tend to dominate the minds of some board members. Yet other aboriginal leaders continue to come forth bridging cultures. Using the incremental process approach to reform, the traditional aboriginal approach, educational decentralization can only be judged a success to date.

Conclusion

Five major conclusions emerge from this study. First, implementation must be seen as an adaptive learning process (Graham, 1990). Government, the Department of Education, and local aboriginal people contributed to the development of DBE over a period of years as they learned to work together and value each other's contributions. The incremental process permitted adaptation.

The second conclusion is that the adaptive learning process was facilitated by strong leadership; leadership from a few political, administrative, and aboriginal people. Without this rather informal oligarchy, decentralization would have been put into question. As well, the process which was spread over many years permitted new leaders to emerge through promotion, transfer, and retirement.

Third, the incubation period, that period when government, Department of Education, and aboriginal people interacted before the formation of DBE, was both functional and dysfunctional. It was functional in that it facilitated learning about the new roles each would play. It was dysfunctional for aboriginal people in that it instilled in some the notion of a DBE as a consultative body rather than a body with powers of its own.

Fourth, when people who held divergent views about education were put together they were adroit enough to resolve what initially were seen as intractable problems. Under the direction of firm leadership cooperative endeavor worked.

Finally, educators realized that the resolution of structural power relationships did not, in and of itself, improve the education of students. Specific goal setting activities by new DBE were required to meet educational ends. For example, a DBE could affirm the importance of their culture by setting a goal of instruction in their native tongue in the early elementary years thereby bringing to life local values.

References

Carver, John. (1990). *Boards That Make a Difference*. San Francisco: Jossey-Bass.

Graham, Katherine A. (1990). Implementing the policy to devolve: Learning by doing. In Gurston Dacks (Ed.), *Devolution and constitutional development in the Canadian north*. Ottawa: Carleton University Press.

Grindle, Merilee. (Ed.), (1980). *Politics and policy implementation in the third world*. Princeton: Princeton University Press.

Hammergren, Linn A. (1983). *Development and the politics of administrative reform*. Boulder, CO: Westview.

Hanson, E. Mark. (1986). *Educational reform and administrative development: The cases of Columbia and Venezuela*. Stanford, CA: Hoover Press Publication, 326.

Hanson, E. Mark. (1989). *Decentralization and regionalization in educational administration: Comparisons of Venezuela, Columbia and Spain*. American Educational Research Association conference, San Francisco, April.

Heymann, Philip B. (1987). *The politics of public management*. New Haven: Yale University Press.

Houle, Cyril O. (1990). *Governing boards*. San Francisco: Jossey-Bass.

Isherwood, Geoffrey B., Sorensen, Knute, and Colbourne, Eric. (1986). Educational development in the north: Preparing Inuit leaders for school board control. *Education Canada, 26*.

Lippett, Gordon L. and Schmidt, Warren H. (1967). Crises in developing organizations. *Harvard Business Review, 45*, 102-112.

O'Neil, John D. (1990). The impact of devolution on health services in the Baffin Region, NWT: A case study. In Gurston Dacks (Ed.), *Devolution and constitutional development in the Canadian north*. Ottawa: Carleton University Press.

Rondinelli, Dennis A. (1981). Government decentralization in comparative perspective: Theory and practice in developing countries. *International Review of Administrative Science, 44*, 133-145.

Rondinelli, Dennis A. (1983). *Development projects as policy experiments: An adaptive approach to development administration*. Toronto: Methuen.

Rondinelli, Dennis A., Nellis, John R., and Cheema, G. Shabbir. (1984). *Decentralization in developing countries: A review of recent experiences*. Working paper, The World Bank, Paper No. 581.

Tichy, Noel M. (1983). *Managing strategic change: Technical, political and structural dynamics*. New York: Wiley.

Special appreciation is extended to Dr. Yvonne M. Martin-Newcombe of the University of Victoria for her comments on early drafts of this work.

4

Shared Services In Isolated

School Districts

A Case Study

Dave Marshall

Introduction

Recent history has not been kind to the small rural school or division. Educators in these settings have been faced with declining enrolments, increasing costs, increased demands for proof of the quality of the type of education they are delivering, increasing awareness of how their schools measure up (in a comparative sense) on a range of variables, and other factors such as parent and teacher militancy. This has led to the critical examination of the delivery of educational services in small rural or isolated school districts and schools.

This critical examination has resulted in three general observations.

First, there is an identified list of the strengths and weaknesses of small and rural educational settings (Marshall, 1985). Secondly, there is a willingness to accept the reality that small, rural, or isolated schools and districts will never be able to deliver all of the educational opportunities that large, urban school jurisdictions can provide. And thirdly, although there are many strategies identified for small schools, these are generally based on the notion that the best overall strategy for small and rural school systems is to amplify the strengths that come with smallness and ruralness while ameliorating the weaknesses associated with the smaller scope of the offerings in such locations. The sharing of services and the development of alternate delivery modes are two of the major strategies in this regard.

While these observations have resulted in the need for more careful consideration of school closures or consolidation, many isolated school districts do not have the option of considering even this possibility. The isolated school districts in northwestern Ontario are examples of such settings. As shown in Figure 1, these 13 school districts are geographically isolated and represent the

Figure 1: Isolate School Boards in Northwestern Ontario

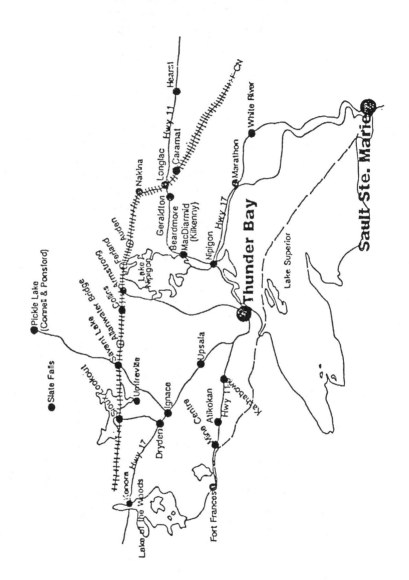

only educational opportunity for students in their catchment area. For instance, Slate Falls is accessible only by air and the option of sending children to residential schools in an urban setting is not seen as a viable alternative. Consequently, these isolated districts are faced with the challenge of amplifying the strengths of the small, isolated school, while at the same time, finding ways of enhancing the educational opportunities available to their students.

In this chapter, the establishment of a shared services operation for these isolated school districts is described and discussed. This case study of an innovative rural educational arrangement is examined in the context of literature and research on organizational change in education and in the consideration of general issues regarding the implementation of shared services in rural educational settings. Criteria for successful sharing of services between educational settings are suggested.

The Case

Northwestern Ontario is still largely an untouched wilderness. Apart from the population centres stretched along the Trans-Canada Highway, most populated areas are small, few, and far between. The provision of educational services to these isolated and sparsely populated parts of Northwestern Ontario has always been a challenge.

There are 17 isolate school boards spread throughout Northwestern Ontario, ranging in size from the Northern District School Area (D.S.A.) Board which operates four schools with approximately 250 pupils to the Collins D.S.A. Board which operates one school with 19 pupils (in 1988). Four of the isolate boards do not operate any schools at the current time. Some of the remaining 13 schools are within a two hour drive of the major population centre of Thunder Bay, while others are accessible only through the northern C.N. rail-line, and still others are only accessible by float plane in the summer and ski equipped plane in the winter. The geography of the area and the location of the schools is presented in Figure 1. A sense of the distances and isolation involved in Northwestern Ontario can be seen by realizing that the distance between Mine Centre and Caramat is approximately 600 kilometres by road, the same distance as driving from Windsor to Kingston.

The challenge of providing efficient and effective educational services to these diverse communities has been enormous. Historically, the Ministry of Education of the province of Ontario has taken a direct role in providing service and assistance to these isolated boards. Ministry officials have acted in the role of board level administrators and provided financial, personnel, and consulting services as required. As early as 1966, the Ministry of Education in Ontario recognized the need for improved education delivery in small, isolated schools and introduced the Northern Core Concept of teacher assistance to these boards. However, after 1969, the Ministry of Education assumed a reduced role in provision of direct services to isolated school boards as many of the smaller school boards were amalgamated into larger units and the board itself assumed greater responsibility for provision of all services, educational and support. In 1970, Steel (1970) studied the problems of isolated school boards and categorized common problems in the small, isolate boards as educational and administrative.

Educationally, it was becoming obvious that isolated single school or two school boards, with teacher populations from two to six, were not able to provide the range of educational services accessible to students in larger urban areas. The small boards did not have the breadth of consulting support, the facility or expertise for hiring, the staff resources to develop curriculum or structures that supported evaluation of programs, teachers, or administrators. For instance, although Slate Falls was considered an independent D.S.A. Board with one two room school and two teachers, it was not capable of carrying out the normal range of educational functions associated with an independent school district.

Administratively, the small, isolated school board did not have the expertise to provide leadership or monitoring in either the financial or management areas. Particularly noticeable was the inability of the local board to provide efficient and appropriate financial services. As independent boards, these units received funding directly from the ministry; however, most of the boards did not have the expertise available locally to assist them in the reporting and accountability procedures required to receive and disperse public funds.

It was recognized (Steel, 1970) that some broader solution had to be devised to assist the isolated school boards. It was felt that any solution must have the potential for improving educational opportunities for children, provide a more efficient business administration and involve more local people in the administration of their school functions. Numerous alternatives were explored as a result of the report of the Steel Committee (1970) but no action was taken until 1976, when the delivery of business services to isolated school boards was at a crisis point. Ministry deadlines for financial reporting, termination of grant advances for non compliance, increases in office expenditures, staff reductions in Ministry offices, spending restraints for isolated boards and staff changes contributed to the proposal to implement a shared services operation in the area of business services. An accountant was hired to work with seven of the smallest and most isolated school boards, and in 1977, the concept of shared services became a reality in Northwestern Ontario.

For funding reasons the shared services operation was established using the shell of a D.S.A. Board that did not have any school or any students. The Umfreville D.S.A. Board became the Umfreville Cooperative Services Unit, and from its modest beginnings in 1977 when it hired one accountant to provide financial services to six isolated school boards, it grew by 1988 to a fifteen person organization offering a broad range of educational, conference, financial, and student counselling services. The current organizational chart of the Umfreville D.S.A. Board Cooperative Services Unit is presented in Figure 2. Figure 3 lists the school boards currently served by the cooperative units and provides some demographics on these boards and types of services that they utilize. It should be noted that the isolate school boards do not uniformly use all of the services available from the Cooperative Services Unit. Some use the complete business and educational services of the Umfreville Unit while others utilize only the territorial student program services and still others utilize only the business support services.

Operationally, the Umfreville Cooperative Services Unit provides service to the isolated boards in five service delivery areas: professional development services; consulting services; financial and business services; territorial student program, and supervisory officer services. These services are offered to the isolated boards on a fee for service basis. That is, an isolate board can choose to buy one or all of the services available. The funding for the cooperative unit comes through the isolated boards. The cooperative unit receives no money directly from the Ministry and receives all of its operating support through the purchase of its services by the isolated boards.

Figure 2: Umfreville D.S.A. Board Organization Chart

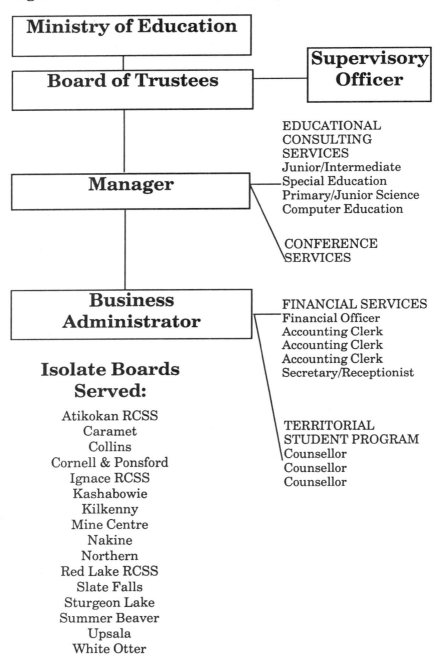

Ministry of Education

Board of Trustees

Supervisory Officer

Manager

EDUCATIONAL
CONSULTING
SERVICES
Junior/Intermediate
Special Education
Primary/Junior Science
Computer Education

CONFERENCE
SERVICES

Business Administrator

FINANCIAL SERVICES
Financial Officer
Accounting Clerk
Accounting Clerk
Accounting Clerk
Secretary/Receptionist

TERRITORIAL
STUDENT PROGRAM
Counsellor
Counsellor
Counsellor

Isolate Boards Served:

Atikokan RCSS
Caramet
Collins
Cornell & Ponsford
Ignace RCSS
Kashabowie
Kilkenny
Mine Centre
Nakine
Northern
Red Lake RCSS
Slate Falls
Sturgeon Lake
Summer Beaver
Upsala
White Otter

ISOLATE SCHOOL BOARDS OF NORTHWESTERN ONTARIO: SUMMARY OF DEMOGRAPHICS - 1988

Board Name	# of Schools Operating	# of Teachers	# of Students	Students per Teacher	Students (%)
Caramet DSA	1	4	42	10.5	0 to 5
Collins DSA	1	2	19	9.5	100
Connell & Ponsford DSA	1	8	95	11.88	20
Ignace District RCSS	1	4	90	15	0 to 5
Kashabowie DSA	0	1	n/a	n/a	n/a
Kilkernny DSA	1	3	43	14.33	100
Mine Centre	1	7	79	11.29	90
Nakina DSA	1	5	83	16.6	0 to 5
Northern DSA	4	17	234	13.76	80
Red Lake RCSS	1	11	166	15.27	0 to 5
Slate Falls DSA	1	3	34	11.33	100
Sturgeon Lake	0	n/a	n/a	n/a	n/a
Summer Beaver DSA	1	7	92	13.14	100
Upsala DSA	1	5	65	13	0 to 5
White Otter DSA	0	n/a	n/a	n/a	n/a

The Components of Shared Service

A review of Umfreville Co-operative Unit (Jones et al., 1988) provided the following observations and recommendations regarding the components of the operation.

✏ *Professional Development Services*

In reviewing the provision of professional development services by the Umfreville D.S.A., it was recognized that professional development for teachers may be one of the most important factors in improving the quality of education in the isolated school districts. Teachers in isolated school boards have a high turnover rate; tend to be newer teachers, working in the isolated community earlier in their career; have not likely had any experience working or and living in isolated communities or with Native populations; and all of the administrators teach as well as run their small school. In addition, the members of the Board (3 Board members in each isolate) are not likely to have had any experience with school systems outside of their isolated school setting.

The Umfreville school unit has been providing the services of a number of professional development activities for the isolates. These activities include: 1) Three days in October for teachers and principals; 2) three days in the Fall for trustees, secretary-treasurers, and principals; 3) three days in February for teachers and principals and 4) two days in March for principals and three days in late spring for principals and secretary-treasurers. In addition, an isolated board Professional Development Committee meets on a regular basis to plan and review the professional development.

Recommendations were made for the development of an orientation program for new teachers and principals, for professional development sessions to pay particular attention to the unique mix of experienced teacher needs and new teacher needs in providing the professional development sessions; for the development of closer links with the provincial professional development program for teachers; and for the further involvement of the local university in assisting with some professional development activities in this regard. In addition, it was recommended that isolate board professional development activities be linked with larger board inservice sessions that could be of value to the isolate teachers.

✎ *Organization and Funding*

Jones et al. (1988) made suggestions regarding the legality of the Cooperative Services Unit and the way in which money is provided. These recommendations attempted to address the confusion with respect to the relationship of the Umfreville D.S.A. to the Ministry of Education. Recommendations were made to clarify whether the Umfreville D.S.A. actually belongs to the isolate boards or is simply a branch of the Ministry of Education. Consequently, the report recommended that appropriate legislation change be effected to allow for the Umfreville D.S.A. to, in fact, act as a school board (called an independent scheduling agency) of the province. They also recommended that the unit be called a Cooperative Services Unit and be eligible for direct funding. Further recommendations were made regarding the nature of the Board of Directors of the Cooperative Services Unit to encourage more contact between the isolate boards themselves and the actual board, the Umfreville Board.

✎ Business Services

The provision of financial services to isolate boards was the original reason for the Cooperative Services Unit's existence in the first place. The Cooperative Services Unit provides a wide range of financial services including processing of invoices and cheques, calculation of payroll and cheque preparation, bank reconciliations, tax collection, accounting, preparation of working papers, budget preparation and other financial reporting. Different isolate boards take different levels of service and there appears considerable satisfaction from the isolate boards with the financial services provided. Consequently, the report recommended the extension of the services to cover the full range of business services normally provided to a school board in a more urban or populated location. The isolate boards themselves need advice in such maintenance areas as appointment of architects, provision of engineering studies, and so on. In addition, the report recommended the possibility of more bulk purchasing of high volume items for the Board.

✎ Supervisory Services

Although the Umfreville D.S.A. had been able to provide direct financial consulting and professional development services, there has been no cooperative service in the area of supervisory services. Each isolate board has traditionally been assigned a supervisory officer from the regional office of the Ministry of Education and links between the Ministry of Education and the supervisory officer and the other aspects of the Umfreville D.S.A. are tenuous.

Consequently, Jones et al. (1988) recommended that the provision of supervisory services be assigned to the Umfreville D.S.A. and removed from the regional Ministry of Education. It appeared paramount that general educational services and supervisory officer services should be delivered by the same intermediary agency.

✎ Consulting Services

The Umfreville Board currently provides curriculum consulting services to the isolate boards in three areas: primary/junior, junior/intermediate, and special education. In addition, special consultants such as computer consultants have been added to this list as Ministry initiatives require. However, the role descriptions and the conditions of employment for consulting positions are varied and primarily incumbent determined. Consequently, Jones et al. (1988) recommended that the isolate boards see a common role description for all of the consultants and that the work of the consultants be guided by a set of annual curriculum objectives. In addition, it was recommended that there be no permanent consultants and that consultant positions be filled on a short term basis of no more than three years. This, of course, recognizes the obvious fact that four consultants cannot possibly cover all of the curriculum areas and priorities will have to be established in a three to five year plan.

✎ *Territorial Student Program*

Finally, with regard to the support for students who leave the isolate school boards to attend education in more urban areas, it has been recognized that a major problem within northern isolate school boards is the tremendous drop-out rate of students who move to the urban centre to continue their education. Efforts have been made for decades to address the concerns of parents and students from isolated boards but the problem still persists. The Territorial Student Program was instituted in 1974 by the Umfreville D.S.A. to assist students leaving away from home in the major centre of Thunder Bay with the hope that this program would assist in their retention and would assist in addressing the problems of culture and educational shock for those students who move from the isolated school and community to the larger urban centre.

The territorial student program assists parents in finding appropriate boarding homes, provides direct counselling services to students, and acts as a liaison between the school and parents. Of all of the services and dilemmas of isolate boards, the issue of students moving to the large urban areas is the most complex, the most perplexing and least easily solved. Despite the best efforts of the Umfreville D.S.A. and its Territorial Student Program, the drop out rates of students (mostly Native students) attending urban high schools in Thunder Bay is almost 100 percent. The whole of this chapter, probably the entire book, could deal with the specific issue of Native students attending schools in a residential setting outside their community. However for the purposes of this chapter, it is suffice to recognize that the cooperative unit has been able to pay attention to the need to support such students and to attempt to develop support programs in the areas of life skills programs, boarding assistance, communication with parents, and so on. This is a service that would not be available were there not some sort of Cooperative Services Unit working with all of the isolate boards on this problem.

The Umfreville concept appears to have proven its viability in meeting many of the needs of isolate boards in Northwestern

Ontario. A unique delivery structure has evolved and it can provide a model for other similar jurisdictions. However, through a further examination of the issues inherent in the Umfreville model, the context of dynamics of change, and the notion of shared services, some suggestions for successful sharing of services are identified.

Current Status and Issues

The Umfreville Services Unit represents a unique model for providing services to isolated school boards. Partly an intermediate unit (Vselka, 1980) and partly a shared services model (Galvin, 1986), it has evolved its unique structure over a ten year period.

However the concept is not without its problems. Umfreville grew out of the most obvious educational needs of the isolated boards; it did not evolve from a planned strategy either from the government's perspective or from the perspective of the small isolated boards.

In 1988, a review of the Umfreville Services Unit was commissioned by the Umfreville D.S.A. Board. Through site visitation, document analysis, surveys, and interviews, the review team (Jones et al., 1988) examined all aspects of the Umfreville Unit in order to provide advice to both the government, to the isolated boards, and the Umfreville unit, itself, on the continuation of the unit. Four issues were seen as providing special concern to the partners in this operation.

Legality: From its very inception, the legality of the Umfreville Cooperative Services Unit has been in question. Regional officials have been repeatedly forced to defend its existence and find inventive ways to fund it. Consequently, the most basic issue with respect to the Cooperative Services Unit has been its very existence, although there appears to be considerable support for cooperative mechanisms such as that provided through the Umfreville D.S.A. Board. However, the existence of a school board in Ontario without any students of its own poses special legal problems. Of special concern is the fact that current legislation in 1988 (under review) did not allow the government to provide funds directly to school boards without student enrolments.

Relationship to the Ministry: The relationship of the Cooperative Services Unit to the Ministry of Education in Northwestern Ontario has always been a question of debate from the very inception of the shared services concept. At issue here, of course, is the concern for control and maintenance of the unit. Should the

Umfreville simply be a department of the regional office of the Ministry of Education? Should the Umfreville Unit belong to the school boards, themselves, since they are buying their services or should the Umfreville unit be an independent agency, not attached to the province or any school boards, simply marketing its services to the isolated school boards and receiving funds directly from them.

Funding: Tied to the question of legality and ownership, is the issue of funding. It is not currently possible (without legislation change) for the Cooperative Services Unit to receive money directly from the government or the Ministry of Education. Consequently, funds are channelled to the Umfreville D.S.A. Unit through the isolated boards that request its services. This poses some dilemmas to the local boards since the funds are never received by the local, isolated boards for subsequent dispersement to Umfreville. Once the board has signed up for the service, although the funds might appear on the isolated boards accounts, the money is sent directly to Umfreville by the Ministry of Education. This appears to be an appropriate way to route the funding through to the Umfreville Unit, however, this poses some political concerns at the isolated school board level.

Needs: The fourth issue of concern is the large range of needs of the isolated school boards, themselves. Clearly the isolated school boards have many of the same needs as the larger school boards in more urban districts. The issue of concern here is whether a Cooperative Services Unit such as the Umfreville D.S.A. is the appropriate mechanism to meet the highest priority needs of isolated school boards.

Criteria for Successful Shared Service Operations

Research and literature on shared service concepts as well as literature on the general issue of change and innovation, combine with the Umfreville issues to suggest some criteria or maxims for successful shared service operations.

✎ *The Whole is Greater Than Its Parts*

This criteria identifies the need for collective agreement among the partners that together they will have access to more services or resources than they would have individually. Tichy (1980) and Corbett and Rossman (1989) refer to this criteria as "The Technical Design Dilemma" where organizations arrange their technical resources so that they can better produce a desired output. The process must be seen as technically advantageous for an organization to pursue a shared model. Furthermore after examining the literature and research on sharing alternatives for small and isolated school districts, Galvin (1986) suggested several perspectives from which both the developing and the maintaining of shared programs could be viewed. In this regard, exchange theory and essentiality (Galvin, 1986) suggests that the need for the services under consideration for sharing must be proven as essential to the operation and attainable through acceptable inter-organizational relationships.

In a situation such as Umfreville, where the partners have the options of buying in or out of the service, accepting that the partnership will result in a better service for resource allocation is crucial.

The continuous growth of the services shared in the Umfreville D.S.A. suggest that the isolate boards have seen that this is the case. Jones et al. (1988) recognized this concern in recommending legislation that would allow Umfreville to receive its funds directly from the Ministry. Consequently, the isolate boards would not actually see the money they provide Umfreville and would eliminate the continued temptation to make comparisons as to what they could have "bought" on their own. However, the Umfreville concept and its success as a shared services operation will continue to depend upon each of the partners in the shared service operation believing that they receive a greater service then they would have received on their own. This is most evident in the Umfreville delivery of the consulting business and conference services.

✎ *A Balance of Power and Autonomy*

Galvin (1986) identified "power dependency" and "preservation of autonomy" as two of the perspectives from which to better understand shared service operations between school jurisdictions. Both refer to the need for partners to develop what Tichy (1980) refers to as appropriate political arrangements or arrangements for the allocation of power between partners.

In the case of Umfreville, the continuation of the shared services concept has been dependent upon the Umfreville unit convincing the sharing boards that control of the unit rested with the individual partners and not with the personnel of the unit. In this regard, Jones et al. (1988) recommended changes to the structure of the Umfreville board of directors to encourage more contact between the actual boards themselves and the board of directors of the

Umfreville unit. The continued life of Umfreville services unit will depend upon its success at communicating and convincing the partner isolate boards that individually they have an appropriate, proportionate voice in defining the services that are provided.

✎ *The Control of Positive External Pressures*

Fullan (1991) suggested that one of the ingredients for successful educational change was the presence of positive pressure and support from peripheral participants in organizations.

In the Umfreville situation, the motivation to establish the shared services model stemmed primarily from administrative and financial dilemmas as observed by or as a result of the Ministry of Education. In fact, many of the services are services devolved from the Ministry of Education to the Umfreville unit. For example, the devolution of business services was a major reason for the initial existence of the Umferville D.S.A. unit. In addition, Jones et al. (1988) recommended that the supervisory officer services currently offered by the Ministry be handed over to the Umfreville unit. Consequently, the issue in the case of the Umfreville shared services unit is not the search for external pressures for change, but a possible excess of this pressure along with an undue association of the change with the outside pressure. Specifically for historical reasons any linkage between the "controlling" connotation of the Ministry and the desired "service" connotation of the shared services unit will be detrimental to the partnership. The shared services unit must be seen as providing service not control and the individual partners must feel that they are in control of the outside forces promoting, supporting, or initiating the shared services model.

✎ *Initiation of Cultural Change*

One of Fullan's (1991) significant contributions to the change literature is the identification of the need to change beliefs and attitudes as a precursor to changes in behavior and action. Corbett and Rossman (1989) recognize this as the ethological or cultural problem that examines the normative glue of the organization and the dynamics of the interaction of beliefs and values by members of the organization.

A combination of factors made and continue to make changing attitudes in beliefs crucial to the success of the Umfreville Co-operative Unit and similar shared services concepts. The isolated school boards are fiercely independent. Their isolation has made them used to operating their own support structures and when outside agencies or individuals have been involved it has been to control service and not to provide or promote it. It is fair to say that there is some justifiable degree of cynicism regarding outsiders and their motives for helping an isolated board.

It has been a slow process for the isolate boards to recognize that people non-resident to their location can provide a better service than can be provided locally and that this can be done without local loss of status or power. Conversely, there have been attitude shifts in those central agencies (Ministry, universities, large school boards, etc.) who deal with the isolates in recognizing that the educational services provided by the isolates is in many ways superior to any other educational alternative for the children in these communities. The changing attitude towards the limits and approaches to the territorial student program and the ongoing recognition of the native language programs are two examples of this attitude change.

The Umfreville case is an example of how attitudes regarding a shared service model can change in a positive way over time and that the best way to insure this change is through incremental successes. Umfreville has had a string of these successes particularly in the business, consulting, and professional development areas and consequently has engendered confidence in its ability to expand to supervisory areas.

Summary

As Fullan (1991:47) suggested that "the myriad of factors that interact and affect the process of educational change are too overwhelming to compute in anything resembling a fully determined way." However the Umfreville case suggests that there are a number of maxims that can increase the odds of a successful shared services operation: the acceptance that the service whole is greater than its parts; the control of autonomy and power; the control of positive outside forces; and the adjustment of attitudes and beliefs.

However as Tichy (1980) points out (and is evident in the Umfreville case) these problems are dynamic and never fully resolved but rather ongoing throughout the life of the operation. Umfreville is dynamic and ongoing. Its careful attention to the need to continually examine these maxims will assist it in remaining a crucial support service to the isolate boards of Northwestern Ontario.

References

Corbett, H. D. and Rossman, G. B. (1985). Beyond implementation series: three paths to implementing change. *Curriculum Inquiry, 15*:2.

Fullan, M. (1991). *The new meaning of educational change*. Teacher's College Press. Columbia University.

Galvin, Patrick. (1986). *Sharing among separately organized school districts: premises and pitfalls*. New York State Legislature, Albany, New York.

Jones, R.; Marshall, D. G., and Yauk, L. (1988). *A review of services provided by the service unit of the Umfreville d.s.a. board*. Umfreville D.S.A. Board, Thunder Bay, Ontario.

Marshall, D. G. (1985). The closing of small schools or when is small too small. *Education Canada*, October, 1985.

Steele, R. R. (1976). *Report to ministry of education*, Thunder Bay, Ontario: November 26, 1976.

Steele, R. R. (1970). Committee report: Paper one: *Isolated school boards*. Ministry of Education, Thunder Bay, Ontario.

Tichy, N. (1980). Problem cycles in organization and the management of change. In T. Kimberly & R. Miles (Eds.), *The organizational life cycle* (pp. 164-183). San Francisco: Jossey Bass.

Vselka, J. (1980). *The delivery of educational services: The small division problem*. A Review of the Literature: Paper Presented to the Faculty of the Department of Educational Administration, University of Texas.

5

Cycles And Crisis Politics In An

Educational Organization – P.E.I.

Parnell Garland

Introduction

The implementation of a human resources approach to the administration of a school district is described in this chapter. The efforts to implement the human resources approach were carried out over a ten year period. The decade of experimentation concluded with a significant political crisis in the school district. The events are described and analyzed in the context of organizational change cycles, political theory, and crisis politics.

Background

The school district, Regional School Unit 3 in Prince Edward Island, was created by legislation in 1972. The predecessor school boards included those of the City of Charlottetown, a regional high school district and a number of elementary districts some of which consisted of single room schools. By 1977 the school district population of 11 000 students was accommodated in three senior high schools and in a number of junior high and consolidated elementary schools. The school district was governed by fifteen elected trustees.

The changes that were required during the first three or four years of the existence of the new school district were substantial. The newly established board and administration were required to establish basic structures and procedures. Principals who had been accustomed to reporting to their own local school board were required to report to a superintendent of education. A new school act was proclaimed in 1972. Also, for the first time, a collective agreement was negotiated with teachers, and teachers were subjected to an individual performance appraisal system which was widely detested. In addition, a number of small schools were closed against the objections of vocal community groups.

The elections of 1975 brought a new group of trustees to the board room table. Their awareness of the reactions to some of the earlier initiatives was obvious. For example, one of their first decisions was to declare a moratorium on teacher evaluations.

At the time that I became Superintendent of Education in the school district in 1976, the significance of the opportunity was obvious. Given the relatively short life of the school district as an organization, policies and procedures were not institutionalized. Vacancies in assistant superintendent positions existed so that there was an opportunity to recruit senior staff. Finally, trustees were interested in improving both internal and external relationships.

Implementation of Human Resources Model

Any individual who assumes the role of chief executive in an organization, school systems and schools included, must accept the responsibility for establishing structures and creating an organizational climate. These acts of the chief executive are, to a large extent, unilateral. These decisions influence the shape and nature of the structure of an organization and impact on the creation of a culture within the organization. Decisions about structures and the design of the decision-making process inevitably flow from the set of beliefs that are held by the individual. In addition, the human resources literature provides a substantial body of knowledge about the structuring and functioning of organizations and the design of motivational forces.

A number of principles were articulated in order to establish a human resources direction for the school district. These included the following priorities for the administration of the school system:

☆ The primary task of the administrator is not to make decisions, but to ensure that the decision-making process is functioning efficiently;

☆ Functional groups whose activities are related in terms of their tasks require the opportunity to develop decision-making skills;

☆ Organizational structures should be designed so that individuals and groups have the opportunity to influence decisions that relate to themselves, their work, and the goals and demands of the school system;

☆ Individual schools are fully identifiable educational units; and

☆ Professional development activities should be structured in a fashion that gives recognition to the concept that schools are the basic units of change.

A number of concepts and beliefs were inherent in the selection of these principles. The recognition of decision making as the central task of administration and the importance of involving people in the process focused attention on the roles of administrators at both the central office and school levels. The identification of the school as a significant entity in the system created the opportunity for school-based staff to take initiatives. Finally, it was recognized that any organization has both formal and informal processes and, in order to achieve effectiveness, it is necessary to harness the energy that resides in the informal system.

During the 1960s, a number of organization theorists made significant contributions to an improved understanding of organizations and of the administrative process. McGregor (1960) identified the importance of the assumptions that are made about people and the implications these assumptions have for administrative styles and organizational effectiveness. Argyris (1964) focused on inherent conflicts that inevitably occur between individuals with their unique needs and organizations with their pressing demands. Likert (1961, 1967) presented a conceptual model of the administrative process along with convincing empirical data concerning the effectiveness of various leadership styles.

The work of these theorists established the foundation for the human resources model of administration. Miles (1971) has articulated a clear overview of the model:

> . . . the human resources model differs dramatically from previous models . . . in its views on the purpose and goals of participation. In this model the manager does not share information, discuss departmental decisions, or encourage self-direction and self-control merely to improve subordinate satisfaction and morale. Rather the purpose of these practices is to improve the decision-making and efficiency of the organization. The human resources model suggests that many decisions may actually be made more efficiently by those directly involved in and affected by the decisions (p. 256).

The human resources model focuses clearly on the development of individuals and the achievement of effectiveness. School systems clearly have a developmental agenda. The model takes account of the need to provide a developmental experience for students, teachers, and administrators. It also provides the framework for a methodology which enables people to become involved and assume responsibility.

Individuals behave on the basis of their beliefs. As social structures, organizations also behave and reflect the beliefs that are of value to individuals who occupy significant roles within the organization. These commonly held beliefs define the culture of an organization and delineate its unique characteristics. Consequently, belief systems of individuals in governance and administrative roles are of particular significance; these values establish a climate and impact upon motivational forces within the organization.

The implementation of a human resources model of administration requires that attention is given to a number of variables including the administrative hierarchy, leadership, the decision-making process, communication, and control processes. Likert's work (1967) is of particular significance; his work provided an operationalization of a number of concepts.

Likert emphasized the importance of leadership and the belief systems of individuals who occupy pivotal roles. His principle of supportive relationships captures these issues succinctly:

> The leadership and other processes of the organization must be such as to ensure a maximum probability that in all interactions and in all relationships within the organization, each member, in the light of his background, values, desires, and expectations, will view the experience as supportive and one which builds his sense of personal worth and importance (Likert, 1961, p. 103).

In his work, Likert (1967) also identified six ingredients of organization: leadership, motivational, communication, decision making, goal setting, and control processes. These processes are common to any organization. However, the style of management that is practiced varies from one setting to another and determines, in Likert's terms, the effectiveness of the organization. Likert identified four distinct management systems: System 1 (exploitative-authoritarian), System 2 (benevolent-authoritarian), System 3 (consultative), and System 4 (participative). The most effective style, System 4, is characterized by a free flow of information, cooperative teamwork, widespread involvement in decision making, group goal setting, and the ready acceptance of responsibility on the part of individuals in the organization.

Likert's analysis (1967) of the process of activity in an organization based on causal, intervening, and end-result variables is instructive. This analysis provides particular insight into the change process and the influence of the needs and styles of leaders. Likert's work provides a useful conceptualization of the administrative process and focuses attention on the impact of causal variables including leadership. His work provides a very useful operationalization of significant variables and offers guidance for the implementation of human resource theory.

Decision making lies at the heart of the administrative process and, as Simon (1947) indicated, the manner in which decisions are made determines the structure of the organization. In the context of a school system, decisions about structuring require that attention is given to the decisions that are allocated to various levels and the role that various role incumbents play in the decision-making process.

In Regional School Unit 3, the responsibility for administration of the school system rested with four individuals, the superintendent of education and three assistant superintendents. Responsibilities were divided into three functional areas: administration, curriculum, and business. The superintendency team was designed to serve as a link between the school board and the school system. Along with the responsibility for planning and for the ongoing administration of the system, the team was responsible for representing the needs of the system and those of individual employees at the school board level.

The pivotal role of administrators at both the system and individual school levels was emphasized. Principals were asked to implement a participative mode of decision making at the individual school level. The objective was to involve, at appropriate stages, individuals or groups who had either expertise to contribute or a stake in the decision. Principals were encouraged to involve both their staffs and parents in appropriate decision issues. The involvement of parents occurred, for example, at a number of levels. Specific provisions were made for teacher-parent discussion regarding the progress of individual children. Eventually, parent-teacher organizations were established at each school.

The implementation of a participative approach to decision making placed significant demands on administrators at all levels of the school system. The time devoted to the decision-making process was increased substantially. In any decision strategy, consideration has to be given to the nature of the problem, the information required, and the available alternatives. The participative approach demands that time is devoted to planning the decision-making process. Issues concerning those who should be involved and the stages at which involvement should occur often receive more time and attention than the decision problem. The approach requires that individuals in pivotal administrative roles consider decision issues so that those who have expertise are appropriately involved in order to enhance the quality of the decision. Also, the involvement of stakeholders is critical in order to facilitate the implementation process. At the administrative level, both within the central office and in principals' meetings, the emphasis was on reaching decisions by consensus. Often, the time required to arrive at a conclusion was extended. However, the result was that additional information received consideration, and there was a stronger commitment to the implementation of the decision.

One of the early initiatives was the implementation of the concept of the school as the unit of education. This decision was based on a growing body of evidence which supported the idea that the individual school had nearly all the ingredients necessary to make education become a reality. The individual school with its principal, teachers, students, and parents was conceptualized as the unit for delivery of programs and of change. Each school was recognized to have a unique culture and tradition. It was felt that the individual school setting provided opportunities for day-to-day interaction among members of a staff. The individual school setting should therefore provide opportunities for a group of professionals to grow together and meet the needs of their students and the community.

The implementation of the concept of the school as the unit of education and change had significant implications for leadership and administrative behavior. First, in cases where the decision was considered to be best made by local school staffs, the Board and central office staff had to be prepared to delegate decision-making functions. This required the development of a spirit of cooperation within the school district and within schools. The approach required regular staff meetings which were devoted to the discussion of substantive issues. It required that staff in the district and in schools had to become committed to improving decision-making processes and utilizing the best knowledge available. The emphasis was on team planning, collegial decision making, and the development of a desire to achieve high levels of performance.

The focus on the individual school was based on a conviction that schools are fully fledged social systems. Development strategies which did not take account of this reality were deemed likely to achieve something less than success. Outer-initiated change approaches which did not take account of the culture of the individual school were discouraged. The challenge was to develop outer-initiated change processes which provided stimulation and alternatives and which were relevant to the needs of the school, its staff, and students. The model was designed to expand roles, enrich positions, and place trust and confidence in professionals at the school level. It was structured to increase the influence that individuals would have on the making of decisions.

In any delegation of decision-making functions, there is always the possibility that fragmentation will occur. The importance of providing for a free flow of information upward, downward, and laterally was recognized as a crucial administrative process. The importance of leadership was also an important consideration. Priority was given to administrator development opportunities which focused on leadership, decision-making skills, participative approaches to the solution of problems, communication skills, and staff development at the school level.

In order to facilitate the implementation of the concept of the individual school as the unit of education and change and provide for coordination, the school district was organized into three families of schools. Each consisted of a high school and its respective elementary and junior high feeder schools. The family structure provided a mechanism whereby problems associated with size were decreased. At the same time, the structure was designed to improve administration and coordination among schools which had responsibility for a child's education. Responsibility for the coordination of activities in each family rested with a chair who was a central office staff person. Frequently, principal's meetings were organized according to a family of schools format.

The definition of the family of schools structure was based on a curriculum and learning rationale. It suggested a need to examine curriculum as a continuum of learning experiences. It was designed to facilitate program development according to a Grade 1 to Grade 12 sequence rather than according to an elementary-secondary model. It provided a forum for the discussion of issues that are unique to feeder and receiving schools: promotion and placement, orientation programs for students before they moved to another level of school, communication among teachers who taught at the exit and entry grades, and professional development activities related to the sequence and continuity of curriculum.

The organization of the district according to a family of schools structure had a number of beneficial outcomes. Principals had a greater opportunity to become involved. The size of meeting groups facilitated participation. The issues which were discussed were more relevant to individuals and their schools, and principals were able to assume higher levels of responsibility for activities within the family of schools.

The family structure also provided a framework for the organization of professional development and in-service activities for teachers. A number of professional development days had a family focus. Teachers had an opportunity, for example, to review curriculum and share experiences within subject areas. Opportunities were provided so that teachers at the exit and entry grades could meet to share information about curriculum and the needs of particular students. Also, teachers organized social events within the family structure. Teachers expressed support for the family of schools structure and felt that they had an opportunity to influence events and share experiences with their colleagues.

The organization of professional development activities was an important initiative in the operation of the district. The initial step involved in the allocation of funds to individual schools and the decentralization of decision making and planning to school staffs. Each principal was requested to establish professional development committees within their school. The composition of professional development committees was left to the discretion of each school staff, however it was recommended that the school administration should be represented on the committee. A number of suggestions were made for the operation of school-based professional development committees; these included the following:

☆ After consulting with the total school staff, establish priorities for the professional development program within the school for the year;

☆ Communicate with the system level professional development committee and the school administration;

☆ Allocate school-based funds to professional development activities;

☆ Accept requests for travel and make recommendations to the school administration;

☆ Plan school and family workshop days that are relevant to the needs and goals of the school and/or the family of schools;

☆ Plan ongoing professional development activities that are relevant to the needs and goals of the schools; and

☆ Evaluate the effectiveness of professional development activities based on the goals and priorities of the school.

The successful implementation of change requires leadership abilities and technical and human skills. The change in approach to the planning for professional development placed new responsibilities on teachers who were members of school-based staff development committees. In order to provide an opportunity for members of school-based committees to develop skills, yearly workshops were held. At the workshops, the emphasis was on process rather than content, and participants were exposed to the theory on which the school-based staff development model was developed. In addition, areas such as needs assessment techniques, and the processes of consultation, planning, and establishing goals were included. The members of school-based committees gained skills in consultation, needs assessment, and decision making, and were able to apply these skills in the planning of professional development programs.

Administrator development activities were planned by a team of principals and central office staff. The focus was on the development of skills in areas such as leadership, decision making, coordination, participative management, and goal setting. Substantive developments and trends in education were also included in administrator development sessions. These programs were organized for principals, vice-principals, and central office staff. The result was that administrators had an opportunity to learn human resource management philosophies and techniques. The administrator development program also had the effect of creating social bonds and a sense of professionalism among administrators.

After years of working on the implementation of human resources theory, it was evident to outside observers and individuals within the system that these efforts had an impact. Principals identified with the approach and often expressed appreciation for the extent of their involvement in decision making. There were genuine attempts to implement a human resources approach in schools. Teachers appreciated the philosophy and often expressed the view that their needs were being represented. The opportunities that were available for teachers to comment on policy proposals gave teachers a sense that their concerns were important.

Objective measures of the perceptions of principals indicated that they perceived the school district to be operating at the lower end of Likert's (1961) System 4 model of organization.

Likert (1967) has described a number of characteristics of the System 4 or participative group system of organization. There is confidence and trust throughout the organization. Group participation is used in goal-setting, improving methodology, and appraising progress toward the achievement of goals. Communication channels are open, and communication efforts are effective. Cooperative teamwork occurs throughout the organization. There is widespread acceptance of responsibility, and individuals have high performance goals.

The implementation of new approaches is never a linear event. In any organization, time and effort have to be devoted to the solution of immediate problems, crises, and the demands of routine administration. During the decade from 1976 to 1986, the school district was presented with many issues. Declining enrollments, the movement of student populations into the suburbs, school construction, and increasing demands for new and improved programs all required time and energy. At times, these issues consumed most of the time and energy in the administrative system of the district. However, there was a conscious effort to apply human resource strategies to the resolution of issues. Consequently, individuals in the system and parents developed a sense of trust and confidence in the decision-making process.

Life Cycle Changes

Individuals act on the basis of their convictions. Differences in beliefs are the fodder for conflict in many human endeavors. Within an organization, the expectations that result from role definitions are also significant determinants of harmony or discord. Each role incumbent enters the position with a set of values and an agenda for action. Expectations are also created by constituencies. These dynamics always present challenges for the functioning of an organization. The risks are increased when role incumbents assume joint responsibility for achieving important objectives in an organization.

The functioning of a school system is often accompanied by some conflict and controversy. School boards are required to make choices within constraints that are imposed by the unavailability of resources. Special interest groups often make demands for consideration. Consequently, during a term of office, a school board and individual trustees have the opportunity to adopt a wide variety of approaches. A school board can be operated as a corporate body; in this case, the board influences events through policy initiatives. Another alternative is to attempt to placate special interest groups and, in the process, become involved in administrative matters.

Individual trustees also have some discretion about their mode of operation. The individual can function as a member of a corporate body and exert influence from a policy perspective. Others may play a more concrete role by representing the demands of special interest groups and the complaints of individual parents. Often, the latter approach is accompanied by lobbying and other attempts to influence decisions through informal channels. In this mode, the potential for the development of misunderstandings and conflict is greatly increased.

One event which engaged the trustees of Regional School Unit 3 in a difficult issue concerned the adoption of a policy on family life education. Following the receipt of a committee report, the board decided to bring forth a policy proposal. This initiative sparked the interest of many parents and community groups. Some argued that the education system could not adequately deliver a family life education program. These individuals felt that the teaching of sensitive value issues should be left to parents and the church. Those who supported the introduction of family life education programs were adamant that the school had a significant role. As Superintendent of Education, I adopted the position that the elected trustees should decide value issues, and that the role of staff was to carry out research and provide information about program alternatives.

The final vote on the proposal for a family life education policy occurred at a public board meeting on April 18, 1984. About 600 members of the public attended the meeting, and a number of individuals, many of whom were vehemently opposed to the proposal, made presentations. The motion to adopt the policy proposal was carried by a narrow margin. Following the meeting, the administration adopted a procedure whereby a family life advisory committee with school staff and parent representation was to be established at each school. The committees were to promote parental awareness, peruse materials, approve supplementary materials, and carry out a yearly review. The establishment of the policy split trustees along ideological lines and created a concerned group of parents. It also placed senior staff in a difficult intermediary position.

In the Spring of 1985, elections were held for seven of the fifteen seats on the board. The issue of family life education and the role of schools in the delivery of family life programs was one of the underlying issues, and a number of individuals who were concerned about the policy were elected. Some of these individuals indicated that they planned to carefully monitor family life education programs.

One of the results of these events was to shift the underlying values upon which the board operated. A coalition of trustees opposed to family life education programming began to work together. Much of this activity was informal, but it was obvious to observers that there was collaboration. A number of trustees appeared to want more control and power. There was increasing involvement in administrative matters, and the demarcation between policy and administration became increasingly unstable. Complaints from parents which, in other circumstances, would have been handled routinely, became major issues which required full scale investigations. The approach that was taken by some trustees appeared to be based on the assumption that the amount of power that was available in the organization was fixed, and that some power had to be taken away from schools, administrators, and teachers. These beliefs were in direct conflict with a human resources approach, one of the underlying assumptions of which is the belief that the amount of power in an organization is variable (Strauss, 1963). In the thinking of human resource theorists, the amount of power that is available is increased as people become more involved in the decision-making process and are empowered to take responsibility for their work.

Tichy (1980) has postulated that there are three interrelated cycles which reflect the ongoing dynamics of the organization as a social system. The three cycles represent problems associated with technical design, political allocation, and ideological and cultural mix. Throughout the 1985-1986 school year, it was evident that, within the operations of the board, the technical design cycle was stable, but that both the political allocation and the cultural mix cycles were beginning to consume more energy, and stress was increasing. The terms of the political allocation cycle, uncertainty developed about whether trustees or administrators had power to make certain decisions. Some trustees became concerned about becoming involved in decision issues which had formerly been settled by administrative staff. Confusion about roles and role relationships occurred, stress increased, and it was becoming evident that a significant problem was developing. Uncertainty was also increasing in the cultural mix cycle. The result of the elections of 1985 was that five of the fifteen trustees were first term incumbents, and a number appeared to represent an ideological position which was antithetical to a human resources approach. Networks and alliances were gradually established and the *modus operandi* of the board changed.

Crisis Politics

After ten years in the role, I resigned from the position of Superintendent of Education on September 9, 1985. The effective date of the resignation was December 31, 1986. The resignation was decided upon after I concluded that the principles of administration in which I believed would be significantly compromised, and that I could not be effective in my role. The final catalyst for making the decision to resign concerned the manner in which the school board executive handled assessment. In 1985, the board engaged an outside consultant to evaluate my performance. The consultant received feedback from trustees, central office staff, and principals. The evaluation included a norm-referenced instrument, and the results placed my performance at the high end in comparison to the normative group. In the Spring of 1986, the board chairman wrote an assessment for the year and documented a number of successful initiatives. However, at a subsequent board meeting, it was evident that a small number of trustees disagreed with a human resources approach to the administration of the system. These individuals prevailed upon the chairman who was persuaded to attempt to have additional comments entered in my personal file. The items concerned day-to-day administrative matters and, in earlier times, would not have been matters of concern to trustees. The issue of greatest concern to me involved process. The manner in which the issue was handled demonstrated to me that the methodologies of administration in which I firmly believed were no longer part of the ideology for a number of the trustees. Trust had been broken, ideologies were at variance, and bias was mobilized against a human resources approach. The conspiracy, conscious or unconscious, bore its fruits.

One week following the resignation, the media reported that the Chairman had stated that I had resigned for personal reasons. This statement, I felt, was capable of many interpretations, and it was not accurate. I had not made any reference to personal reasons in the letter of resignation. Following consultation with a legal advisor, I determined that the public record had to be corrected. Consequently, I issued a statement in which I indicated that I had made no reference to personal reasons as being the cause of the resignation, and that I stated in the letter that the resignation was based on matters of principle.

In retrospect, it is evident that these early events had a significant influence on the development of a long and difficult crisis for the school district and for the individuals involved. Until the occurrence of these events, the issues were a matter for only a small number of individuals, the trustees and senior staff in the central office. The theatre quickly became much larger. A number of groups with the option to remain fascinated as spectators choose to become involved. The entrance of the larger audience, school district staff, parents, and the provincial teachers' organization was to have a significant impact on the development and resolution of the crisis. The spectators are "a part of the calculus of all conflicts," (Schattschneider, 1960, p. 66) and, in this case, had a significant impact on the development of events.

One week after the resignation, the central office staff and the principals in the district presented separate Briefs to the Board. In both presentations, concern was expressed that the resignation signaled a change in philosophy and direction. The Board was asked to clarify its position and affirm its belief in the philosophy of administration under which the system had operated.

Within a short time, the issue became front page news. Speculation about the resignation and questions about the manner in which the Board was functioning began to appear in newspaper articles and on television reports. One editorial called on the Chairman to clarify the issue and provide an adequate report to the public. A few days later a trustee issued a prepared statement which was critical of the manner in which the Board had functioned. Throughout the crisis, this individual would continue to play the role of the loyal opposition. In the meantime, the Board made no attempt to clarify the reasons for the resignation. This decision was apparently taken after the Board had received legal advice. It was a decision that was likely motivated by a fear that the Board could split into factions, and that the procedures and processes which the Board had been employing would not stand up to public scrutiny. At the least, it represented an attempt to control the agenda and prevent issues from becoming issues.

The annual meeting of the Board was held in one of the district high schools on October 1, three weeks after the resignation. Typically, annual meetings attracted only a small representation from the public and a few members of staff. On this occasion, over 500 people attended the meeting. There was extensive media coverage. Briefs were presented by the local teachers' organization and by the provincial organization. These presentations called for a clarification of the Board's position. In the Brief from the provincial teachers' organization, it was suggested that the Board was not following its own policies, that the failure to deal publicly with the issue was destroying confidence, and that trustees were engaging in teacher bashing. Finally, the Brief suggested that, if the rumors that were circulating in the educational community were founded, the Board Executive should resign. In total, eighteen members of the public made presentations to the meeting.

Eight days after the annual meeting, the Board sent out replies to all the parties who had made written submissions. In these replies, it was stated that the Board would not discuss the reasons for the resignation. Furthermore, in the reply to the provincial teachers' organization, the statement included an assurance that the philosophy of the Board was intact. In each case, the reply concluded with a statement that a committee composed of community, staff, and trustee representation would be established. This Committee was given a mandate to study roles, rebuild a viable communication system, and study the philosophy, direction, goals, and objectives of the school district. The Board appointed a well-known member of the local clergy to chair the Committee. The intent of the individuals who drafted the terms of reference for the Committee appeared to represent an effort to buy time for a cooling off period. The plan was that the Committee would not examine the resignation, but would engage in a period of study.

The appointment of the Special Committee did not have the effect of containing and settling the crisis. On the contrary, a number of the events which occurred over the next few months brought the Board into a deeper crisis. One of these involved the resignation of a second senior staff member. On December 10, the Superintendent of Administration submitted his resignation. This second resignation was announced without explanation. This event refueled speculation about the functioning of the Board and, once again, brought the issue back into the headlines. One trustee again publicly criticized the Board for its silence on the resignation. Individual parents and home and school organizations began a campaign to have the Board explain its actions.

The Board was faced with another issue which required resolution by the end of December. The legislation under which the Board operated mandated that school boards were required to have a superintendent of education in their employment. My resignation was effective on December 31. Consequently, it was necessary to effect an appointment before that date. The Board decided to engage an out-of-province consulting firm to advertise and create a short list of applicants for the position. The teachers' organization criticized the decision. They argued that the decision should be delayed until the Special Committee made its Report and that teachers had not been consulted about the decision. Teachers and principals subsequently declined when the consultant sought input concerning the qualities which would be desirable in candidates for the position. Time was not adequate for the recruitment and selection of a candidate prior to the end of year deadline. With time running out, the Board made arrangements with an individual to assume the position on an acting basis for the balance of the school year.

Eventually, following the Board's rejection of a request from the teachers' organization that a teacher be placed on the interviewing panel for the selection of a superintendent of education, the teachers' organization applied to the Supreme Court for an injunction to restrain the Board from proceeding with the selection. The organization also requested that its members and those of other teachers' organizations refrain from submitting applications for the position. These events led to charges and counter charges which were played out in the media for a fascinated public.

In the meantime, the Special Committee proceeded with its work and, over objections from the Board, decided to investigate the reasons for the resignations. Although there were initial disagreements between the Board and the Special Committee about the mandate of the Committee, the Committee proceeded to hear private submissions from individuals including board members. The Committee sat for over fifty hours and gathered over 170 pages of notes and evidence. The Report of the Special Committee was presented at a public board meeting in February, 1987.

The Report was immediately endorsed by the provincial teachers' organization, but the response of the Board was the opposite. The Board attacked the Committee and its Report. In a prepared release, the Board called the Report "biased" and "vindictive." The Committee, which included two trustees among its nine members, was also reprimanded for failure to address two of the three terms of reference in its mandate. There was also a strong reaction to the fact that a section of the Report which dealt with my resignation had been vetted by me prior to the board meeting. In fact, such consultation is considered appropriate when individuals are named in a report, and no change of substance occurred as a result of the consultation. Nevertheless, the Board used the incident in an apparent attempt to discredit the Report of the Committee.

Iannaccone (1967) has observed that, in the typical political crisis, governments are often called upon to settle disputes when there is public controversy about ideological assumptions. In junior governments, with delegated powers, the intervention of the senior government can be expected. In this sense, events proceeded in a predictable fashion following the release of the Board's reaction to the Report of the Special Committee. Increasingly, pressure was mounting for the Minister of Education to intervene. Within hours after the release of the Board's comments, the Minister of Education issued a public statement which called for the resignation of all trustees in the district. Only two of the fifteen resigned. The remainder argued that the Minister of Education had no legislative authority to intervene, and that the action was undemocratic. Within days, the Lieutenant Governor-in-Council ordered a public inquiry.

The Order of the Lieutenant Governor-in-Council provided for the appointment of a Supreme Court Justice as Commissioner and directed an inquiry and report upon the circumstances leading to the erosion of effective relationships within the school district, how these relationships might be re-established, and ways in which roles might be better defined. The Commissioner was given wide powers to call evidence and witnesses, engage staff, and exercise all the powers conferred under the legislation concerning public inquiries.

The staff of the Commission proceeded by carrying out a study of relevant legislation, minutes of school board meetings, policies, the Report of the Special Committee, and other documentary materials. The Commission staff undertook interviews of a large number of persons including current and former trustees, central office staff, principals, some teachers, and representatives of teachers', trustees', and parents' organizations. After completing these activities, the Commission decided to produce a Report (1987) of their investigation and to recommend that public hearings were unnecessary. They reported that the public concerns arose when the Board did not make an accounting to the public when the issue became one of public concern. The Report did outline a chronology of events over the preceding months and obtained agreements from the parties to refrain from using the media to resolve their disputes and to begin the process of establishing relationships. The Board gave an understanding to implement the recommendations contained in the Report of the Special Committee. The teachers' organization withdrew its application for a court injunction to restrain the Board from engaging a superintendent of education. The Minister of Education withdrew the request for the resignation of trustees. In the meantime, another senior staff person resigned and accepted a position with a university. A crisis that had developed in the early part of the school year survived and intensified for some nine months until the Report of the Commission was published in May, 1987. The quantification of the long term impact of the crisis may be difficult.

Discussion

Explanations of the change process in an organization require the use of concepts that transcend an analysis of roles and the study of individual personalities. Tichy's concepts (1980) concerning technical, political, and cultural cycles provide a rationale for the explanation of events in the life cycle of an organization. The school district example provides an opportunity to review the application of the theory and suggest possible additional considerations.

In an educational organization, there is always some instability in the technical cycle. Cause-effect relationships between teaching and learning are always at issue. There are various competing theories about the means that should be used to achieve results. Individual differences among clients complicate the issue immensely. These characteristics are, however, typical of educational organizations, and the case under discussion did not exhibit any evidence of a peak or high level of uncertainty in the technical cycle.

The cultural cycle did exhibit signs of uncertainty for a period of time before the crisis. A change in the cultural mix occurred about a year before the crisis when school board elections changed the mix of trustees. Values and ideologies are not always immediately evident. Consequently, these subtle changes were unnoticed by most observers and many of the participants. However, subtle changes in values can be pervasive. Furthermore, a change in the cultural mix problem is perhaps the most difficult to influence because of its ideological roots.

The peak in the cultural mix cycle provided a navigation route for the development of uncertainty in the political cycle. The transition from ideological differences to a shift in agreement about the functioning of the organization was relatively easy and perhaps inevitable. Requests from trustees for additional information, the increasing involvement in administrative matters, and the tendency to set aside information and recommendations provided by staff were all indicators of an increasing level of stress. Tichy (1980) hypothesized that one of the triggers for a change in the political cycle is a shift in agreement over methods. However, cycles trigger other cycles. In this case, the peak in the political cycle was preceded by a peak in the cultural cycle. The peak in the cultural cycle did not subside when the political cycle began its incline. The consequence was that there was concurrent action in two change cycles, and the organization came under heavy stress. In fact, the cycles remained at a high level of uncertainty over a period of time while the crisis was gathering momentum, and the organization almost unraveled.

While it is evident that change cycles take on a life of their own, it is also obvious that cycles are influenced by the participants and the problem solving skills of the players. The skills that are appropriate for the solution of technical problems are of little value in the solution of problems in the cultural and political allocation cycles (Iannaccone & Cistone, 1974; Tichy, 1980). The uncertainty that occurs in the technical cycle is the result of problems with production and effectiveness. This type of uncertainty is best managed by maintaining an equilibrium between the information required to complete the task and the information that is actually available. The use of human resources administration with its emphasis on information, flow, and involvement in decision making is an illustration of the skills that are required to maintain certainty in the technical cycle. On the other hand, the political cycle is managed by negotiation, compromise, and the sharing of power. Furthermore, technical problems generally fall within the jurisdiction of administrative roles, and administrators can more easily assume leadership roles in matters related to the technical cycle. Leadership and preventative action in matters concerning political allocation problems or the ideological and cultural mix dimension cannot be assumed as easily by individuals in administrative roles. These cycles involve wider issues which are concerned with goals, the allocation of resources, and the representation of values. Consequently, these issues are more significantly influenced by those in governance roles.

Responsibility for governance in most school systems rests with school boards. Therefore, the manner in which school boards are constituted and function in an important consideration. Trustees are elected to an office which bestows position power. The qualifications for the position are limited to matters such as age and residency. The trustee usually does not have experience in educational administration and teaching. Furthermore, incumbents do not have the opportunity to gain experience incrementally. Legislation concerning the functioning of school boards is usually general, and there is a lack of clarity in role definitions. Roles and guidelines have to be invented and are subject to drift. This creates a vacuum in the structure, and encourages the promotion of individual agendas. Typically, there is inadequate time for the appropriate study and consideration of issues. In this climate, the use of formal rules of order and the resolution of issues by formal voting often leads to win-loss decision making. The use of consensus decision making and win-win decision strategies would have a beneficial impact on the health of school organization.

The question of mandate is also relevant. In many instances, there is a high level of voter apathy, and trustees are elected by a small percentage of the population. Often, the electorate is unaware of the qualifications and beliefs of candidates. Once elected, there is little in the way of a system of checks and balances. Parents generally ignore the operation of a school board unless there is a crisis or a specific issue which has direct impact. For the most part, the media give more energy and resources to the coverage of higher levels of government. Finally, there is the absence of a legitimate, loyal opposition. Consequently, there is no formal mechanism by which to channel dissenting views, force the articulation of beliefs, and resolve conflicts. Indeed, it is a tribute to many of the individuals who are elected to school boards that the system works as well as it does.

A common response in the management of a crisis is to close ranks and attempt to create a cohesive group. It has been argued that the decisions of the governance system, in the end, serve the interests of those who hold the power. If there is a tendency toward the "Iron Law of Oligarchy," (Michels, 1966) a crisis in governance will tend to accelerate the process. In these situations, energies are devoted to the survival of the governance structure and the protection of the reputations and careers of those who control the structure. Dissension, if it is tolerated, is scorned. However, the tendency toward the "Iron Law" often moves in the direction of a polyarchy when the audience decides to participate and exercise their dispersed power.

A critical element in the events which occurred in the school district was the fact that staff had developed a set of expectations as a result of their exposure to human resources administration. Over the years, administrators, teachers, and other staff had developed a sense of confidence and trust in the administrative process. A common set of values and beliefs had developed. Individuals in the system had expectations about involvement in decision making, open communication, and the sharing of information. Inadequate responses from the Board in the early stages of the crisis confirmed suspicions about a change in ideology and direction. Sensing that this was an issue of significance, staff and their supporting organizations joined with conviction.

Parents also have a significant stake in the operation of their schools. Parents delegate some of their responsibility to an institution of the state with the expectation that their children will have an adequate opportunity to succeed. Given the aspirations that parents naturally have for their children, it is not surprising that parents expect that resources and energies will be devoted to the primary task of the school. The diversion of time and energy to a crisis in political processes is a strategy that is certain to increase interest and concern. In fact, in this case, the concerns became sufficiently persistent and intensive to cause a higher level of government to intervene. The mode of the intervention, the request for resignations, was dramatic. The fact that it was done in the absence of legislative authority provided a demonstration of the willingness of the senior government to respond to concerned public.

The events which occurred in this instance are not predicted by human resources theory. On the contrary, human resources theorists hypothesize organizational health and productivity. Why, in this case, did the attempt to implement human resources strategies coincide with a crisis? The answer can be discovered by considering the nature of organizations and the differences that often exist among levels of an organization. In this instance, the use of the human resources approach had been attempted over a period of time at the administrative level. However, at the governance level, another set of assumptions applied, and win-lose strategies were in evidence. It is also probable that the techniques that are at the core of the human resources approach are less applicable to the resolution of crises that have cultural and ideological foundations. In fact, in this instance, the fact that human resources theory had been accepted by many people in the organization intensified the crisis.

Conclusion

The experience in the school system provided a demonstration of an attempt to implement human resources theory. Over a period of time, professionals in the system developed a strong allegiance to the approach. However, the case did provide an illustration of the fact that it is possible to have variant beliefs and approaches at different levels of an organization and the consequences which may result from such differences.

When school board elections resulted in a change in board membership, prevailing values were changed, and the cultural mix cycle began to peak and cause stress. This event triggered a peak in the political allocation cycle. With two organizational cycles peaking and creating high levels of uncertainty, the organization was vulnerable. A political crisis ensued following the failure of governance processes.

The depth of the crisis was intensified by two characteristics of the organization. The human resources approach was widely embraced within the school district. The possibility of change created anxieties for staff and their professional organization. This reaction placed additional pressures on the governance system. Consequently, the stress in the political cycle was intensified beyond the level that might be expected. Another contributing factor to the depth of the crisis was the inability of the Board Executive to apply appropriate strategies such as bargaining and compromise to the solution of issues as the political cycle began to peak. The result was loss of control and intervention by a higher level of government. The events were influenced by historical antecedents in the organization. The system administration which had been implemented impacted on the dynamics of the crisis. The case suggests that the dynamic interplay among life cycles in an organization are dependent upon the individual history and circumstances of the organization.

Epilogue

Elections for eight of the fifteen positions on the Board were held in the Spring of 1987. The Chairman did not reoffer. The Vice

Chairman reoffered and was defeated. The trustee who played the role of the loyal opposition and resigned in response to the request from the Minister of Education, reoffered, was re-elected, and became Chairman of the Board. Most incumbent trustees did not reoffer. The trustee who had been Board Secretary during the crisis did not reoffer at the expiration of his term in 1989.

References

Argyris, C. (1964). *Integrating the individual and the organization*. New York: Wiley.

Canada, Province of Prince Edward Island. (1987). *Report: Public inquiries act, commission of inquiry on regional administrative school unit 3*. Charlottetown, PEI: Author.

Iannaccone, L. & Cistone, P. J. (1974). *The politics of education*. Eugene, Oregon: ERIC Clearinghouse on Educational Management.

Likert, R. (1961). *New patterns of management*. New York: McGraw-Hill.

Likert, R. (1967). *The human organization: Its management and value*. New York: McGraw-Hill.

McGregor, D. (1960). *The human side of enterprise*. New York: McGraw-Hill.

Michels, R. (1966). *Political parties*. New York: Free Press.

Miles, R. E. (1971). Human relations or human resources? In D. A. Kell, I. M. Rubin & J. M. McIntyre (Eds.), *Organizational psychology* (pp. 253-264). Englewood Cliffs: Prentice Hall.

Schattschneider, E. E. (1960). *The semisovereign people*. New York: Holt, Rinehart and Winston.

Simon, H. A. (1947). *Administrative behavior: A study of decision-making processes in administrative organization*. New York: Free Press.

Strauss, C. (1963). Some notes on power equalization. In H. J. Leavitt (Ed.). *The social science of organizations* (pp. 45-59). Englewood Cliffs: Prentice Hall.

Tichy, N. M. (1980). Problem cycles in organizations and the management of change. In J. R. Kimberly, R. H. Miles & Associates (Eds.), *The organization life cycle: Issues in the creation, transformation and decline of organizations* (pp. 164-183). San Francisco: Jossey-Bass.

6

Parent Participation in Rural Schooling

Peter Bruce Wiebe and Peter James Murphy

Introduction

Over the next decade, Canadian provincial school systems are going to be subjected to substantive social forces which will require them to modify many functions. In fact, the public schools of tomorrow will differ significantly from those of today. Until recently, public schools throughout the country provided children with a rather standardized education which satisfied adequately most of their immediate needs. This basic schooling has evolved gradually from the beginning of the century when the small, white school house in many areas of the country provided sound instruction in the three Rs. An incremental approach to policy making has undoubtedly characterized Canadian public schools. Consequently, many people find it difficult to believe that schools of tomorrow will differ very much from these of the present. This rather myopic view of society fails to give due consideration to the dynamic forces operating in our contemporary world.

Most school districts in Canada, until the late fifties, were flat organizations with well established chains of command and frequent professional interaction between field-based staff and senior control office administrators. As course offerings diversified and support services expanded, many school districts developed into tall organizations, usually comprising of a substantial number of central office staff. Over a relatively short period of time, these school districts have evolved into complex bureaucracies with all the advantages and disadvantages of this type of organizational structure.

Since the early sixties, Canadian public schools have undergone many reforms, but very few have continued for any extended period of time. Of the reforms which have survived, child-centred learning has been one of the most significant. Most learning experiences, as a consequence of this pedagogical focus, have become more personalized. If children are viewed as individuals, then learning experiences must be designed to accommodate their unique needs.

When funds for schooling declined during the late seventies and early eighties, most learning experiences continued to focus on the child as an independent learner. In fact, children with special needs, namely the gifted and the handicapped, were provided with additional services in this period of constraint. Consequently, child-centred learning can be expected to be the focus of public schooling in Canada for several decades to come.

Most Canadians have enjoyed a high standard of living for many years. This prosperity has enabled individuals to satisfy many of their personal desires; a situation which has resulted in the consumer market becoming more and more sophisticated. Many companies will now provide, if requested by customers, specially designed products. People appear to want more choice when they go shopping and companies are endeavoring to respond to this desire.

Greater choice, specialized goods, and customizing of products has recently become apparent in the service sector of the Canadian economy. Parents now desire, more than ever in the past, that their children receive special instruction or special services while attending school. Quite naturally, this change in demand for schooling has had and will continue to have a significant impact on Canadian provincial school systems. Both educational programs and support services are being diversified as conditions permit.

The supply side of education has been similarly subjected to substantial social forces. Of these forces, tight fiscal policies have had the greatest impact on school systems and individual institutions. Simultaneously, demands for all types of school services have intensified, which has increased the competition among agencies for federal and provincial government funding. Since school systems do not usually compete very successfully with other social service organizations, most of them have received fewer resources than they have requested in recent years. Also, continued inflation has reduced in "real" terms the value of the funds which provincial school systems have been allocated.

Greater demands for accountability generated by public resistance to additional taxes has required school systems to report achievements, costs, and activities in more precise terms. A new era of "payment by results" appears to be emerging. The resultant outcome has been slow growth in the supply of special learning experiences and support services offered by public schools.

The discrepancy between the supply of and the demand for new learning experiences and special services in Canadian provincial school systems is increasing, possibly at a geometric rate of growth. To avoid a political crisis, provincial governments have been recently encouraging a greater decentralization of school governance through a variety of forms of school-based management. This more democratic form of governance encourages both parents and teachers to become more involved in school affairs which not only assigns them greater decision-making powers, but usually delegates to them more responsibility for financial matters. The new school councils which have been formed to facilitate parents and teachers becoming involved in managing schools are required to allocate effectively funds schools receive via the school districts from the provincial government. Any additional resources schools may desire usually have to be obtained from other sources, more specifically, the local community or the "users" of the school system.

Parental Involvement in Schooling

Parent participation in Canadian public schools is not something new. For decades parents throughout the country have participated in various ways in the schooling of their children. Most of this involvement, as everyone is aware, has been primarily concerned with school activities of marginal importance. The "real" parent participation in provincial school systems has been at the school district level where elective officials, known as trustees, perform a variety of governance functions. School boards, as Wiebe (1989) notes, "are expected to answer parent questions and are ever increasingly being held accountable for the assessment and improvement of programmes" (p. 30). Therefore, school trustees not only represent parents, but are responsible for directing and shaping the future direction of the public schools in their educational jurisdictions.

Recently, trustees have encountered increasing difficulty performing their duties in a manner which seems to satisfy adequately many people in the local community. This phenomenon is occurring as a consequence of the dynamic social, economic, political, and cultural forces operating in contemporary society. People want more customized learning experiences for their children, as mentioned earlier, which large school districts have difficulty providing. Greater adversity between school trustees and the public whom they represent can be expected to arise in the future as the desires of various interest groups and individuals are thwarted. This conflict can be reduced substantially by the introduction of some form of school based management which transfers the responsibility for many school functions from central office staff and trustees to school based administrators, teachers, and parents. A smaller organizational unit, as in this case the local school, is able to respond more effectively and promptly to changing societal conditions than a larger one.

As school governance becomes more centralized, Canadian provincial school systems will evolve into organizations characterized by small autonomous units, shorter chains of command, regular interaction among staff at all levels, a more rapid response to consumer demands and a higher level of collaboration between the user and the supplier of educational services. The new autonomous, locally managed school which will emerge as a consequence of dynamic societal forces, will develop and grow in accordance with the desires of the school staff and the local community. Toffler (1980), in his well known text *The Third Wave*, speaks of the "electronic cottage;" here we have emerging the "autonomous school" as a consequence of the same forces. Both these institutions are products of a technologically complex and socially diverse society characterized by continuous change.

Are teachers prepared to open their classroom doors and share responsibilities with parents? Di Silvestro (1985) perceives the issue is not whether parents should be involved in school affairs, but how they might be encouraged to become effectively involved. Furthermore, as this scholar emphasizes, parents who volunteer to participate in the schooling of their children are one of the most enduring sources of support for a school.

For the new management partnerships to be effective all interest groups associated with schooling must be committed to the concept of participatory decision making. Without this commitment, these partnerships are reduced to making decisions on marginal school activities. Another factor which has a significant impact on the effectiveness of the new partnerships is the attitude of the principal. As Sills (1979) so astutely notes, "the success of change-oriented parent association groups is so often dependent upon the degree of support received from the principal of the school in question" (p. 45). When initiating new ideas in schools, principals by virtue of their pivotal role in the system, knowledge, and interaction with all interest groups often decide whether a proposed intervention will be accepted or not.

Recent research on effective schooling seems to suggest that a greater involvement of parents in the management of a school has a very positive impact on the effectiveness of an institution (Leithwood & Montgomery, 1985; Long, 1986; Maurer, 1985; and Moles, 1982). However as Sandfoot (1987) points out, parents tend to become less involved in school affairs as their children move from elementary school to junior high school to senior high school. According to Wiebe (1989):

> Complexity of subject matter and a greater generation gap between parents and their teenagers . . . have increased the walls that separate home and parent involvement in the high school classes (p. 39).

How to encourage parent groups who traditionally have not been involved in school management to become more active participants in school affairs needs to be investigated before school-based management becomes applied more extensively.

No reform is without some shortcomings. Many people may become members of a school council because they have a specific "axe to grind." Parents from lower socio-economic groups may be reluctant to seek election because of limited knowledge of the public school system, a lack of confidence, and attending meetings is difficult. Similarly, certain ethnic groups may not become involved in school management because their culture has never encouraged or supported parent involvement in schooling. These circumstances may produce a school council which is not representative of the socio-economic milieu and cultural mix of the local community. Hence, the socio-economic groups on a school council may advance their own interests at the expense of others.

If parents are to effectively perform a variety of managerial tasks, they quite naturally require special training. To expect individuals with limited knowledge of public schooling and management to complete satisfactorily complex tasks is unrealistic. Yet many parents are, in fact, performing their duties without appropriate training. This "muddling through" approach to decision making is unsatisfactory and usually generates high levels of frustration, anxiety, and conflict. What is more serious for children is that inappropriate management can result in valuable and limited resources being wasted unnecessarily.

As the School-Based Management Movement gains momentum and autonomous schools become more common, rural school districts in northern Canada will want to experiment with this new form of school governance. Traditionally, small rural communities have been characterized by a unique culture and community spirit which will strongly support any schools interested in acquiring greater independence and autonomy. In a rural area, as Wiebe (1989) notes: "Just as the community depends on the school, so the school depends upon its parents" (p. 19).

Rural schools, due to the unique conditions under which they operate, must function as open social systems encouraging and facilitating interrelationships among staff, students, and community members. The special culture of rural schools and their geographical isolation has resulted in many of them functioning as independent education entities. Consequently, the introduction of school-based management will legitimize an organization's structure and mode of governance which has been existing in many rural communities for several decades in a simpler form.

A review of professional literature reveals that research on rural schooling in Canada is rather limited. Even more scarce is research in the management of rural schools and parent involvement in school affairs. Therefore, any initiatives to introduce some form of school-based management in the rural schools of northern Canada will be at risk. Although conditions appear conducive for establishing autonomous schools in rural areas, insufficient knowledge and lack of training opportunities for participants may result in experimental ventures concluding in failure.

The Collaborative Management Cycle

Most rural schools in British Columbia are usually at a distance from urban centres of large rural communities. This isolation produces communities with many unique characteristics. The small school which provides local children with numerous educational services plays an important role, as one might expect, in the life of a community. Riedl (1988) believes that a rural school, since it acts as a resource to the community as a whole, "should be an agent of change and prompt local development rather than just react to it" (p. 33). School and community must complement each other and build upon, as Maxwell (1989) emphasizes "the unique opportunities and natural advantages inherent between them and their communities" (p. 24).

To facilitate interaction between schools and communities, a number of boundary-spanning organizations have been established over the past fifty years. Of these organizations, the most well known, and perhaps the most effective over an extended period, have been parent-teacher associations, school councils, and school management committees which have brought parents, teachers, and the general public together on a regular basis to discuss school affairs. Through these organizations, values, concerns, and expectations are voiced which enable schools to be more responsive to the changing needs of society.

Most parent-teacher boundary spanning organizations in the past have involved themselves in issues of marginal importance in the operation of a school (e.g. bake sales). Since the early eighties, this situation has changed drastically in many countries. Presently, school systems throughout the world are being encouraged to experiment with school-based management or have been directed through legislation to facilitate a greater involvement of teachers, parents, and the general public in school management. These new partnerships differ from those of the past in many ways. Of these differences, one of the most significant is that parents and teachers with administrators, and sometimes government officials, will be responsible for making decisions that may have a direct impact on the quality of learning experiences offered to children (e.g. establishing budget priorities).

Professional literature and research on effective schooling suggests that by involving a wide cross-section of a school's community in decision-making activities, the achievement of students is usually enhanced substantially. Participation in the management of a school, as Wiebe (1989) notes, appears to generate for the individuals concerned a sense of responsibility, a commitment to approved policies, and a feeling of personal ownership in the success of a school. The conducive climate for learning which this participation in school affairs creates, as might be expected, has a very positive impact on children.

Recently, Caldwell and Spinks (1988) developed a model, known as the Collaborative Management Cycle, to extend our understanding of the various activities associated with school-based management. This cyclical process, as shown in Figure 1, consists of six distinct decision-making centres, namely: (1) Goal-Setting, (2) Policy Making, (3) Planning, (4) Budgeting, (5) Implementing and (6) Evaluating. To facilitate the prompt and effective completion of various tasks associated with managing a school, the decision-making centres are assigned the responsibility of two distinct groups.

The first group, known as the "policy group," consists of parents, teachers, administrators, and members of the general public. These individuals are responsible for providing a school with

Figure 1: The Collaborative Management Cycle

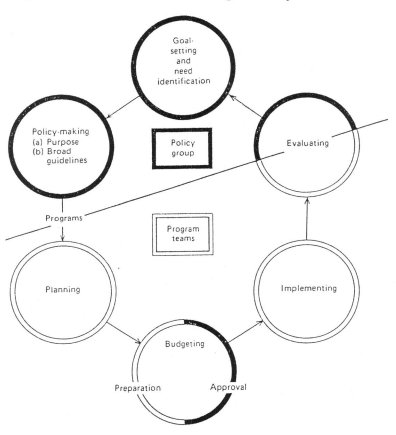

direction. Consequently, the "policy group" usually addresses politically sensitive, value-laden, administrative issues. The second group, known as "program teams" is responsible for implementing the decisions of the "policy group." Most of the issues which confront these program teams are technical and managerial in nature. Communication between the two groups is maintained by individuals who have dual membership. One of the most appealing features of this model is flexibility which is essential for coping effectively with the demands of a continuous changing society.

Since the rural communities possess many unique features, the nature and scope of school-based management can be expected to differ from one rural school to another. Caldwell and Spinks (1988) address this circumstance with a second model identified as "Levels of Collaboration." This model, as shown in Figure 2, consists of eight levels of collaboration. At one end of the continuum, a low level of collaboration (Level 1) is where the principal acts autonomously; while at a high level of collaboration (Level 8) a democratic council manages a school. As Riedl (1988) accurately points out, "a school and community [will] seek the level they perceive serves their needs the best" (p. 54).

A comprehensive review of the professional literature indicates that the models developed by Caldwell & Spinks (1988) possessed the greatest potential for studying and initiating greater school autonomy in rural areas. Recently, this model was modified by Murphy and Holt (1991) to study parent participation in school management in several Local Education Authorities in England and Wales. These modifications enabled issues concerning communication, personnel management, and curricula development to be addressed.

Rural Schools

The professional literature on school-based management, participatory decision making, and contemporary school governance seems to increase annually as more and more attention is focused on how schools may function effectively as self-managing entities. Although there is ample discussion on the pros and cons of this new form of governance, actual empirical research tends to be rather scarce. Consequently, our knowledge of parents' thoughts on involving them more in school affairs is limited.

Many governments continue to provide a greater decentralization of school governance, numerous school systems endeavor to facilitate parents becoming more involved in the schooling of their children and a variety of agencies endeavor to offer a miscellaneous selection of training experiences for parents either involved or willing to become involved in the management of a school. Without an adequate knowledge base all these activities are fraught with instability, compromise, and potential disaster. Regretfully, financial constraints, political pressures, and popular support for perceived progressive innovations are overriding sound judgement.

If our knowledge of this new form of governance is not extended quickly chaos may occur in the educational community. Schools will compete aggressively with each other for resources. The less fortunate socio-economic groups will find themselves even more disadvantaged than in the past, educational administrators will flounder in their efforts to cope with the demands of numerous

Figure 2: The Collaboration Continuum

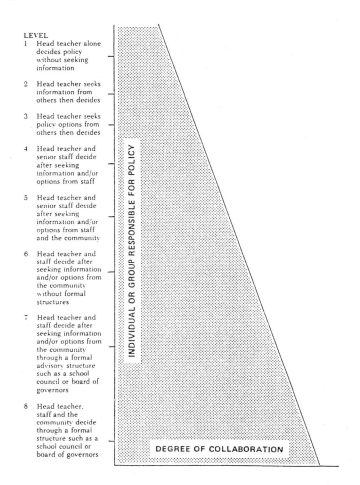

interest groups, and parents will become frustrated in their efforts to grapple with difficult managerial and administrative issues. Some people will be winners and others losers in this dynamic zero-sum game.

Most school systems, as well as many individual schools would undoubtedly benefit from being granted greater autonomy. Encouraging parents, teachers, and the general public to participate more in school affairs would have a very positive and long term impact on school relationships. The new partners which evolve possess the potential for benefitting everyone.

Canadian rural schools have traditionally developed, as noted earlier, strong affiliations with their local communities. Often a "rural culture" particular to each community exists, a culture which is reflected in the activities of local schools. These small, independent, tightly knit, rural communities of Canada, as one might expect, solicit numerous services from these schools. Similarly, these institutions reach out to local residents for support and assistance. The white school house, often along with the church, is usually the hub of social life in a small community.

An awareness of government initiatives to decentralize school governance has promoted a number of field practitioners from northern Canada to investigate parent involvement in school affairs in a rural context. Although these studies were small exploratory enquiries, valuable information was obtained which offered useful insights concerning the increased participation of rural parents in school management.

The Yukon Survey

Due to the vastness, physical geography, climate, and settlement patterns of the Yukon, communities in this northern region of Canada tend to be small and unique in character. Most schools in these isolated communities have much in common with the local communities which they serve. Riedl (1988) asked principals and school committee members in each of these schools to comment on parental involvement in school affairs. Prior to the survey being initiated, the schools chosen to participate in the study were classified into two groups, namely: 1) Type 1 Schools where Native students were the majority and 2) Type 2 Schools where Native students were in the minority.

Of the 18 principals and 43 school committee members invited to participate in the enquiry, 13 principals (87 per cent) and 23 committee members (47 per cent) completed the survey document. The language and format of the questionnaire were found difficult by some of the school committee members which resulted in a lower response rate than anticipated.

Among the respondents, there was general agreement that schools should communicate with parents on a regular basis. Creating a comfortable and familiar atmosphere for parents was considered to be second issue of importance to principals. Principals in Type 1 Schools assigned a high level of importance to encouraging parents to share skills and knowledge at school. Their colleagues in Type 2 Schools considered this issue to be of much less importance.

After regular communication with parents, school committee members considered that teachers and parents should have the same goals for children. The school committee members agreed with the principals that parents should feel comfortable in a school. However, in contrast to the principals, the school committee members perceived parents should have input into school policy.

Committee members from Type 1 and Type 2 Schools assigned different levels of importance to parents being encouraged to share skills and knowledge at school. The parents from Type 1 Schools, where Native Students were in the majority, perceived this issue should be viewed as very important.

When requested to comment on "what was" actually happening in the rural schools of the Yukon, the principals considered that parents were involved more in school affairs than parents perceived themselves to be. Accessing parents to school activities through pre-schoolers was viewed as occurring by all respondents. Principals and committee members from Type 1 Schools considered that many parents were not comfortable in schools while their colleagues from Type 2 Schools perceived most parents were comfortable when visiting schools. All respondents were in agreement that parents were not attending school committee meetings frequently enough.

After reflecting upon the findings yielded by analysis, Riedl stated a number of significant conclusions regarding parental involvement in the rural schools of the Yukon. These conclusions included:

1. Very few, if any, written policies concerning parental involvement exist at the Department of Education level or in the rural schools.

2. More consensus exists among parents than principals about attitudes and perceptions concerning parental involvement in schools.

3. Native parents are not represented on rural school committees to the extent that the Native pupil population warrants.

4. Matters nurturing a good relationship and familiarity with the school and teachers were considered very important by all respondents.

5. Principals feel parents have more input into school policy than school committee members perceive.

6. Parents seldom attend school committee meetings.

At the conclusion of his report Riedl captured the essence of his enquiry when he noted:

> Parents and professionals are just beginning to collaborate on matters of schooling, Economic circumstances, growing political interest and a reawakening to responsibilities are all forces that have combined to make the parent-teacher partnership inevitable (p. 88).

The Prince George Survey

School District #57 (Prince George) in British Columbia serves a large northern urban centre and a number of small rural communities. If the distance from the District Board Office, physical geography, climatic conditions, and community demography are taken into account, the rural schools of this isolated educational community differ significantly from each other.

A small scale, but very interesting enquiry concerning parental involvement in rural schooling was completed in this isolated school district by Wiebe (1989). More specifically, this study analyzed school district policies and procedures concerning parental involvement in school affairs, examined current parental involvement in rural schools, obtained parents' satisfactions and desires regarding their involvement in the schooling of their children, and proposed recommendations for improving school district policies and procedures related to parent participation in rural schools.

All the small, rural schools (n=10) outside the city of Prince George and other northern communities in the area with a population of 250 people or more, were invited to participate in the enquiry. At each school the principal and five parents actively involved in school affairs, selected at random, were extended invitations to comment on the present and future participation in the schooling of their children. Of the 50 parents invited to participate in the research study, 40 individuals completed the survey document, representing an 80 per cent response rate. In the administrator group nine principals out of the ten school leaders approached returned a completed questionnaire, representing a 90 per cent response rate.

Although requested, none of the principals sent policy statements, written or unwritten, regarding parental involvement in school affairs. Yet all the administrators emphasized that parents were involved actively in their schools.

Most of the parents contacted considered themselves welcome and comfortable in their childrens' schools, and furthermore stated that they were very satisfied with their reception. Similarly, regular communication between home and school, invitations to school activities, parents assisting with sports days, and teachers reporting to parents their children's problems were rated as occurring frequently. Parent participation in policy making, planning, student discipline, and school management were all considered to have occurred very seldom. These issues were ones most of the parents reported they were least satisfied with at the moment. Many of the parents appeared to be rather dissatisfied with their present level of involvement in the governance of the schools which their children attended.

When invited to comment on the future involvement of parents in school affairs, most of the parents wanted a school to be an enjoyable place for them to visit. Of equal importance to parents was being informed when their children were having difficulty at school. The majority of the parents appeared interested in becoming more involved in many aspects of schooling.

Only a small number of rural parents participated in this enquiry, which means that the findings should be viewed with discretion. However, consensus among the respondents regarding their desire to participate in school affairs, although they were dispersed over a wide region, was very evident.

A number of conclusions were proposed by Wiebe after completing this enquiry. Of these conclusions, several of the most interesting ones were:

1. Very few, if any, clearly written policies regarding parental involvement at the school district level and rural school level existed.

2. Parents felt that they should have more opportunity to participate in various aspects of schooling.

3. Rural parents and principals were aware of the important role parental involvement in schooling has in effective education.

4. Parents felt that their involvement in parent advisory councils did not give them enough control in school governance matters such as developing policy and budget direction.

5. Opportunities for parents to share skills and knowledge were judged as very important.

6. Parents considered regular communication by a school a very important issue.

At the conclusion of this report, Wiebe acknowledged the importance of the new partnerships evolving in rural schools, as follows:

> As educators our goal has been to provide the best learning opportunities for our students. There is little doubt that the same is coveted by parents for their children. Through collaboration, cooperation, and sincerity, parents and professionals can become true partners in education. Only then, will students reach their full potential as learners (pp. 99-100).

The Nechako Survey

School District #56 (Nechako) is a large rural school district located in the centre of the Province of British Columbia. The physical geography, climate, and vastness of the region served by this school district has had an adverse impact on settlement in the area. Although the school district is approximately one fifth the size of France, less than 25 000 people reside within its boundaries. Major employers in this region, as one might expect, are resource-based industries. More recently, tourism has been flourishing as a growing number of people have been attracted to the excellent natural recreational facilities in this locality.

Approximately 3 000 children from a catchment area of 11 000 square kilometres are provided with educational programs and support services by twelve schools. The majority of these institutions are located in or near four small communities. Of these schools, six institutions, selected at random, were invited to participate in a small, but very interesting investigation, conducted by Gregg (1989), on the involvement of parents in rural schooling. Scholarly work of Owens (1987), Caldwell and Spinks (1986), Arnstein (1976), and Tannenbaum and Schmidt (1973) provided a theoretical base for this enquiry.

After approval had been granted to undertake this study, a small group of parents (n_p=66), teachers (n_t=45), and administrators (n_a=6) were invited to complete a special survey document developed for the investigation. The members of all three groups were asked to comment on the role of parents, the role of teachers, and the role of administrators in schooling. In addition, parents were asked to answer specific questions regarding their own personal involvement in school affairs. Since the language and format of the survey instrument could have a significant impact on how participants responded to questions, the survey document was pilot-tested with a small group of parents and teachers. This enquiry was reported by Gregg to be of significant importance locally, as well as nationally and internationally because "it offered a starting point for dialogue and for sensitizing administrators, teachers, and parents towards their changing roles in school governance" (p. 62). Due to the scarcity of research in this area, Gregg perceived his study would offer rural school districts "a base from which to explore their own involvement in collaborative school management" (p. 9).

Administrators seemed to possess a more tolerant attitude towards parents as partners in education, while teachers tended to view parental partnerships less favorably. However, both these groups of educators perceived parents to presently have limited involvement in school affairs. In contrast, most parents considered their current participation to be higher than the professional educators. All three groups were in general agreement that parents were and should be involved in establishing, modifying, and implementing school goals and objectives. This input was not to be undertaken without some accountability. Parent participation in school affairs was perceived by the majority of the parents, teachers, and administrators as requiring regular evaluation for it to be effective.

Teachers were considered by all three groups as having a more important role in school management than parents. Input into school goals and objectives was ranked the most important duty performed by teachers of those examined in the survey. Most parents perceived teachers as being concerned primarily with the learning environment in the classroom. The management responsibilities of the teachers were considered of less importance. Yet, all three interest groups perceived teachers should participate more in managerial activities having direct impact on instruction or the learning environment in a school.

Of the interest groups participating in the enquiry, the administrators were considered to have the greatest role in school management. Among the many roles performed by educational leaders, many respondents maintained the following to be of greatest importance: (1) setting the goals and objectives of their school, (2) staffing their schools, and (3) evaluating staff. Parents specifically perceived administrators to be responsible for translating their expectations (values and priorities) into action strategies.

After completing this small but valuable study on parental involvement in rural schooling, Gregg deduced a number of conclusions, including:

1. Written policies concerning the role of parents, teachers, and administrators were almost non-existent at both the school and school district level.

2. Parents, teachers, and administrators all agreed that parents' most important role in school governance was the establishment and revision of school goals and objectives.

3. Many schools in this rural school district had established parent advisory groups, but their principal responsibilities were mainly fund-raising, operating school canteens, and supporting school special events.

4. Teachers, parents, and administrators all perceived that teachers should have a greater role than at present in school management.

5. Administrators were perceived by all interest groups to play a vital role in all areas of school management.

6. Parents had little opportunity to interact with educators in situations that were not related directly to their own children's' educational progress.

Before rural parents become more involved in school management, Gregg recommends that formal policies and philosophical statements regarding the role of parents and parents advisory groups in school governance are necessary. This practitioner/scholar emphasized that these policies and statements should be developed collaboratively by parent groups, teachers, administrators, and school trustees. Without a sound foundation of this kind, any initiatives to increase the participation of parents in school affairs will be characterized by "muddling through" which will generate unnecessary adversity.

Concluding Comments

Due to a multitude of societal forces, public schools in Canada are going to be granted greater autonomy during the present decade. Traditionally, Canadian educational institutions have been very conservative organizations. Consequently, this transfer of power will occur incrementally. Initially, public schools will appear to differ marginally from those of the past. However, by the turn of the century, most schools will differ substantively from those institutions which children presently attend. Corporate sponsorship of school activities, events, and materials, as an illustration of the possible changes, might be a common practice in schools of the future.

Most parents and teachers will be naturally hesitant about becoming involved actively in school affairs. For decades, members of both these interest groups have been discouraged from participating in important aspects of schooling. Although some government officials, school trustees, and educational administrators would deny this fact, very few parents and teachers have had a significant impact on decision making in schools. Exceptions to the norm always exist, but for the majority of parents and teachers "real" participation in school affairs has been a myth rather than a reality.

Due to the placation which has characterized school management in the past, as well as the present, we should not be dismayed that parents and teachers are not rushing to become more involved in school affairs. However, conditions in the educational community are changing rapidly. In the new future, as schools are granted greater autonomy, many interest groups will want to exercise their right to shape and to direct the destiny of local schools.

A transfer of power from school trustees and school district staff to parents, members of the general public, and school-based staff is going to occur. Thus change will quite naturally have far-reaching consequences for everyone associated with schools. If substantial conflict is to be avoided, this local management of schools must be characterized by high levels of collaboration, communication, and consideration.

Parent participation in school affairs has been more common in rural areas than in large urban communities. This phenomenon is well known and recognized as a special feature of rural life. The local school is a "corner-stone" of any rural community since it maintains and nurtures the unique culture of the local area as well as providing access to residents to the continuous changing conditions in contemporary society. In fact, if a school closes, a community quite naturally becomes concerned about its future survival. One of the principal institutions for presenting community life has disappeared.

Many people maintain that new government legislation to increase the autonomy of schools is merely legitimizing what has been happening in rural areas for years. Unfortunately, this perception is not completely accurate. Traditionally many parents in the rural communities of Canada have had special relationships with the schools attended by their children. The partnerships which have evolved over time usually have been temporary, simple, and concerned with marginal school activities. Under the new conditions, emerging rapidly in Canada, partnerships are going to be more dynamic. Members of school councils are going to find themselves socially, fiscally, and legally responsible for their actions. Differences between previous partnerships and new ones are going to be significant.

Since educational reforms in Canada tend to occur incrementally, there appears to be sufficient time for parents, teachers, administrators, and other potential participants (e.g. business people) to familiarize themselves with the special responsibilities associated with a self-managing school. This assumption may not be true. Time tends to pass very quickly when innovative changes are introduced into an organization or social system. Often it appears that within only a short period of time a proposed reform is being put into practice. Yet, two or three years may have passed.

If collaborative school management is to benefit all schools and all children, this new form of management needs to be studied comprehensively and promptly, otherwise equal educational opportunity may no longer exist in Canadian provincial school systems. In fact, many children could be placed at risk by a reform designed to make schools more responsive to their needs. As schools become more self-managing and resources for education more limited, a situation can quickly emerge which promotes the "survival of the fittest."

The present era is characterized by rapid advances in technology, economic instability, political stagnation, and dramatic changes in social behavior. A turbulent milieu exists which impacts on all aspects of peoples lives. Provincial schools, whether they are located in rural, urban, or inner-city areas are going to play an important role in assisting Canadians, both young and old, to cope effectively with the many challenges confronting them in this "brave new world."

How schools respond to these new conditions will be influenced significantly by the leadership provided by administrative teams and the parents, teachers, and members of the general public empowered to participate in school management. The research studies undertaken by Riedl (1988), Wiebe (1989), and Gregg (1989) all indicated that very few, if any, written policies concerning collaborative school management existed at the school district or local school levels. Without appropriate policies and procedures the effective participation of various interest groups in school management and associated new partnerships will not be feasible. Similarly, parents, teachers, and members of the general public cannot be expected to manage schools without appropriate training. As Murphy and Nixon (1992) emphasize, "new infrastructures and delivery systems have to be developed for providing professional people, [as well as parents and members of the general public], in remote, rural and northern communities with high quality learning experiences" (p. 18).

The rural schools of Canada are known to be special in many ways. One of these unique features has been the close relationship which exists between school and community. Parents are viewed as partners in their childrens' education. Also, teachers are considered important and vital community members. Such an environment is conducive for establishing new collaborative partnerships for managing schools. Consequently, as Canadian provincial schools acquire greater autonomy, new school-community partnerships emerging in rural areas should be studied and considered as models for establishing new school management partnerships in different settings. The small, rural schools of Canada have always made and will continue to make important contributions to the economic growth and social development of the nation.

References

Caldwell, B. J. and Spinks, J. M. (1986). *Policy-making and planning for school effectiveness*. Hobart: Department of Education.

Di Silvestro, F. and Di Silvestro, R. (October, 1985). Room mothers are great, but today's parent volunteers can do so much more. *American School Board Journal, 172*, 10 p. 26.

Gregg, D. A. (1989). *Collaborative school management in School District #56 (Nechako)*. Victoria: Faculty of Education, University of Victoria. Unpublished Master of Education Project.

Leithwood, R. and Montgomery, D. (1986). *The principal profile*. Toronto: OISE Press.

Long, R. (1986). *Developing parental involvement in primary schools*. London: MacMillan Education.

Maurer, K. H. (April, 1985). A seven course strategy to entice parents to school. *American School Board Journal, 172*, 4, p. 36.

Maxwell, C. (1981). Quality in the absence of quantity: Education in sparsely populated areas of developed countries. In F. Darnell and P. M. Simpson (Eds.), *Rural education: In pursuit of excellence*. Nedlands: University of Western Australia.

Moles, O. C. (November, 1982). Synthesis of recent research on parent participation inchildren's education. *Educational Leadership, 40*, pp. 44-47.

Murphy, P. J. and Nixon, M. (1992). *Beyond the ivory tower: Professional development at a distance*. Paper presented at the 1992 Conference of the Association of Teacher Educators in Europe. Lahti, Finland.

Murphy, P. J. and Holt, A. (1990). *School effectiveness in the future: The empowerment factor*. Victoria: Faculty of Education, University of Victoria. An Unpublished Manuscript.

Riedl, W. (1988). *Parental involvement in Yukon rural schools*. Victoria: Faculty of Education, University of Victoria. Unpublished Master of Education Project.

Sandfoot, J. A. (February, 1987). Putting parents in their place in public schools. *NAASP Bulletin, 71*, 496, pp. 99-103.

Sills, J. (Fall, 1978). The school principal and parent involvement. *Contemporary Education, 50*, 1, pp. 45-48.

Wiebe, P. B. (1989). *Parental involvement in Prince George rural schools*. Victoria: Faculty of Education, University of Victoria. Unpublished Master of Education Project.

7

Implementing Parent Involvement in Northern Manitoba Schools

The Principal's Role

W. A. Gulka & B. Knudson

The educational scene of the 1990s is characterized by a number of uniquely "modern" phenomena. Among these are educators' attempts to cope with the "knowledge and information explosions;" alternate theories on the ways in which children learn; changes in parenting approaches and skills; complex social forces, challenges, and concerns; new concepts of organizational structures, processes, and behavior; and a reconceptualization of the change process and the manner in which innovations are implemented. In response to these at times "bewildering" developments, fundamental changes are under way in educational systems – a reform movement (if not a revolution) is occurring.

One significant aspect of the educational changes under way is the increased attempts at involvement by non-school constituencies and agencies in the affairs of the school. Prominent among these are parents. While parents have historically had some measure of formal "democratic" influence and voice in school affairs, it has generally tended to be of an arms-length, representative nature. However, the nature and intensity of this involvement is changing. Smith (1988) makes this observation:

> The role of parents in the education of their children has become one of the most prominent aspects in the reform movement in education. That attention often thrives under the amorphous terms of 'parental involvement'. Whether at home, in the school, or at school board meetings helping to shape education policy, parents are encouraged to get involved (p. 68).

The educational experiences of Canada's aboriginal people have historically been much different from those of the majority culture. While their involvement and influence were not encouraged, aboriginal people are quickly realizing and appreciating the fact that the education of their children is an important avenue by means of which they can enhance and preserve their cultural identity, participate meaningfully and effectively in the social, economic, and political affairs of the mainstream and global societies, and attain self-determination. With Indian bands increasingly adopting band-controlled schools or aboriginally-dominated and directed educational systems, aboriginal people are beginning to determine and influence in a very direct way the education of their children. The concept of parental involvement sweeping across the schools of the global community is not passing them by.

The findings of a recent study (Knudson, 1990) which looked at the principal's role in one successful effort of a large northern school system in the province of Manitoba to introduce, promote, and encourage the involvement of aboriginal parents in the educational affairs of their children is presented in this chapter. To place the findings and discussion in a proper perspective, it is useful to present a brief overview of the nature and extent of parental involvement in school affairs as it has evolved up until the present time. This is followed by a description of the setting in which the study took place and the methodology that was employed. The findings are then analyzed in terms of Corbett and Rossman's (1989) triple perspective of implementing changes in educational settings. The authors' personal experiences with and knowledge of the educational system in the Northwest Territories are included for comparative and illustrative purposes.

The Nature of Parental Involvement

For as long as there have been schools, people have always known and appreciated the fact that the home and the school are educational partners (Pearson, 1990) interested primarily in and concerned exclusively with the raising, rearing, and welfare of the community's children (Seefeldt, 1985). Successful education has always been defined and understood in terms of the cooperation and collaboration of parents, the community, and the school exerting a united effort towards the educational and social welfare of children.

While parental involvement in schools is beginning to assume new forms and pursue hitherto little-touched or unexplored areas of concern and interest, Brandt (1989) and Epstein (1987) have identified five major areas in which parental involvement has seen expression both historically and in more recent times. A number of other writers have discussed these individually or in selected groupings. Table 1 illustrates these five types of parental involvement, indicating specific activities exclusive or appropriate to each type, the major initiators of each form of involvement, and examples of writers who have discussed each type of parental involvement.

It is probably accurate to say that traditionally, school-based and home-based activities have been most frequently utilized and preferred formats for any parental-school involvement that could be classified as resembling a partnership venture to any extent. While parents have always had some role to play in educational governance, this has traditionally been one of a representative, arms-length nature, with the "silent majority" being excluded from any direct or meaningful involvement. However, this has changed dramatically in recent times, particularly in the last decade. Many more parents are more actively involved in school affairs in an ever-increasing variety of ways and roles.

While this increased involvement can be at least partially attributed to changing social standards and expectations, provincial educational agencies are responding in a positive way as well. A good example of this is Saskatchewan's Education Act (1978) which mandates local boards of trustees in rural school districts and permits local school-level advisory councils in urban centres.

In the Northwest Territories, schools are urged to implement and maintain a community vision, reaching out to the community and becoming a part of it by providing opportunities to involve family and community members in school activities. Further, one of the primary goals of the Territorial Department of Education is for schools, in partnership with families and communities, to be key players in helping young people develop the characteristics they will need to fulfill their roles as adults in the twenty-first century (Northwest Territories Department of Education, 1991). Schooling should respond not only to the goals of the larger society but also to the particular goals of the Northwest Territories communities and their residents. Consequently, parental and community involvement in education is essential.

In Canada, the involvement of Indian parents in educational affairs has generally been minimal. One historical factor is the residential school system through which many aboriginal people received their education. Even with the establishment of federal schools on Indian reserves, parental involvement likely occurred much less frequently for them than for parents in the majority culture. As so often happened in the schools of the majority culture, parents would typically become involved in school matters only in times of crises, the annual Christmas Concert, or Education Week.

FORMS OF PARENTAL INVOLVEMENT IN EDUCATION			
Major Initiators	Form of Involvement	Specific Parental Activities	Authors
Home State	–parenting –welfare	–raising/rearing children	
School	–communication	–information –schedules –announce- ments	–Beale (1985)
School Home	–school-based	–volunteering –audience –co-learner –support –aides/ assistants	–Beale (1985) –Pearson (1990)
School Home	–home-based	–extension –enrichment –law suits –home work	–Pearson (1990)
State Home School	–governance/ advisory	–school board –advisory council –committees –planning –representation –advocacy	–Beale (1985)

In spite of the fact that the benefits of a home-school partnership are as beneficial for Indian people as for others, Davis (1986) notes "very limited success in achieving reform for Indian and Metis students" (p. 37) in terms of parental involvement in schools. Notwithstanding this less than desirable state of affairs, he reiterates the "value of participation of native people in the educational process" (p. 32).

With the increasing number of band-controlled schools and aboriginally-controlled school systems that are occurring, a whole new development is unfolding in terms of the involvement of native parents in their schools. In a very real and direct sense, aboriginal parents are taking charge of the education of their children. Through the avenue of autonomy, aboriginal people are "establishing systems that depend, for the most part, on total parent involvement" (Richardson & Richardson, 1986, p. 25), enabling them to pursue "self-determination in education through local control" (p. 25).

Richardson and Richardson (1986) identify two formal approaches through which limited parental involvement in education has until very recently been realized: parent advisory committees and home-school programs. Davis (1986) adds teacher aides/assistants and school trustee roles as two more recent forms of parental involvement in aboriginal schools.

Important as these local level participatory initiatives are to aboriginal parents, Davis (1986) identifies three new approaches or directions in which aboriginal people are being provided with enhanced and sophisticated opportunities for participating in educational affairs. Through the formation of parent action groups in urban centres (e.g., Native Survival schools), parents are becoming less dependent on the mainstream public school systems for their survival. Through Indian and Metis branches of mainstream cultural, political, educational, and women's organizations, they are able to work through these established organizations towards their own particular ends. Finally, formal educational institutions such as the Saskatchewan Indian Cultural College and the Gabriel Dumont Institute provide training in skills and a knowledge base for culturally focused programs.

Frontier School Division

Frontier School Division is located in northern Manitoba. The Division was created in 1965 by the consolidation of remote, northern schools previously operated by the Manitoba Department of Education as special schools, independent school districts, church administered schools, and some federally operated schools. The Division consists of 37 schools in 34 communities spread over an area of 177 000 square miles (one-half the area of Manitoba). The professional and support staff are offered competitive salaries, a generous benefits package, subsidized housing, and travel allowances. In addition, a comprehensive range of professional support services is available to all staff.

Communities within the Division range in size from Norway House, with a student population of nearly 1000 enrolled in three schools, to Red Sucker Lake with a total of nine children in a one-room multigraded facility. Students in the Division are primarily Indian and Metis, although in centres such as Gillam, the majority of the people are non-Indian. The September, 1989, student enrollment of the Division was 5443. Teaching staff totalled 385.5 teacher-equivalents with an additional support staff component of 353.5 people. Despite the varying degrees of isolation and remoteness, Frontier schools are generally similar in appearance to schools elsewhere in the province. They are well-equipped modern facilities with all the necessary materials and resources. The Manitoba provincial curriculum is followed in all schools, although a great deal of adaptation, modification, and supplementation is required to make the curriculum relevant to student needs.

The five schools that were visited during the course of this study ranged in size from 100 to 500 students. All school facilities included a gymnasium and library. Special programs were offered in all schools, the number of which depended upon the size of the school. Course offerings included music, Cree, French, industrial arts, home economics, art, business education, Native Studies, special education, and alternative vocational education programs. Four of the schools offered kindergarten to grade eight programs, while the fifth school was a senior high school. School staffs ranged from 21 to 41 people; these numbers included both teaching and support staff.

The economic bases of Frontier communities vary. Some communities rely on fishing and trapping, others derive their livelihood from the forestry and logging industries, while others function as service centres. Some of the communities owe their existence to the construction or maintenance activities associated with hydro-electric projects. Tourism and local business ventures are important to this region as well. All communities are accessible by road with two communities having daily scheduled air service. Charter air service is available in all communities.

Local School Committees (LSCs) are elected in each community to provide guidance, support, and advice to teachers and administrators in the school. Area advisory committees are elected by the school committees in each of the five geographical areas of the Division to assist the area superintendents. The Division Board is elected by the area committees. In accordance with the Manitoba Public Schools Act, the Board develops and evaluates policy, establishes and evaluates educational goals, adopts a budget, and attempts to keep its citizens informed.

Students attending school away from home require additional support, encouragement, and assistance from parents. The Division Student Placement Program places Frontier students in suitable educational programs when such programs are not available in the local schools. Information, assistance, orientation, consultation, counselling, and personal support are provided.

Frontier School Division leaders believe that parents have a key role to play in the education of their children. "Not every teacher is a parent but every parent is a teacher" is a motto the Division leaders advocate. High on the list of priorities for Frontier School Division is meaningful parental involvement in education. Staff in the Division are expected to give their time and energy in order to work with parents to offer the best possible education for the students, and to make their contribution to the quality of life in their respective communities. Frontier School Division leaders pride themselves on bringing parents, communities, students, and staff working together as partners in learning. They believe that informed and involved parents are valuable players on any educational team. The logo on the *Parental Involvement Handbook* – "Frontier Schools . . . Partners in Learning" – reflects this philosophy and belief.

The Study

The purpose of this study was to investigate change strategies utilized by school principals to bring about increased parental involvement, with particular attention being given to the role of the principal in the change process, and the factors related to context. An effort was made to examine the perceptions of principals in planning for change, namely, that of parental involvement in education, and more specifically, in their schools and communities. Particular attention was given to initiatives, supports, strategies, cultural factors, and implications. A deliberate attempt was undertaken to gain an understanding of contextual factors, especially in relation to the aboriginal culture and the large number of local staff involved in the school.

A naturalistic field research method which utilized an inquiry approach was employed for this study. Qualitative data were gathered by the researcher in an attempt to understand the subjects' world as related to the inquiry.

The subjects of this study consisted of twelve school principals from Frontier School Division, selected in consultation with the chief superintendent of the Division. These schools were selected because of the success that was experienced in enhancing parental involvement at the local level. The sample also included the division board chairperson and the chief superintendent. The relatively small sample allowed for the utilization of an ethnographic-descriptive approach to interpretations utilizing participant perspectives and meanings.

The instruments utilized for data collection consisted of questionnaires and semi-structured interviews. The questionnaires consisted of open-ended questions concerning the principal's role in planning for change in parental involvement. These items were based on the literature and the researcher's past experience as principal of northern schools. Semi-structured interviews were utilized to further explore the responses of five of the participants who responded to the questionnaires. Observations were also noted during the site visits.

Parental Involvement From a Triple Perspective of Change

All change initiatives are complex, complicated, multi-variate events with a multiplicity of participants, perspectives, and related supporting and constraining variables. In discussing the findings of this particular study, the role of the principal and the attendant school-level contextual factors (i.e., human, organizational, physical, and political factors) are highlighted as they related to the successful implementation of a parental involvement program in a number of selected schools in the Frontier School Division. As well, the school board, community, superintendents, and, of course, the parents, are integrally involved in everything that happens, both by circumstance and by design. Seefeldt (1985) offers a short quotation which captures the essence of what it is that Frontier School Division's parental involvement program is striving to attain:

> When parents are knowledgeable about events that occur during their children's day at school, they can intelligently discuss school with their children. They are able to reinforce the work of the school while gaining a measure of control and confidence as parents (p. 100).

The principal's role in the implementation of the Frontier School Division parental involvement initiative is described in terms of Corbett and Rossman's (1989) "Three Paths to Implementing Change." The Political Path arbitrarily forms the starting point for this story, primarily because of the high priority and emphasis that the school division leaders placed on initiating and supporting the program. The Cultural Path is examined next because the reconceptualization and redefinition of how teaching, schooling, and education relate to the profession and to the community served, in the final analysis, to make the program work successfully. Finally, the Technical Path is considered. Without implying that this is the easiest path to describe, many common and proven techniques were employed to enhance parental involvement in these schools. The cultural and political variables served to make these strategies "the right things" to do.

In reality, these three paths are interactive and quite complex. The segregation and isolation of these paths is maintained solely to facilitate understanding and discussion. While concentrating on a particular path, the interrelationships and interactions with the other paths are interjected where appropriate. References are made to the literature to support important concepts and themes that emerged from the study.

The Political Path

While limited forms of home-school "partnerships" existed in varying degrees within all of the school communities in Frontier School Division, the school board and system-level administration identified greater parental involvement as a goal and initiative worthy of pursuit. Reference to the current literature on parental involvement in education confirmed their belief that there were many benefits to be gained by involving aboriginal parents in the educational endeavors of their children (Frontier School Division, No. 48, 1989, pp. 3-1 to 3-4). As a result, parental involvement was identified and adopted as a system-level priority, receiving support over other competing demands and priorities. This initiative thus became a favored recipient of fiscal resources, time, personnel, and attention.

Key decision makers were vital to making the program work. These included the school board, superintendents, the Local School Committees (LSCs), and the principals. The nature of their positions and responsibilities ensured the important role and influence that principals would play in the process. The political importance of this "coalition" was reflected in a number of important ways. The LSCs and principals were represented on the school-based Parent Involvement Committees (PICs). The school board adopted a policy mandating formal parental involvement initiatives at each school. This had the effect of informing reluctant staff members of the seriousness of the board's intentions, the importance attached to the effort, and the system's expectation for each staff member to get involved in his/her school's initiatives (Pearson, 1990).

The importance of the principals was critical to the success of the parental involvement initiative. It was ultimately their responsibility to make the program work. As Principal Bea stated, "People are looking at the principal to establish something in the line of parental involvement." In all the schools studied, the principals' enthusiasm was reflected in their membership in the coalition, offering active support, and assistance and encouragement during trial activities. This visible enthusiastic administrative support and involvement extended into the Cultural Path in that an important matter – parental involvement – was being stressed, new ways of doing things were being encouraged, and new norms and values were being introduced, promoted, and established. The principals played the very critical role of reiterating and stressing a system-level goal and vision that they identified with and personally valued and deemed important enough to "bother" and remind their staff members about.

The Cultural Path

In contrast to the integration of authority and support (Fullan, Anderson & Newton, 1986) that was evident in the Political Path, the Cultural Path involved reconciling personal beliefs and values with new expectations and norms, accommodating and fitting new practices and ideas into established routines, and altering current practices to allow new techniques to be established and incorporated. Symbolic gestures and activities assumed importance in establishing new values, beliefs, and norms in the individual school communities. The Cultural Path impacted upon everyone involved in the school community: teachers, students, division-level personnel, parents, and members of the community.

Like their underprivileged counterparts in urban settings, the parents of Frontier School Division had very limited school involvement experiences prior to the initiation of the parental involvement program. Home-school relationships were characterized by apathy and passivity, stemming in part from many of the parents' experiences as students in residential school settings. At the system level, the school board and superintendents realized that this lack of involvement at the local level required changing. As a system goal and priority that was reflected in a policy mandate, the principals of these schools were expected to become advocates for this goal, translating it and promoting it at the school level. At the school level itself, positive, supportive staff attitudes established a school climate willing to give parental involvement a try.

Many of the activities and strategies that were employed in the trial and skill development activities of the Technical Path can be interpreted in terms of important symbolic gestures that served to foster parental involvement. The superintendents' visitations to these communities afforded them opportunities to articulate and manifest their belief in the importance of parental involvement, and to explain how they were attempting to accomplish this. That the residents perceived these officials as credible individuals was attested to by the fact that these meetings were invariably extremely well-attended. In Principal Al's words:

> Whenever he (chief superintendent) comes to speak, people want to go and listen to him. He's a very good friend for the Division, for education, for this whole aspect of involving parents. When he talks to people, they listen to him so he's very, very important.

The principals extended these gestures of system-level symbolic leadership to their schools, sending a clear and unmistakable message to their staffs, the students, the parents, and the community.

Parental involvement has become an important and desirable school norm and activity for Frontier schools. With its elevated priority and status, many concrete strategies were attempted to lure parents into the school. As Principal Cal says, "It doesn't really matter how they come in, just get them coming." The formation of the PIC with its LSC, school staff, and parent representatives portrayed a partnership and coalition that was serious about parental involvement. The specific activities attempted were all intended to send a message to the students, the community and the school staff that parental involvement was sought, desired, and deemed to be important. These school events, which were deliberately structured to involve the parents, included Open Houses, orientations, Open-Door Policies, advertising of school events and activities in the community, with particular emphases on welcoming parents when they came to the schools.

Pearson (1990) and McLaughlin and Shields (1987) state that any efforts at enhancing the home-school partnership need to accommodate and reflect the norms, values, and the political reality of the local community. The parents of these schools were most anxious and concerned that their cultural knowledge, abilities, and beliefs be incorporated into and taught as part of the total school social-educational program. To achieve this, two very important clusters of activities occurred. First, new staff interaction patterns typically emerged in these schools. These included matching new staff members with someone who had acquired community status either by birth or by tenure, encouraging staff members to participate in extra-curricular community events, and matching teachers with students in a form of mentorship. The ultimate goal was to change the existing passive home-school relationship into an active parent-teacher partnership/coalition.

The school staff members, many of whom are local community members and residents, played a particularly important support role for the parent involvement initiative. They served as a bridge and link between the school, and the parents and community, and functioned as a vital and influential communication conduit for these sectors. Principal Al stresses the importance of these staff members in this way: "People look upon them as insiders who really know what is going on in the school and give credence to what they say." They also served to introduce and establish these "outsiders" into the community.

The second important result that was evident was the acceptance and establishment of new norms by the entire school community. The school climate served to shape the expectations and attitude of the staff members to accept parental involvement as the proper and necessary thing to do. Principal Al commented, "Input by parents in whatever ways you can think of is important." This was reinforced, no doubt, by the various successes that the students attained, and the home support that began to become more evident. Parents began to assume meaningful and active roles in the affairs of their schools, while staff members became conscious of their accountability to the community for the school's educational program. Principal Deb stated, " With parents likely to drop in on a classroom teacher, the teacher likes to be a little more prepared, thereby making her more accountable for the education of their children."

The official proof of this new partnership/coalition was evidenced in the many ways in which the provincial curriculum was adapted and modified to reflect and incorporate the community-cultural beliefs, knowledge, and abilities that were important to the parents as part of their cultural heritage. Finally, more than anything else, the schools began to understand and accept the philosophy that they needed to work and do things *with* rather than *for* the parents. Principal Deb's observation that "the school must work towards doing things with the community rather than for it" was strongly supported by Principal Bea.

The Technical Path

The Technical Path reflected an effort to try things out, to introduce novel approaches to involving parents in school-related activities. While the traditional parent-teacher meetings and contacts, and annual events such as the Christmas Concert were not abandoned, the system-level administration and key decision makers realized that they had "everything to gain and nothing to lose" by encouraging and mandating a more sophisticated and enhanced form of parental involvement in school activities. While the concept of training parents (Cervone & O'Leary, 1982) was an important underlying purpose in Frontier schools, the teachers were not excused from learning activities either.

An important step that occurred early in the process was the formation of PICs at each school. Representing the main constituents of the school community, they served as temporary systems (Hopkirk & Newton, 1986) which formally planned and initiated the activities that were engaged in by individual schools. Among the activities and events attempted were parent workshops, orientations, advertising school events in the community, newsletters, informal parental involvement in the schools that utilized specific talents and abilities that individuals could confidently and competently contribute, open houses, and open-door polices.

Both school staffs and parents required a lot of encouragement to "keep the ball rolling." The school division personnel compiled the *Parental Involvement Handbook* which was distributed to each school, and updated periodically to maintain its currency. This handbook served as a valuable resource for suggesting activities and ideas that individual schools could adopt or adapt to their local situations or circumstances. The superintendents' visitations and system-wide communications to both the schools and the communities served to assist and encourage individuals in their respective capacities to become better at bringing about a new home-school partnership. While the school division personnel offered symbolic support and encouragement, the principals, LSCs and PICs encouraged and promoted parental involvement initiatives at the local level. It was here at the local level that the principal's advocacy, support, and encouragement served to foster successful initiatives in a very real way.

Good will and noble intentions of themselves do not assure the implemention of a change in a meaningful way. McLaughlin and Shields (1987) also remind us that pressure alone is insufficient to bring about a willingness on the part of staff members to participate in parental involvement initiatives. Teachers and administrators require support encouragement, and motivation to try new practices and strategies. Assistance of various kinds was required as well to support and sustain local efforts.

At the school level, the principal, with the assistance of the PIC, offered symbolic and personal support, assistance and expertise to make things happen. At the system level, support, and assistance were evident in a number of ways. Through the handbook, communications, and community visits, the administration and school board not only set a direction for the school communities but as well indicated their encouragement and support for local efforts. The school board and LSCs translated this assistance into concrete measures such as allowing local transportation arrangements to be made to enable parents to attend and participate in school activities, and approving the use of local school facilities for community functions and extra-curricular activities open to the community. The school board also had personnel and consultants available to assist individual schools with difficulties which they may have encountered, or to provide specialized assistance.

Summary

The story of the successful introduction and implementation of a program to involve aboriginal parents in the educational affairs of their children in Frontier School Division is an example of what is possible and what can be done. What happened here is really an example of forming partnerships for a common cause. The system-level leaders' important role as advocates, initiators, and supporters of this program is eloquently echoed by Principal Ev in this way: "Like all good policy makers the board and the senior administration have enabled the schools to have meaningful parental involvement . . . The Division has made it possible for parents and schools to get together." At the local level, the principals were the key to implementing parental involvement programs and stimulating activity in this regard. Principal Cal says it simply: "If the on-site administration – if principal and vice principal don't want it to go, it's not going to go."

The formal, deliberate, and defined approach to parental involvement in Frontier School Division required that attention be devoted to a significant aspect of the implementation process. A fit or degree of coherence between the concept of parental involvement and the specific strategies through which this would be accomplished, and the context, cultural values, and ways of doing things in the local community needed to be established at each local school site. For the school administrators, Principals Bea and Deb stressed that schools must do things with, not for, aboriginal parents and their communities. Principal Al stated, "If people from two different groups are willing to work together on a project or work in close association with each other, then there usually is mutual respect and understanding."

Teachers and principals need not view parental involvement as threatening to their jurisdiction or an abdication of their powers. As long as both sides adhere to current legal definitions of their own rights and powers, jurisdictional conflicts need not arise. In the final analysis, meaningful involvement and roles for parents based on honesty and a climate of trust and acceptance are essential.

The parental involvement initiative in Frontier School Division appears to be off to a good start. Principal Deb reflects the serious, meaningful approach that typifies, at the very least, those schools where parental involvement has been successfully implemented in this way: "You have to know how to pull your strings . . . one person is strong here and the other one is strong there so you make sure you tap their strengths, allowing them to have a lot of input." Yet, in the final analysis, she believes that there is only so much that the school can do; the initiative will ultimately be successful if the parents are serious about involvement and display the will and desire to maintain their involvement. In her words, "There's a point where you gotta get your hands off. You have to see if it flies or not."

It is imperative that the aboriginal people in their communities become good at parental involvement. Although influential formal Indian-Metis organizations and institutions currently exist to champion the educational aims of aboriginal people, Davis (1986) alerts us to a potential problem that needs to be carefully considered. Because of their reliance on professionals, consultants, and skilled people, there is a danger that these formal groups may adopt advocacy rather than advisory roles. Historical evidence indicates that low participation, top-down bureaucracy, and public apathy are the results when the common citizens are excluded or omitted from the process.

Meaningful parental involvement with Indian and Metis people requires time and effort on the part of parents and school personnel. In many cases, parents and teachers have been estranged for so long that mutual trust and respect must first be established, and then remain the foundation of a successful working relationship between both parties. Similarly, programs must be given time to develop before being evaluated as successful or unsuccessful. There must be sincere commitment on the part of both the parents and school personnel to work effectively.

The approach being used in Frontier School Division is a successful step in developing active constituents and empowering aboriginal people to become good at doing things for themselves and with others. Cervone and O'Leary (1982) write that "a good parent involvement program therefore includes strategies for keeping less visible parents 'connected' as well as strategies to stimulate and tap the potential of highly visible parents" (p. 49). It appears that this is indeed happening in this northern Manitoba school system.

References

Beale, A. V. (1985, January). Toward more effective parent involvement. *The Clearing House*, 213-215.

Brandt, R. (1989). On parents and schools: A conversation with Joyce Epstein. *Educational Leadership, 47* (2), 24-27.

Cervone, B. T., & O'Leary, K. (1982, November). A conceptual framework for parent involvement. *Educational Leadership*, 48-49.

Corbett, H. D., & Rossman, G. B. (1989). Three paths to implementing change: A resource note. *Curriculum Inquiry, 19* (2), 163-190.

Davis, S. (1986). The participation of Indian and Metis parents in the school system. *Canadian Journal of Native Education, 13* (2), 32-39.

Epstein, J. L. (1987, January). What principals should know about parent involvement. *Principal*, 6-9.

Frontier School Division, No. 48. (1989). *Parental involvement handbook* (2nd ed.).

Fullan, M. G., Anderson, S. E., & Newton, E. A. (1986). *Support systems for implementing curriculum in school boards*. Toronto: The Ontario Institute for Studies in Education.

Hopkirk, G., & Newton, E. (1986). Reconstructing educational organizations: Reason and foolishness. *Canadian School Executive, 6* (2), 3-12.

Knudson, B. (1990). *A study of the principal's role in planning for increased parental involvement*. Unpublished master's project, University of Saskatchewan, Saskatoon.

McLaughlin, M. W., & Shields, P. M. (1987, October). Involving low-income parents in the schools: A role for policy? *Phi Delta Kappan*, 156-160.

Newton, E., & Wright, R. (1987). Forces affecting change in small rural schools. *School Organization, 7* (3), 357-366.

Northwest Territories Department of Education. (1991, March). *Our students, our future: An educational framework.*

Pearson, N. L. (1990). Parent involvement within the school: To be or not to be. *Education Canada, 30* (3), 14-17.

Richardson, D. T., Richardson, Z. A. C. (1986). Changes and parental involvement in Indian education. *Canadian Journal of Native Education, 13* (3), 21-25.

Seefeldt, C. (1985). Parent involvement: Support or stress? *Childhood Education, 62* (2), 98-102.

Smith, C. B. (1988). The expanding role of parents. *The Reading Teacher, 42* (1), 68-69.

8

Program Equity in Small Rural

Schools in Alberta

Lynn Bosetti & Tom Gee

Introduction

Education has been on the brink of change for the past decade or more. A number of attempts have been made to change the educational paradigm that has existed since formal schooling was introduced into the western world over a hundred years ago. The educational system, designed initially to meet the needs of a rural agrarian society, and modified for an industrial urban society, had as its main purpose the acculturation of immigrant children into society, and the selection and sorting of children in terms of their potential for carrying out work roles in the urban industrial economy (Schlechty, 1990). Emerging social and economic realities now require significant changes in our educational system in order to prepare students to function effectively in, and to contribute to, an emerging information-based global economy. Communications technology has the potential to be used to lead education into the new reality of the twenty-first century.

In 1987, in an attempt to solve problems of program equity in small rural schools, where the need for fiscal responsibility has increasingly come into conflict with educational needs, and where the retention of families in rural communities is often concomitant with improving school programs, Alberta Education introduced distance education as a pilot project to thirteen small high schools in ten southeastern Alberta jurisdictions. Within one year the number of participating schools had increased to twenty-eight in sixteen school systems. A second project was introduced that brought distance education programming to an additional twenty-four schools in the northwestern quadrant of the province. By the third year, one hundred and thirty-nine small schools throughout rural Alberta were offering some, and in one case all, of their high school program by distance education.

The purpose of this chapter is to describe the development and implementation of distance education in the province of Alberta

163

and to discuss, from the perspective of those involved in its management and delivery, how it works in practice.

Genesis

If teachers can no longer be reasonably expected to know everything about everything and impart that knowledge to their students; if it is too expensive to train teachers in sufficient numbers so that every school has specialists in every subject; if the subjects that schools are being asked to teach (environmental education, computer literacy, Career and Life Management, electronics, foreign languages, and so on) are beyond the knowledge base of most or all the teachers on staff; if parents are asking for the moon in a time of fiscal restraint; if one or two students in the entire student body want to take Beauty Culture; if thirty students want conversational French and a dearth of French teachers in rural areas prohibits hiring even when the school board is prepared to do so, then a new paradigm for education seems warranted. Distance Education, and more specifically the technology associated with distance delivery, is changing the conventional educational paradigm. Education, through the influences of technology, is moving into the age of information.

In Alberta, the rural population and the agrarian lifestyle have been in a state of decline for several decades due to the demise of the small farm and the rise of corporate farming, as well as the general movement toward urbanization. As a result, student enrollment in rural schools has also been declining steadily. The solution to this problem from the 1950s to the 1970s was the amalgamation of school districts and the busing of students, often over long distances to regionalized schools (Clark & Schieman, 1988). Every rural school system in Alberta owned a fleet of buses, maintenance garages, and bus compounds, or the service was provided under contract by private companies.

But closing small schools and bringing students to centralized educational services had inherent limitations. Eventually the distances and time spent getting to and from school were too great. Political representatives realized the prohibitive expense of transporting students and heard the outcry from parents that their children were spending too much time in transit. As well, the closure of small schools had a detrimental effect on the cultural identity of rural communities. The school was often the only visible symbol of community, and school closure was perceived as an attack on the community structure itself (Clark & Schieman,

1988). Thus, the Government sought new delivery systems that would facilitate its goal of providing equitable educational opportunities for all students irrespective of their ability, circumstance, or location, and would permit small rural schools to remain open by enhancing their course offerings in a cost-effective way (Secondary Education Policy, 1985; The School Act, 1988). Consequently, in the late 1980's distance education came into its own.

Since the 1920s, the Alberta Correspondence School (ACS) had provided a conventional form of distance education to students in the remote parts of the province of Alberta. By the 1980s, ACS was serving over 30 000 students. A third of these were adults who were upgrading their education and had neither the time nor the inclination to go back to school to do it; or they lived in rural communities and had no easy access to community colleges which offered after-hours adult upgrading courses. The other two-thirds of the student body served by the ACS, with the exception of a handful of elementary students and students overseas, were high school students attending schools which did not have the teacher expertise to provide them with all the subjects they wanted, or which were too small to establish economically viable class sizes in all the courses that were needed. Most of these schools were in the rural areas of Alberta, and these students were expected to work on their ACS courses after hours at home, where print material was delivered and returned by regular mail. Problems of declining motivation and isolation resulted in less than thirty percent completion by students involved in ACS courses (Haughey, 1990; Alberta Education, n.d.). It became apparent that when compared to students in large urban high schools where a variety of courses were available through conventionally delivered classes, rural students were not receiving equitable educational opportunities. In 1987, in response to these inequities, the Minister of Education introduced the Distance Learning in Small Schools (DLSS) Project.

The Project

The DLSS project was conceived over a three month period during the summer of 1987. The project design was guided by the following statements from the Secondary Education Policy in Alberta: "The remote or small rural school, limited in teacher personnel and/or resources, could use distance education to offer a broader choice of courses" and "alleviate the need to close small schools and the negative effect this has on communities." As one of its main principles, the policy states that "The secondary education system must use technology to enhance and to facilitate access to equitable educational opportunities for all students, regardless of ability, circumstance or location." These directives, combined with the economic reality of fiscal restraint in funding education, required innovative approaches to allocating educational resources, particularly in small rural schools.

The DLSS project was designed to incorporate the following seven purposes: equity of access and flexibility for rural students in terms of program offerings in small rural schools; improvement in quality of course delivery and support services to distance learners; promotion of resource sharing among jurisdictions and/or schools to provide high quality, low cost educational services to larger groups of students in small schools; decentralization of correspondence course marking and tutorial services to create a more effective learning environment at the local level; development of regional or school-based resource services to enable students to access materials, information, and human support; application of technology in the delivery of distance learning; and establishment of a new course design system that incorporated effective techniques for independent learning and the appropriate use of technologies (Alberta Education, June, 1987).

Ten school districts from the southeastern quadrant of the province were invited to participate in the project. Within these districts, 13 schools, separated by as much as five hundred kilometers, with fewer than 50 students in their senior high grades ten to twelve, were selected. While Alberta Education provided funding for the three year project, the intent was that if the project was successful, the participating school districts would continue the distance education program on their own, sharing administrative and instructional staff (Alberta Education, June, 1987).

Challenges and Constraints

After consultation with numerous rural small school administrators, the DLSS Project Director was confronted with a number of challenges and constraints in the design and implementation of the project. The first challenge was to adopt only those communication technologies that had proven themselves in distance delivery, and would not jeopardize the advancement of high school students. For example, consideration was given to the level of computer literacy of students and their ability to keyboard their lessons onto the computer in order to then transmit their work to a subject teacher at another location. One distance education teacher (tutor-marker) commented on her experience with computer transmission:

> I tried having my students do their lessons on the computer on an experimental basis to eliminate the exchange of paper, to make reading their lessons easier, and to make it easier to keep track of their work and progress. It was a wonderful idea but the students weren't ready for it.

Due to such constraints, the DLSS project was initially based on the transmission by facsimile of materials prepared by the Alberta Correspondence School and augmented by additional personnel and communications technology (Clark & Schieman, 1988).

The second challenge that restricted the kinds of communication technologies that could be used for program delivery was one posed by some of the principals of small schools in rural Alberta. These principals were initially opposed to implementing synchronous (real time) delivery technologies such as teleconferencing, audio graphic conferencing, and satellite broadcasts, that would require common time tabling of courses between participating schools. In the scheduling of the school day, these principals already had to take into consideration such factors as busing schedules with other schools, itinerant teachers, gymnasium and shop schedules, and kindergarten hours, to name a few, making common time tabling for distance education an added burden. The alternative would be to provide release time from other classes for students to attend distance education sessions. The Project therefore adopted communication technologies such as telefacsimilie (FAX) machines, tele-tutorials between the tutor-markers and students using long distance telephone exchanges, and telephone answering machines. The purpose of adopting these technologies was to facilitate asynchronous delivery, but also to ensure that students had their lessons marked and returned, or their questions that were either Faxed or left on the telephone answering machine, answered by the tutor-marker in a turn-around time of 36 hours or less.

To determine which courses would be offered through the DLSS project, the participating school superintendents identified courses, from the 323 listed in the Alberta Program of Studies, that they would like offered as distance education courses. They identified 65 courses which were then grouped into ten subject areas: English, French, German, Sciences, Social Sciences, Mathematics, Business Education, Industrial Education, Home Economics, and Art. It was apparent that ten teachers would be required to implement the program.

Implementation

✎ *Technology and Support*

Nine teachers were hired, one by each of nine participating boards (the tenth board assigned one very small rural school to the project for the receipt of courses only). One board hired a retired English/French teacher. One board hired a home economics teacher who lived in a small town which had no school, so a FAX and answering machine were installed in her home. Another board hired a business education teacher who wanted to stay at home to look after her preschool child. One board hired a local farmer who was also a certified industrial arts teacher. After he had harvested his crops in the Fall, he had time on his hands until Spring planting. Throughout the Winter he could feed his stock and deliver industrial art courses from his ranch house. The art teacher and the German teacher taught in elementary schools and were given some time from their regular elementary teaching to provide tutorial-marking services to high school students through distance education courses. FAX and answering machines were placed in their schools. The social science teacher was given time from her regular high school assignments in a very small rural school to offer social science courses by distance education to the "consortium" or "network," as the project schools were collectively being called. A mathematics teacher was likewise given time from his high school teaching assignments to serve the math needs of the consortium. The science teacher taught part-time for a local community college and also for the consortium. A FAX and answering machine were installed in her home. In each case where the teacher was in a school, the school was one of the thirteen participating schools, and the FAX machine used by the teacher to deliver out to other schools was also used by students in that school to send and retrieve their own course work to and from their distance education teachers located elsewhere.

✎ *Tutor-Markers*

The distance education teachers were called "tutor-markers" and were expected to mark and provide feedback on student's assignments and examinations, be available for telephone tutorials with their assigned students, initiate teleconferencing with students in accordance with perceived needs, develop materials and tests as required in addition to those supplied by the ACS, and maintain a tutor log which recorded all individual and collective tutor/student conferences. The French teacher explains how she views her role as a tutor-marker:

> To teach at a distance you have to have a real feel for kids. I get along pretty well with them. I teleconference on a regular basis – usually three or four times a week for French. I like teleconferencing because the students get to talk to each other and we get to know one another. I don't actually teach the course, rather I supplement it. The kids do the lessons and then I take their lessons and look at their difficulties, arrive at some conclusions and then discuss these problems during our teleconference. If I don't have time during the teleconference to adequately handle a problem, I then encourage them to phone me individually.

Not all tutor-markers, however, were able to accommodate teleconferencing in their courses because of differences in class schedules among the participating schools. Some of these teachers became frustrated by the limitations of the FAX machine, telephone, and telephone answering machines. The DLSS Project Director explains:

> A student from Acme School would reach a point in his course where he encountered a problem. He would telephone or FAX a message to his distance education teacher and receive a reply. A few days later a student in Altario School, three hundred miles to the northeast, would reach the same point in the lesson and encounter similar problems. He too would contact the tutor-marker for assistance. The distance education teachers found themselves repeatedly answering the same questions as their students arrived at these points of difficulty in the lessons.

During the second phase of the DLSS project, a principal was seconded from his school system to network the twenty-eight schools and the five distance education teachers who worked out of their homes into a DLSS computer network. The solution to the problem of one-to-one instruction by FAX or telephone was a computer bulletin board system (bbs) and electronic mail which would permit multi-point asynchronous delivery. A set of subject forums were set up on a computer bulletin board system on ASPEN, the Alberta Special Education Network, for each of the ten course areas offered through distance education. When students reached a problem they could ask a question on the appropriate subject forum and the tutor-marker would respond to it (asynchronously), usually in less than thirty-six hours. The question and answer would reside there until all the students had reached or passed that point in their lessons. Teachers could also leave directions on the bbs for the entire class. The system also provided a teacher-talk forum and a test forum accessible only to teachers, as well as a student chat forum. One tutor-marker commented on her use of the bbs:

> There is so much you can do with a computer bulletin board. Some schools were just wonderful, every Friday morning they'd log in, so there would always be interesting messages or notices. My French students would exchange messages in French with their fellow students in the consortium. I would leave messages reminding students when their reports were due, and for those of my English students having difficulty finding an essay topic, I would leave a number of suggested topics on the bulletin board.

The teacher went on to say that when the bulletin board went from being accessible to those in the DLSS Project consortium to being open to all consortia as these evolved across the province, teachers and students tended to stop using it.

> I'd pull up the bulletin board and see maybe fifty messages, none of which related to me or my students. It became too impersonal. I didn't want to put my English 23 essay topics on the bulletin board for everyone to look at. I felt a little foolish. I didn't feel like informing the world.

The evaluators of the DLSS project reported that, in regard to electronic mail the major advantage was that the intended recipients did not have to be present when the message was sent, but could read and respond to the message at their convenience. However, this same feature was also viewed as a disadvantage by the tutor-markers because they had to rely on the intended recipients, their students, actually accessing the system and reading the messages. As a result, this communication system was slow to catch on due to the general lack of confidence that the messages would actually be read (Clark & Schieman, 1990, p. 40). Students, however, used their "chat" forum excessively, and the evaluators saw potential in bbs/electronic mail, and felt that its place in distance education was still emerging (p. 41).

✎ *Coordinator*

In each participating school a "Distance Education Coordinator" was identified, who in some cases was the school principal, but usually, and more effectively, was an interested teacher who was given some release time to coordinate the program. In schools where the principal was involved in and supportive of the distance education program, cognizant of what was happening and monitoring it closely, the program was most successful. However, in schools where the principal was not personally involved in the program, it did not run as smoothly (Alberta Education *Monitoring Report, 1989/90,* p. 2). A principal explains some of the problems in managing a distance education program in a small school. His concern is a result of his desire to have each off-site tutor-marker meet the expectations of the school, and to have consistency in the practices among tutor-markers and the regular teaching staff with regard to grading and penalizing students for incomplete or late assignments.

> With the cooperation of the teachers — and the distance education teachers would be an extension of this — I like to have a sense of control over what happens in my school. As principal I am the one who is ultimately responsible for the operation of the school program. A problem exists when the distance education teachers want to have the same sense of ownership over the students that are taking their course as they would if they were teaching that course on site. What I would like is to have a marking service and a consultative service, and the ownership remain with us. That is, we set the contracts with the students as to when they are going to complete their lessons, we monitor them and carry them through, and if there are to be penalties attached for not getting their work in on time, we will set them. The problem is that these tutor-markers are not here at our staff meetings and are not involved in the informal interchange with the teachers, so they don't necessarily play by the same rules.

A tutor-marker comments on how she deals with school principals in the monitoring and evaluation of students:

> I view the principal as having supreme authority. If there is a decision to be made regarding the progress of a student, I recommend action rather than demand it. I always contact the school supervisor and the principal, and then I document every bit of it. Sometimes I even tape our conversations so I am sure of what has been said.

The findings of the evaluation of the DLSS project (Clark & Schieman, 1988) identified matters of consistency and lines of authority with respect to tutor-markers as an issue that required policy guidelines. The evaluators reported that tutor-markers sensed themselves being responsible to 13 school principals who operated under different philosophies and jurisdiction policies (p. viii).

The school's distance education coordinator was officially responsible for ensuring that distance education students in the school were properly registered in their distance education courses; had time allocated in their daily course schedule to work on their distance education course(s); had adequate supervision for their distance education classes; received their course materials on time; Faxed their lessons on schedule to their tutor-markers; and received assistance as necessary to contact their tutor-markers. Finally, the coordinators were responsible for the administration and processing of all correspondence course examinations for the school. It was soon determined that the better the coordination at the school level, the better the distance education program worked in the school.

✎ *Scheduling Distance Education Courses*

While one of the central values in distance education is the flexibility inherent in an independent study approach, by the end of the second year of the DLSS project most of schools had forsaken this approach in favor of ensuring course completion through closer monitoring of students' progress (Clark & Schieman, 1990). The scheduling of distance education classes in schools varied in the extent to which they were formally scheduled, ranging from no designated classes, to some assigned, to all assigned (Clark & Haughey, 1990).

Professional supervision was often rotated among members of the teaching staff; however, this was not always the case. In one school the supervision of distance education students was assigned to an interested local resident with a high school diploma, who spent a great deal of her time reading books in the subject area she was supervising in order to be of more assistance to the students. In another case the supervisor was a lawyer with three degrees. Depending on the distance education coordinator of a particular school, who was frequently the distance education supervisor as well, the role of the supervisor would vary. However, supervision at the school was deemed to be essential. In most cases, the supervisor was responsible for discussing with students their responsibilities for learning/working at their own rate, including reviewing the sequence of the course content, the number of units or modules, matters of testing and evaluation, and the importance of working consistently to finish the course in the time provided. The students would then establish a contract with their distant tutor-marker in which they would determine how they would complete the course assignments in the given time. For the remainder of the course the supervisor's responsibility would be to monitor student progress, answer student questions or assist them in contacting their tutor-marker or another teacher with the appropriate subject area expertise, distribute materials and mark assignments, ensure assignments were Faxed to the tutor-markers, distribute and supervise examinations, update student progress records, and generally supervise the distance education classroom. Many supervisors developed a timeline for certain subject areas "based on completion dates for the units at that grade level, and made wall charts identifying dates so that students could easily calculate the differences between where they were and where they were supposed to be" (Clark & Haughey, 1990, p.16). In some schools the supervisor recommended ten percent of the course grade because he or she had direct contact with the student. In all cases, the effective supervisor remained in close contact with the tutor-markers, particularly in the case of students encountering difficulty completing the course. A supervisor explains:

> I spend a lot of time on the telephone just letting the tutor-marker know if the kids are having some trouble in certain areas or with certain concepts, or if they're going to be late with their assignments, of if they are having family problems that are influencing their ability to do their work.

The key problem that most supervisors faced was ensuring that the students complete their assignments on time.

Distance education coordinators have experimented with a number of different ways to assign teaching staff to the supervision of distance education classes. In one school, each distance education student was assigned to a member of the regular staff who was to serve as their on-site mentor/monitor (Clark & Haughey, 1990). Because of low pupil-teacher ratio, another school integrated distance education students into existing courses so that teachers taught their regular course and, at the same time, supervised students engaged in distance education courses. A principal shares the following example:

> A teacher supervisor may be teaching a chemistry 10 class, but have students working on science 14 and chemistry 20 through distance education in the same room. The teacher would teach the chem. 10 lesson, and while those students

were working on their assignment she would go around and help the distance education students.

In general, students and supervisor preferred to have some scheduled time and an assigned classroom for distance education classes because many students did little homework and seldom used their spares to meet the unit dates necessary for course completion. At scheduled periods during the week, all distance education students were assigned into this room irrespective of the distance education courses they were taking. In the evaluation of the distance education project, the evaluators found that it was beneficial to limit distance education classes in any one of these periods to a reduced range of possible tutor topics for the supervising teacher. They recommended confining these classroom periods to one grade level ideally, and to no more than three different subjects or courses in the room (Clark & Haughey, 1990, p. 16). In practice, however, there were often as many as three grade levels and up to ten different courses/subjects represented in the distance education classroom at any given time.

Impact on Students

The success of distance education is to a great degree contingent upon the ability and level of motivation of the students. Individual learning skills are needed to succeed in distance education because students have to take more responsibility for their own learning. For some students, using distance education materials increased their opportunities for success because the Carnegie time unit was not as strictly adhered to as in conventionally-delivered courses. There was more time tabling flexibility which allowed students to pick up courses after the conventional registration period (suggesting the possibility of multiple entry points), and there were more courses available to them (Alberta Education *Distance Education Monitoring Report, 1989-90*, p. 2).

In their evaluation of the distance education project Clark and Haughey (1990) found:

> The transfer of students from a system where the teacher provided the impetus through class lecture and sustained the focus through seat work, to one where students had to obtain all the information from written booklets and provide their own motivation with limited teacher assistance was a difficult transition for many students (p. 18).

They found that while students of all levels of ability did well using a distance education format, the key factor was the level of motivation. The less motivated students required support and structure to assist them in coping with their new found freedom and to guide their learning. These students were the biggest challenge for supervising teachers because they required longer explanations and were easily distracted (p. 19). Conversely, the motivated students used the system to accelerate their progress, and enjoyed the freedom and challenge of setting their own pace. Clark and Schieman (1990) recommended that schools carefully screen students who they counsel into distance education. They found students with low ability and low motivation were often put into distance education courses because they constituted the smaller course group. However, in some cases, these students were the least able to handle the level of abstraction and the level of reading required.

Results

The real success of distance education still remains to be seen as more schools become involved in offering courses through this approach, and as more learning resources involving alternative technologies are developed. Small rural schools are still discovering the potential of distance education technology for addressing problems such as small class sizes and declining numbers, the dearth of subject specialist teachers in rural high schools, the limited range of courses available to students, the limited choice in how and where students complete their high school education, and the decreasing viability of rural schools and their communities. However, the potential of distance education to increase effectiveness in such areas will be realized only as teachers and administrators are willing to entertain the possibility of computer terminals and computer linked networks replacing the classroom as the venue for instruction. The educative relationship between students and teachers must also change to accommodate the reality that distance education technology not only allows students to take more responsibility for their learning, but also allows them to engage in cooperative learning through communication networks that move them beyond the boundaries of the school (Levinson, 1990). In distance education, teachers are no longer viewed as the sole basis of information, especially when students who have a particular interest will be able to pursue, on their own, information which is current. Teachers will be facilitators of learning, and will teach students how to access, manage, and make sense of current information. They will be more involved with how students learn than with what they learn.

There is a beguiling temptation to assume that distance education technology, or the perfect packaging of distance education curriculum materials, will resolve the problems of teaching at a distance (Batey & Cowell, 1986; Haughey, 1990). The focus of distance education must remain on enhancing and facilitating student learning, and not on the transmission of content. Batey and Cowell (1986) caution that to embrace technology as a panacea would create problems – technology is not the curriculum:

> Distance education must be separated in our minds from the technology which delivers it. . . . At it's best it can stimulate the students, energize the teaching staff and solidify the community while delivering exciting learning experiences to all three of these groups (p. 31).

Conclusion

In conclusion, what was learned in Alberta's Distance Learning in Small Schools Project? Technologically, the systems that worked the best were those which disrupted conventional classes the least. These were asynchronous technologies such as the FAX machine, the telephone answering machine, and the computer bulletin board system. Synchronous teleconferencing was essential to the language courses for their oral component and, therefore, was accommodated, in some cases reluctantly, by the participating schools. Satellite television broadcast, when attempted, was only accessible interactively by those students free of conventional classes at the time of broadcast; otherwise, it was dubbed off air for asynchronous use of the tape. Videotape libraries began to evolve in the schools as teachers discovered the wealth of satellite programming available.

Academically, the Project demonstrated that rural school course offerings could be more than triple those available by conventional delivery, and at no more cost per unit. Pedagogically, students learned as well as students engaged in education delivered through conventional means. The completion rate of the distance education courses increased to nearly ninety percent, whereas the completion rate of conventional correspondence courses was only thirty percent. This increase is attributed to the closer contact between students and their supervisor and a faster turn-around time in marking and returned assignments from the tutor-marker. Relative to conventionally delivered courses, student averages in distance education were not significantly different. Heuristically, distance education has had a significant impact on education in Alberta. Distance education technology has the potential to connect students globally, to provide students with skills and experience in accessing information from people or systems with that information, and to foster the acquisition of knowledge by those who need to know. As society moves into the information age and as communication technologies become more sophisticated, geographical boundaries will have little meaning to students in small rural schools. It may be that the current trend of declining populations in rural communities will end as communication technology gives people the option of maintaining their rural lifestyle while, at the same time, connecting to the global information network. By 1990-91 in Alberta, five large consortia of school systems and numerous smaller networks connected all small rural high schools for the delivery of courses by distance education.

Finally, the impetus for the development and implementation of the DLSS Project can be summarized with reference to the conceptual framework developed by Tichy (1980) to explain how organizations change in response to the dynamic contexts in which they are embedded. Tichy argues that organizations change in an attempt to resolve three interrelated ongoing dilemmas related to technical design, political allocation, and ideological and cultural mix (p. 165). The genesis of the DLSS Project can be viewed as the Government's attempt to fulfill their political goal of "providing equitable educational opportunity for all students regardless of their ability, circumstance/location" (Secondary Education Policy, 1985; School Act, 1988). This problem of program equity was compounded by the reality that there was an apparent shift in the cultural values and lifestyle of people residing in rural Alberta. Distance education technology was viewed as a means of maintaining the cultural identity and social and economic viability of rural communities where the school and perhaps a grain elevator may be the only visible symbols of the community. Through distance education small rural schools could remain open, enhance their course offerings in a cost effective way, and provide the opportunity for students to complete the course requirements for a high school diploma. Finally, distance education provided an efficient and effective means to address the technical and human resource problems of operating small schools. The central problem being that it is not feasible for small schools to employ adequately trained teachers (meaning specialists) to teach the required core and complimentary courses necessary for a high school diploma. Real constraints such as low student enrollment, budget and time tabling constraints, as well as the cost and time involved in busing children to consolidated/regional schools created the need for alternative means of providing quality education to students regardless of their geographic location. Thus, the development and implementation of distance education was a means of addressing political and technical problems related to program equity, as well as the cultural problem of maintaining life in rural Alberta.

References

Alberta Education. (n.d.). *Distance education in Alberta*. Edmonton, AB: Author.

_____ (n.d.). *Distance education monitoring report 1989-90*. Edmonton, AB: Author.

_____ (n.d.). *Distance learning in small schools: An action research project, 1987-1990*. Edmonton, AB: Author.

_____ (1987). *Distance learning in small schools: An action research project (Project guidelines)*. Edmonton, AB: Author.

_____ (1990). *1988/89 annual report*. Edmonton, AB: Government of Alberta.

Batey, A. & Cowell, R. N. (1986). *Distance education: An overview*. Portland, OR: Northwest Regional Education Laboratory. (ERIC Document Reproduction Service No. RC016071).

Clark, W. B. & Haughey, M. L. (1990). *Evaluation of year one of distance learning project north*. Under contract to Alberta Education, Edmonton.

Clark, W. B. & Schieman, E. (1988). *Evaluation of phase 1 of the distance learning in small schools action research project*. Under contract to Alberta Education, Edmonton.

_____ (1990). *Evaluation of phase 2 of the distance learning in small schools action research project*. Under contract to Alberta Education, Edmonton.

Elliot, O. (1991). Project north: A model for distance learning became a model for frustration. *Spectrum*, June, 4-5.

Gee, T. (1991). Program equity in Alberta's small rural schools. *Distance Education, 12* (2), 170-190.

Haughey, M. (1990). Distance education in schools. *The Canadian Administrator, 29* (8), 1-9.

Levinson, E. (1990). Will technology transform education or will the schools co-opt technology? *Phi Delta Kappa, 72* (2), 121-126.

Schlechty, P. (1990). *Schools for the 21st century: Leadership imperatives for educational reform*. Oxford: Jossey-Bass.

Tichy, N. (1980). Problem cycles in organizations and the management of change. In T. Kimberly and R. Miles (Eds.), *The organizational life cycle*. San Francisco: Jossey-Bass.

9

Distance Education Technology

Equalizing Educational Opportunity for Students in Small Schools

Don Downer and Wynanne Downer

I know of no more encouraging fact than the unquestionable ability of man to elevate his life by a conscious endeavor.

Volkman, A.G. (1960). *Thoreau on Man and Nature*

Introduction

The term "distance education" refers to the development of especially designed instructional materials and their structured delivery to individuals separated from their institution by space and/or time. An alternative definition is that distance education learning involves live, simultaneous transmission of a master teacher's lessons from a host classroom or studio to receive site classrooms in distance locations (Barker, 1987). Moore (1973) gave a more comprehensive definition: distance education is "those teaching methods in which because of the physical separation of learner, and teachers, the interactive, as well as the proactive phase of teaching, is conducted through print, mechanical, or electronic devices" (p. 5).

> Distance education media involves a full range of technology including audio teleconferencing, audio graphics, audio tapes, video tapes, television via satellite, two-way interactive television, and microcomputer links and networks. Rural schools . . . especially in Australia, Alaska and Canada . . . are becoming innovators in applications of technology and in networking. The emphasis is on the use of multiple technologies, collaboration, and coordination as important steps in addressing the needs of rural schools (Hobbs, 1985).

Canada with a small dispersed population separated by climatic and geographical barriers is well suited for a distance education program. Learners in small and remote communities are the main beneficiaries of such a program. Newfoundland and Labrador with its characteristic climatic and geographical barriers and a sparse population has proven to be fertile ground for the development of distance education. With the reality of a large number of small isolated fishing settlements scattered along a vast coastline, the province has had a long struggle to equalize educational opportunities for students attending small schools frequently in remote areas.

Since 1961, Memorial University of Newfoundland, in conjunction with a number of other agencies including Newfoundland Telephone, has been in the forefront of the development of distance education in the province serving mainly adult audiences using tele-communications technology. The following is an excerpt from a speech delivered by V. G. Withers, President and CEO of Newfoundland Telephone on March 25, 1992, at the Interactive Television Tele-communications Demonstration at Memorial University of Newfoundland:

> The application of technology, in particular telecommunications technology, to overcome the special difficulties of the Newfoundland environment is one of our strengths. Over the past 10-15 years we have proven that by working together we can use leading edge telecommunications technologies to find innovative and cost effective solutions to the difficulties presented by our environment, and become world leaders in the process (p. 4).

The distance education program, which serves high school students in small and remote schools in the province of Newfoundland and Labrador, was established by the Department of Education in 1988 as a pilot project. One cohort of students have completed three levels of Advanced Mathematics, the first high school courses to be introduced. The distance education program offering will include Physics and French during the 1992-93 school year. In 1991, there were 31 distance education centres operating in the province (Figure 1).

In this chapter an outline of some of the cultural, technical/organizational, social/political pressures which have been associated with the development of distance education efforts in small and remote schools in the province will be examined (Tichy, 1980; House, 1981; and Corbett and Rossman, 1989). There will also be an effort to examine some of the positive and negative aspects of the current Advanced Mathematics program which is being offered to students in small schools through the distance education program. Enrollment numbers of males and females in the Advanced Mathematics will be compared to determine if there are any gender differences for students opting to do the program.

Distance education efforts elsewhere in North America will be examined by a review of available literature.

Development of the concept of distance education in the province will be looked at mainly by an assessment of available research data collected from the people currently involved: the students and their parents in the small communities; school principals and teacher coordinators at the schools level; distance education instructors and the administrative personnel at the Department of Education; and school board personnel. Data collection has been mainly by extensive personal interview.

Setting

The island of Newfoundland has a coastline of 6000 miles; when the coastline of Labrador is included, the length almost doubles. In 1949, the year of Confederation with Canada, there were 1187 schools in the province in communities mostly stretched along this vast coastline. A total of 778, or 66.5%, of these schools were one-room or "sole charge" with multi-graded classrooms and largely untrained and often inexperienced teachers (Rowe, 1964, p. 156).

Newfoundland is a province of small schools. During the 1960s more than half of the approximately 1300 schools in the province were one- or two-room schools administered by some 270 small school boards. In 1972 27.1% of the total number of schools in the province had two rooms or less (Fisher and Warren, 1972, p. 36). In 1989-90 there were 543 schools serving 130 109 students in approximately 302 communities. Although resettlement and consolidation of schools has substantially reduced numbers, in 1992 there are 531 schools and 27 school boards; 80 of these schools are still considered to be small schools concentrated along the coast of Southern Labrador but scattered along the full length of the long coastline of Newfoundland and Labrador as well. A total of 16 621 of the student population attended 249 schools funded under the small school regulations in 1992; that is, the schools were allocated extra units based on their small size (Royal Commission of Inquiry into The Delivery of Programs and Services, 1992, p. 134).

Sixty percent of the school boards are rural and approximately one-half of the students are in areas predominated by a rural lifestyle. Since 1969 and the implementation of several recommendations of the Warren Royal Commission Report, the number of school boards in the province has been substantially reduced. From almost one board for every small outport school of a partic-

Figure 1: Distance Education Sites in Newfoundland/Labrador

Distance Education Sites
1990-91

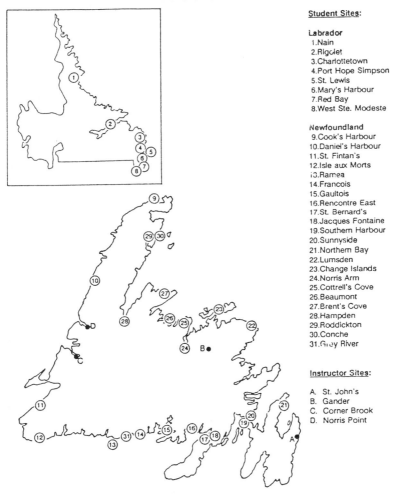

Student Sites:

Labrador
1. Nain
2. Rigolet
3. Charlottetown
4. Port Hope Simpson
5. St. Lewis
6. Mary's Harbour
7. Red Bay
8. West Ste. Modeste

Newfoundland
9. Cook's Harbour
10. Daniel's Harbour
11. St. Fintan's
12. Isle aux Morts
13. Ramea
14. Francois
15. Gaultois
16. Rencontre East
17. St. Bernard's
18. Jacques Fontaine
19. Southern Harbour
20. Sunnyside
21. Northern Bay
22. Lumsden
23. Change Islands
24. Norris Arm
25. Cottrell's Cove
26. Beaumont
27. Brent's Cove
28. Hampden
29. Roddickton
30. Conche
31. Grey River

Instructor Sites:

A. St. John's
B. Gander
C. Corner Brook
D. Norris Point

ular religious denomination the number was initially reduced to thirty-two boards. Beginning again in the late 1980s this number has now been reduced to just twenty-seven boards consisting of one run by the Pentecostal Assemblies, one by the Seventh-Day Adventist, sixteen by the Integrated denominations (Anglican, United Church, Salvation Army and Presbyterian Churches), and nine by the Roman Catholic Church. In May, 1992, the William's

Royal Commission of Inquiry report, *Our Children, Our Future*, recommended that the number of school boards in the province be reduced to nine regional boards which would be non-denominational.

F. W. Rowe, Minister of Education in 1958, stated the average child in the one-room schools of Newfoundland was sentenced to semi-illiteracy unless drastic and radical steps were taken to provide some means of giving a high school education to the pupils in these schools. He added that of the 2810 children who were in the second grade in 1949 only four matriculated or passed grade eleven in 1958. Rowe considered that the chance of a child in a one-room school achieving matriculation was about one-sixth of one percent (Perlin, 1959).

A government resettlement program during the 1960s resulted in the demise of hundreds of small communities scattered along the coastline of Newfoundland and Labrador. The program, although it uprooted thousands of families causing them to relocate into larger communities and some "growth" centres, was successful in drastically reducing the approximately 1300 schools in the province at that time.

During the 1980s the closing of small schools in both urban and rural communities became a big issue across Canada. Deane (1992) states that a small school in New Brunswick today can be defined as a school with an enrollment of 200 or fewer students and/or a teaching staff of 10 or fewer. In New Brunswick 28.5% of the schools meet this criterion. The escalation of emotions generated by the proposed closing of small neighborhood schools is well illustrated across Canada in both urban and rural areas.

Cartwright School, in the tiny community of Cartwright in Southwestern Manitoba, for example, is well known nation-wide because of the media coverage given to it in recent times (Langton, 1992). The School Board in the region proposed in March, 1991, to transfer grades 10-12 students to Killarney School, 32 km to the east of Cartwright. After five months the issue was resolved and the community was permitted to retain its K-12 small school status but the high school section became an independent private school.

The closing of S.D. Cook School, an elementary K-6 school in the relatively large community of Corner Brook, Newfoundland, generated almost as much furor. The debate flared on two occasions over some four years beginning in 1985 with the School Board's decision to close the neighborhood school. Many of the parents with children attending S.D. Cook were people with professional positions in the community. They argued strongly and presented data to support the position that their children would receive a better education in the smaller school rather than in a substantially larger school nearby. The parents lost the argument when the School Board closed the school in 1989 in a cost-cutting measure.

Not all parents have lost in the volatile debate over the closing of schools. A decision by the Inverness County School Board on Cape Breton Island, Nova Scotia, was rejected by parents and local citizens (Gilles, 1992). The plan was to close Margaree Forks District High School as well as Whycocamagh, Port Hood, and Judique schools and to bus the students to a new collegiate at Inverness in September, 1992. The strategy in this case was to elect candidates to wards of the office of trustee, or the local school board, and to overturn the decision of the previous school board. The plan worked: the decision was overturned and the schools remained open.

Parents and the general public across Canada have become more sophisticated and adept at defeating unpopular decisions by school boards and governments concerning the closing of small schools during the past decade. Political skills have become finely honed in the process. Governments and government agencies in recent years have become wary of this and are often reluctant to take potentially unpopular decisions about closings of small neighborhood schools and schools in small communities.

While the closing of certain small schools, especially those which necessitate the busing of children over long distances, frequently during severe winter conditions, has resulted in much opposition across Canada and in Newfoundland and Labrador; the reality of the small school remains. Small schools which are located in small communities generate a multitude of associated problems including the difficulties of attracting qualified staffs, offering as wide a range of programs as can be offered in larger schools and providing adequate resources.

Various means have been adopted in an attempt to address the problem of inequality in the educational system over the years. In 1938, for example, the Correspondence Division of the Newfoundland Department of Education was established to give children in small isolated settlements access to an education by correspondence since they could not attend any school. This scheme was partially abandoned during and following the war years with the building of more schools, resettlement in the 1960s, and improvements in employment opportunities. Itinerant teachers, bursary programs which brought students from small schools into larger high schools, additional teacher allocations to small schools and a resurgence of correspondence courses have been some of the schemes tried by governments to combat the problem.

Crocker and Riggs in their Task Force Report (1979), *Improving the Quality of Education*, stated that there was a substantial variation in the high school programs offered in different schools throughout Newfoundland and that school size affected the variety of program options available to students. Following introduction of the reorganized high school program in the early 1980s, many educators and parents in the province felt that this innovation accentuated the differences between small and large schools and rural and urban areas. This probably resulted in one of the recommendations of the *Report of the Small Schools Study Project* (Small Schools Project, 1987), addressing the need for all senior high schools to have the ability to offer all courses prerequisite to entry into post-secondary institutions either by "direct classroom teaching or by distance education" (p. 62). The report specified the date for first introduction as well as the specific courses which should eventually be offered through distance education: first year chemistry and first year physics. The report also addressed the technology to be used, the organization of a distance education school and its structure, the creation of mobile laboratories in Industrial Arts and Home Economics and the creation of a Coordinator of Small Schools position at the Department of Education.

Distance Education: The Concept

Hansen (1987) considered that educational decision makers must make a conscious endeavor in developing a distance education program of quality to preserve the small school as a first step. Following this they must capitalize on delivery systems, prepare teachers to use distance education, allocate instructional resources to distance education, assign responsibilities for materials and media selection, simplify logistics, and nurture partnerships.

Barker (1987) stated that in remote and isolated schools where certified teachers are not always available, or in small schools where limited student enrollments make it cost prohibitive to hire teachers for low incident courses, instruction by means of distance education may be the next best thing to being in the classroom. McCormick and McCormick (1982) supported this saying that the problems associated with smallness (costs, range, and quality of the existing programs, and special services to special populations) can be overcome by utilizing various electronic technologies in rural schools. Hobbs (1985) considered that the characteristics of the new telecommunications and computer technologies have the potential to transcend space, to network, to redefine learning as dynamic and interactive, and to stimulate innovations and creativity. The rate of creative application to small rural schools is dependent upon whether the technology can be tried first on a small scale, is compatible with existing behaviors and practices in small schools, is simple and easy to use, has low cost and high effectiveness, and has a support system externally and within the local school.

Hart (1990) linked the success of "Independent Learning Courses" delivered to students in five small Ontario schools via distance education to several factors including the structure of the program, counseling of students involved, screening services provided to select students going into the program, student progress monitoring, and the adequacy of time available to teacher coordinators for completion of the program. Distance education also provides a means to move away from mass schooling towards individualization of instruction (Swanson, 1988).

The idea of technology aiding in instruction in Newfoundland is not new. Memorial University has had a long and successful involvement in distance education efforts in the province. The first efforts to provide delivery of programs to distant adult audiences was provided by the Extension Service of Memorial University. In 1961, two years after the Service was formed, 26 one-half-hour and 20 quarter-hour radio programs were delivered via the CBC National Network in Home Economics, Accounting, Art, Music, Drama, and Foreign Languages; this was later extended to television (Balsom, 1982).

In 1967, Educational Television at Memorial University produced televised lectures to permit television to "help professors cope with numbers in less than ideal spaces" (Starcher, 1982, p. 26). By 1969 Educational Television was capable of coping with distance as well as with numbers since they then had their own private distribution system for distance education. Audio teleconferencing, computer teleconferencing, and video teleconferencing as a form of distance communications mode involving three or more people has been used in Newfoundland since 1972.

House (1982) indicated that the earliest participants and pioneers in distance communications in the province have been

Memorial's Faculty of Medicine. He stated that not only can the technology be used to provide continuing medical education within the province but also large numbers of students take regular university credit courses via this medium and "that these students perform just as well as colleagues taking the course in a classroom" (p. 50).

Beginning in 1990 the Centre for the Development of Distance Career Counseling of the Faculty of Education at Memorial University began a project called CAMCRY in conjunction with other areas across Canada. CAMCRY refers to Creation And Mobilization of Counseling Resources for Youth and is funded by the Canadian Guidance and Counseling Foundation. The programs developed include a career awareness program for career drifters, career education and counseling for parents, a computer-assisted vocational life skills program for offenders, an occupational integration program for women, a career counseling intervention program for teenage mothers and pregnant teens, and dial link: a peer career counseling outreach program for grades 10-12 students. At Memorial, CAMCRY is a three-year program which began in April, 1990, and has currently gone through the development and pilot stages and is moving into its final field test period. All programs have been developed to be offered through distance education in rural and remote areas in the province.

There are three main components of the distance education high school program equipment configuration: the teacher site, Telemedicine located at Memorial University, and at the students' sites (Figure 2) (Distance Education and Learning Resources, 1991, p. 21). Each distance education student work station consists of the following equipment:

✔ one IBM compatible computer and modem;

✔ one Telewriter II (electronic blackboard);

✔ one audio-teleconference convenor kit;

✔ one facsimile machine.

Students have immediate two-way audio interaction using the teleconference equipment and visual interaction using the Telewriter. Facsimile machines permit students to electronically transmit handwritten assignments or tests to the teacher and vice versa. The curriculum consists of modified materials based on the existing Department of Education course materials.

Figure 2: Distance Education Equipment Configuration

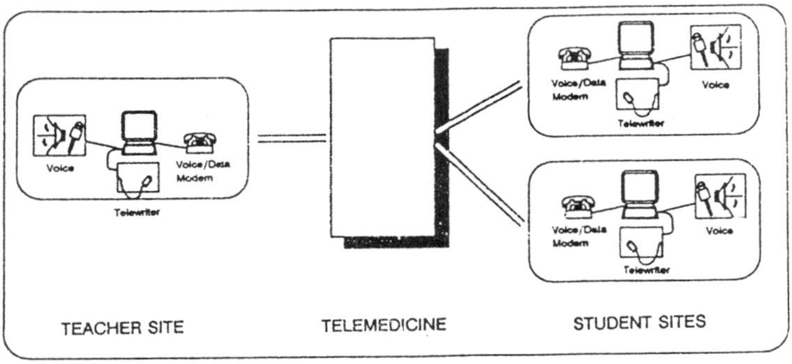

| TEACHER SITE | TELEMEDICINE | STUDENT SITES |

Precedents have therefore been set on many fronts in distance education. When the Department of Education in Newfoundland and Labrador began its efforts in 1987 to offer Advanced Mathematics to high school students in small schools through distance education, many of the technology problems had already been addressed with adult learners and with others in the community. The demographic, climatic, geographical, and cultural realities in the province made it imperative that inequality of educational opportunity for high school students be addressed in more creative and effective ways than had previously been attempted. It was an opportune time for the introduction of distance education at the schools level in the province.

The Distance Education Program: Perspectives on Innovation

Tichy (1980), House (1981), and Corbett and Rossman (1989) refer to cultural, technical/organizational, and socio/political pressures which start and affect a change process throughout its history. These three perspectives can be applied to an analysis of the implementation of the distance education program in Newfoundland and Labrador.

✎ *Cultural Considerations*

Corbett and Rossman (1989) consider cultural perspectives to be "socially shared and transmitted definitions of what is and what ought to be . . . and the symbolic meanings practitioners, students, and the community attach to the change efforts" (p. 165). House (1981) considers the cultural perspective to be the context of the innovation or change effort.

The government and school boards in the province have had a long history of struggle to address the marked differences between urban and rural parts of the province in terms of educational opportunities for children. Geography, history, and climate have given rise to varied problems including isolation, difficulty of travel, and the ubiquitous small school. Uncertainty as to how to address these problems manifests itself in the many and varied schemes which have been in place over the years. The distance education program, therefore, began with cultural or contextual pressures uppermost (Corbett and Rossman, 1989). The dominant cycle at start-up was the cultural cycle (Tichy, 1980) (Figure 3).

Riggs in the *Report of the Small Schools Study Project* (Small Schools Project, 1987) makes the following recommendation:

> That by direct classroom teaching or by distance education, all senior high schools should have the ability to offer all courses which are prerequisite to entry into post-secondary institutions and the ability to accommodate particular course requirements of small numbers of students (p. 26).

A second recommendation in the report was that first year high school chemistry and physics be made available to small high schools by September, 1987. The recommended mode of delivery was computers, audio-video tapes, or by "other means of distance education" (p. 27).

A final recommendation was that a Distance Education School be established and that a principal and teachers be employed to assume responsibility for the development and administration of the distance education courses (p. 28).

The Williams Royal Commission of Inquiry Report (1992) endorsed these earlier recommendations. The report states that newer telecommunications and computer technology had now made it possible to reduce or eliminate many of the inequities in the school system so that the needs of learners can be met regardless of location.

Thirty-five students in thirteen small or remote schools were given access to the first high school Advanced Mathematics course in the fall of 1988. Beginning in September, 1989, the second high school Advanced Mathematics course was offered to 28 students and 55 students enrolled in the first year course. In the fall of 1990 there were 22 students in the third year Advanced Mathematics course, 45 in the second year course and 90 in the first year course

Figure 3: Graph showing peaks and troughs of presssures from the Cultural, Technical/Organizational, and Socio/Political perspectives of the Distance Education Program (Secondary Advanced Mathematics) in Newfoundland & Labrador.

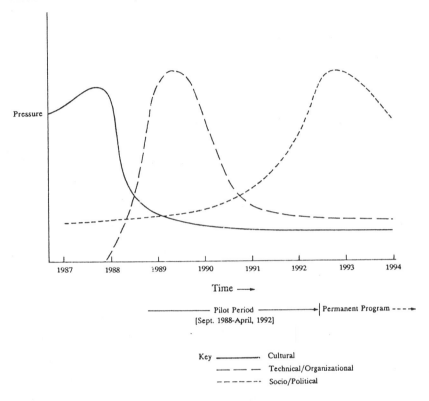

(Young, 1990a). The first students graduated in the spring of 1991: twelve females (57%) and nine males (43%).

In 1989, seven new small schools were added to the existing thirteen distance education sites for a total of twenty schools. Ten more sites were added in 1990 and one more in 1991. During the 1991-92 school year there were 31 distance education sites.

Distance education, however, has not been perceived as the final answer to the problem of the small school. Doug Young, Consultant at the Department of Education and one of the pioneers of the distance education program in the middle 1980s reported in early 1992 that "something that started with very meager beginnings is now beginning to take off." He contends that distance education's major problem is that it has been perceived by all the main players as a temporary or stop-gap measure until a more secure and more permanent solution to the problem of small schools is found.

Despite this perception, students in one school who were involved in the program explained that to be part of a province-wide class is very interesting and exciting. They placed a high value on the experience which seemed to break down barriers of isolation that have long been a part of the reality of living in a Newfoundland and Labrador outport. School personnel interviewed reported that parents for the most part are also proud to have the distance education system in their communities. Parents and students felt that it was tangible evidence of attempts to address the problem and, symbolically, it represented a very real attempt by government to come to grips with the problem of equalization of educational opportunity across the province.

Teacher coordinators, parents, students, and principals constantly referred to the challenging nature of the Advanced Mathematics distance education program. One parent had this to say about her daughter:

She wasn't interested in it at first . . . didn't think she could manage it. But, I thought she could give it a try anyway.

Another parent explained:

There have been times when I would rather she (daughter) had not done this program but then there are times when I see the value of it.

A student remarked:

(S)ometimes I get so frustrated. I'll sit down with twenty problems and can only do two. I get so fed up, I just want to throw it all away. Then, I'll phone [the teacher] and tell her I have twenty problems I can't do. . . . She'll talk to me and tell me to come first thing in the morning to give me a hand.

Although the difficult and challenging nature of the program was emphasized, at no time did any of the people interviewed think it was difficult enough that it should be abandoned. A student in one school commented:

Doing this Math course puts pressure on us. When we get to university, we will know how to handle it (the pressure) better; if not, we might flunk out.

All seemed to realize that it would be an advantage later in university for the students who were successful in the course. For students who remained with the program and their parents the Advanced Mathematics offered through distance education represented a chance of success at university. It also, ironically, offered these young people the opportunity to leave their small communities and, indirectly, would likely lead to the demise of these communities.

It also appeared that those who were engaged in the program (particularly the administrators and teacher coordinators) were responding to the accusation that there were low expectations of students in many of the high schools in the province, particularly those in smaller rural schools. A vice principal/teacher coordinator referred several times to accusations of low expectations of students in schools in the province. He observed:

> (O)ur students generally aren't challenged. I don't know how many students are (challenged) these days . . . . We do have low expectations here. I'm not sure if it's the wrong thing in our school from what we have to deal with . . . . We have to go back further than just say we have to change our expectations. There are a lot more things that have to be changed other than our expectations. Simply jacking up our expectations would just create more failure.

The majority of others interviewed (principals and teacher coordinators) spoke with pride about the challenge of the Advanced Mathematics distance education program for their students and how they rose to the challenge. This success seemed for them to be a rebuttal to the arguments of low student expectations.

The Vice-Principal elaborated further on the problem of a community with a mixed native and white population:

> We are a multicultural, bilingual community. Most of the parents are not really supportive of school in general, not to be actively supportive. They don't take active interest in their child's education; they might say, "yes, I want my child to finish high school" . . . but they don't come in to us and say, "my child needs extra help," or "what can you do for him?" We get very little communication from the parents.

The problems as articulated by this vice-principal have to do with the culture of native Labradorians living in a white man's world. The problems of native children in school and of their feeling frustrated and uncomfortable with the interactive learning medium which is distance education have to do with a culture in which learning for centuries has taken place by listening without much response to stories passed down by way of the elders. These aspects of the culture are deeply entrenched, somewhat unique, and perhaps different but not absent in similar communities with a predominance of white inhabitants.

In most isolated Newfoundland and Labrador communities story-telling, learning by listening, and quiet shyness in the presence of strangers are characteristic of people within the white culture. A particularly skilled communicator, perhaps one born and bred into such a situation, would be necessary, perhaps essential, for students to have success in distance education in these circumstances.

Learning through distance education, therefore, represents a solution to inequality of educational opportunity in small schools located in small, sometimes isolated Newfoundland and Labrador communities; but, cultural barriers exist. While distance education is recognized as a challenging program for students and as providing increased opportunity in higher education, the interactive nature of the telecommunications technology involved runs contrary to native cultures and to some extent to the culture of many small Newfoundland and Labrador outport communities with predominantly white populations.

✎ *Technical/Organizational Perspective*

The technical/organizational perspective interprets innovation implementation problems as the products of the failure of systematic planning (Corbett and Rossman, 1989). Goal ambiguity, the unavailability of important resources such as staff time, inservice activities, efficiently operating equipment, lack of opportunity for instructors to discuss and share ideas, and less than maximum use of available equipment could be considered negative technical/organizational pressures which together could cause this cycle to peak.

Although cultural or contextual pressures were the reason why distance education was initiated, the technical/organizational cycle (Tichy, 1980) very quickly peaked shortly after the beginning of the program (Figure 3). Proper planning and the proper introduction and use of the specified sophisticated equipment at various sites became essential. It is important, therefore, to consider issues related to start-up of the distance education program including equipment malfunctions, less than adequate telephone-line service and instructor/teacher coordinator inservice (Corbett and Rossman, 1989). These generated technical/organizational problems which probably contributed to the peaking of this cycle in less than a year after start-up of the program.

At least one teacher adviser is located in each small school. The principal in most cases is the person responsible for the school becoming a distance education site and in many cases has become the student adviser. There appear to be two requirements for the on-site student advisers: technical expertise often in the area of computers; and the need for someone with a Mathematics background to provide tutorial help to students.

The format of instruction which has been adopted for the Advanced Mathematics course involves a Thursday mathematics lesson taught by the distance education instructor during which all school sites are on-line. On Friday students are invited to ask questions about problems which have developed; all sites are again on-line. On Monday, Tuesday and Wednesday the instructor assigns one on-line time period for three or four sites during which students are encouraged to question the instructor in a tutorial setting about difficulties they are having.

Equipment malfunction was cited by several people interviewed as a major problem in the first year of the distance education pilot. This coupled with a one-day inservice for beginning instructors caused much frustration in the fall of the first year. Students at one school reported: "someone else on the computers the first year slowed us down . . . and breakups (of voice transmission) was frustrating." The principal of the school supported these statements.

A teacher sponsor noted that her school had four students begin the program in the fall of 1990 but three subsequently dropped out. She commented:

> I think it (the student drop-outs from the program) was a combination of several factors. Number one, the equipment in the beginning . . . was a bit frustrating. It wasn't difficult to learn the operation of the equipment; but just the fact that they were being left on their own was the second factor. I don't think they were mature, independent workers . . . . I think that was a major contributing factor.

A principal / teacher coordinator added:

> We were in Gander for one day and that's all the inservice we got, that one day. We came out and we had a few problems

with the equipment. I think it was because of the phone lines. We got through it and now it gets easier each year because the students teach each other.

A more optimistic note was sounded by another principal:

The equipment arrived in mid-summer and when we got back this teacher (who had attended an inservice in St. John's) began to set it up with the manuals and with the training that he had and with discussion by telephone with me and the coordinator in St. John's. After that with the teacher who would be teaching the course we got some scheduling and everything fixed up and the two students just went on the system. I must say it was really easy . . . . There was nothing complicated about it.

Students generally made light of any start-up frustrations with operation of the equipment. A distance education student on the south coast of Newfoundland, when asked about problems and frustrations responded: "No, not at all. It was quite easy." It is evident, however, by the rather large numbers who dropped the Advanced Mathematics program in the first year of start-up in 1988 that strong negative factors were operational and that frustrations and a lack of familiarity with the rather sophisticated equipment by everyone involved likely contributed to a peak in the technical/organizational cycle during the first six months of implementation of the pilot.

A number of teacher sponsors and principals mentioned problems of start-up associated with the telephone lines, necessary for two-wire transmission (as opposed to four-wire transmission which takes place using dedicated lines). Transmission break-up and sudden shut-downs of the system were the most common occurrences. Other less prevalent and more isolated problems noted by those interviewed in the schools involved: difficulties with fax machines including slowness of repairs and replacement with "loaners" in more remote areas; over-loaded lines when fax and teleconferencing equipment were operating simultaneously; and difficulties in getting students to fully utilize the telewriter capabilities of the system.

A teacher coordinator cited some of the frustrations experienced throughout the period his school had been involved:

Our fax machine hasn't worked properly since we put it there . . . . It was the wiring . . . . The wiring is multicord and if you leave the distance education machine plugged into the two-wire system with the fax machine, there is an over-load.

Several principals and teacher coordinators mentioned the one-day inservice for coordinators in beginning schools as a serious problem; some of the people equated this with the problem of student drop-outs from the program in the first year of operation in 1988. A principal stated:

> I think there is a need for students to spend more time on-line with the instructor. I also think there is a great need for instructors to be inserviced. From talking with instructors, . . . they went into this particular system in the fall cold . . . . There was no inservice provided beforehand; they walked in one day and there was a computer system, telewriter and everything else in front of them . . . . Students are not meeting with success when they have instructors who have not been inserviced in this particular type of teaching.

According to Doug Young, inservice of both instructors and of teacher coordinators in the schools was a problem. He felt that one or two weeks at Telemedicine with much on-line experience prior to commencing a distance education program in a school for all teacher coordinators was necessary. He also said that, since most of the instructors in 1992-93 would be located at one location in St. John's, this should solve the problem of instructor isolation and the sharing of ideas and professional development which could not take place while they were located throughout the province.

The quality of instruction and the characteristics of an instructor for students to have success in the distance education program were emphasized by those interviewed. One student said:

> I have problems with it (the distance education program). We don't have enough time to ask questions . . . . This year I find it really bad . . . . He goes too quickly; he's always talking . . . during the whole time he's on-line . . . . You never get a chance to ask questions . . . . Oh, I'm getting 80s but we are doing it on our own.

Students were quite concerned about this and on occasion expressed considerable frustration. A group of seven students commented as follows on the approach of one instructor:

> (He is) always in a hurry like the world is coming to an end or something . . . . You can cope with it after a while (but) it gets on your nerves . . . . (He goes) straight to a page number like it's all programmed.

Students appeared to relate well with some instructors but not with others. They were most frustrated by instructors who monopolized on-line teleconference time without providing time for student questions and who rushed through the material without pausing occasionally for some informal chatter and to create a climate on-line which would be conducive for student-instructor and student-student interaction. Instructors who took time with informal banter at the beginning of a teleconference, for example, and who showed understanding, were generally accepted and rated highly by students. Committed teachers appear to be the vital key to both program development and program effectiveness (Strasheim, 1989).

Students also gave an indication of the kind of student whom they thought would do well. A student enrolled in the third year Advanced Mathematics course had this to say:

It is really a good program. You get prepared for university; you have to work on your own and you more or less teach yourself and you get more responsibility. . . .You learn to be independent.

Another student commented:

You need to know how to plan your time and you've got to be independent. A person is just not able to pick it up and work on their own and not be afraid. You have to be outgoing. It is a challenge and you have to know that you can do it. You have to have a lot of self-confidence.

A science/mathematics program coordinator with one school board gave a character sketch of the student whom he believed would be successful in the distance education program:

One who learns to accept responsibility . . . . One who takes a hold of things, becomes familiar with the technology of the equipment to the extent that they can set it up on-line and use it . . . . Engages in discussion, competes to get the answer to the instructor. I find that they have to do that or they're left out . . . . They are in a room by themselves; the teacher is just a voice; so, they have to learn responsibility and . . . that's been good for them . . . . They become their own source of information and they become self-starters.

Initiators made an attempt during the first year of the pilot to compare instruction through distance education with instruction by means of conventional methods but the results were not conclusive. The most that could be said was that the retention rate for students in distance education was the same as that for students taught by conventional methods in the first year.

The technical/organizational problems associated with distance education expressed by individuals in Newfoundland and Labrador may in fact be minimal as compared with problems associated with distance education offered by other means, such as correspondence. Winders (1988), for example, writing about the British experience said:

> In distance learning the interaction between students and tutor or between students themselves is often minimal. Written correspondence is limited and slow. The learner is often unable to obtain help or advice at the moment when needed. Information technology offers a variety of possibilities for presentation and interaction (Preface).

The technical/organizational pressures associated with the initial introduction of the distance education technology in the schools surfaced in almost every conversation with principals, teacher coordinators, and instructors. It became evident also that pressures from this source of frustration were largely corrected during the second year of the pilot. The peak of stress in the technical/organizational cycle (Tichy, 1980) for all participants in the distance education program probably took place during the latter part of the first year and the early part of the second year and the stress reached a trough during the 1991-92 year. Most of those interviewed during the spring of 1992 seemed to have moved well beyond the technology problems of start-up and were now considering other problems of program and instruction.

✎ *Socio/Political Considerations*

Corbett and Rossman (1989) consider the socio/political perspective in analyzing a particular innovation implementation to be the less optimistic perspective since it recognizes limits to rational behavior and focuses attention on the interplay of divergent interests among participants in the change process. Power and power brokerage become matters of major importance. Socio/political considerations may be thought of as both the change effort and the context of the change (House, 1981).

The distance education program as described has the potential for almost complete paralysis since it ostensibly involves five diverse groups all with their own vested interests. In reality the two main players have been the Department of Education and the school boards since the other three players only are involved with the telecommunications delivery system which is used by the Department of Education on a user pay basis. Since the distance education program was established and known as a pilot project through four years, the socio/political cycle remained in a trough during this period (Figure 3).

Doug Young identified the most serious drawback to the distance education program as the fact that it has been seen as a temporary or experimental program by both the Department of Education and the school boards. This is underscored by the fact that the two most recent studies of school programs in Newfoundland, the Crocker Task Force on Mathematics and Science Education (1989) and the William's Royal Commission of Inquiry (1992), presented contradictory recommendations with respect to distance education in the province.

While Crocker recognized the inherent difficulties of offering a diverse range of programs in a small school and the impossible expectations which are frequently placed upon teachers in such situations, his solution to the problem was to reject distance education as a solution to recognized problems in mathematics and science. While he considered that "on the surface, distance education has some attractions" (p. 157), he stated that it is "essentially experimental" and that mathematics and science may be the wrong subjects for such experimentation. The teaching of such courses using existing technology may appear to be successful on the surface but, he believes, it is possible to modify the courses to accommodate the limitations of the technology. Williams, on the other hand, took a much more optimistic view of the potential of distance education to equalize educational opportunity for all students in the province but particularly for students in small and remote schools. Recommendations in the report call for the expansion of the program and the establishment of a Provincial Advisory Committee on Distance Education and Technology and a School of Distance Education and Technology for the delivery of the program throughout the province.

This kind of ambivalent thinking in the province has been the chief reason for the less than whole-hearted commitment of resources to distance education by either the Department or the school boards. It has resulted in schools assuming that temporary accommodation in libraries or corners of laboratories or classrooms is quite sufficient. Since the instructors get no sense of permanence to the program, they have been reluctant to commit time or money to courses for upgrading in the field. Their knowledge and know-how in the area, therefore, has been very much "learn as you go," instinctive and intuitive. Since they have operated in the past from separate centres in larger communities in the province, there has been very little opportunity for learning from each other, sharing of expertise, and professional growth.

The Department of Education in April, 1992, made clear to superintendents of school districts the Department's perception of the role of each of the two main players, school boards and the Department of Education, in distance education. The intention of the Department to expand beyond Advanced Mathematics in the 1992-93 school year into Physics and French was conveyed to district superintendents. The move marked the evolution of distance education from a pilot project to a continuing initiative. Concurrent with instigation of a new grant system would be a division of contributions of each of the two main participants. School boards participating in the program under this new scheme would be required to pay for fax machine maintenance, to supply fax paper, to provide a computer of pre-determined specifications, to provide a video cassette recorder where needed, to purchase specified lab equipment for Physics, and to purchase an audio cassette recorder for French.

The contribution of the Department of Education would be to pay for all teleconference costs; all long-distance costs; all print materials; all video, audio, and computer software; digital interface equipment and software for Physics, and the salaries of all distance education instructors. This policy statement is concurrent with the Department of Education's position on all such initiatives which have moved from pilot status to one of some permanence after having had a relatively long period of phase-in of the innovation.

The response from school boards to the proposal by the Department of Education has been somewhat overwhelming. During the spring of 1992 school boards applied in record numbers for the right to establish new distance education sites within their jurisdictions. They agreed in all cases to provide the required input of resources to qualify for the requested new distance education sites. Some boards even agreed to provide everything needed to set up a new site including the instructor. This situation has created pressure to have Telemedicine (at Memorial University) install a new circuit to serve the additional sites.

Added political pressure in the province to expand the distance education program has come from parents and the general public.

The Minister of Education, Dr. Phil Warren, for example, was a guest on an open-line program in May, 1992, during which he received numerous telephone calls demanding the establishment of additional distance education sites in several small communities. A senior official of the Department of Education indicated that there would be 53 sites offering distance education during the 1992-93 school year. In matter of weeks the distance education program had been given a much higher profile within the province.

Hansen (1987), in a paper dealing with development of a distance education program in Oregon, said that the educational decision makers must make a conscious effort to preserve the small school as a first step. Considering efforts of various governments spanning several decades in Newfoundland to do away with small schools as well as in many cases the small communities themselves, prior to May, 1992, it was unlikely this would become a reality. The recent political pressure, however, may have some impact in reversing this trend. Over-all political pressure within the province, therefore, seemed to peak during the summer of 1992 (Figure 3).

Local political pressures surfaced periodically as well. One good example of local area politics and non-rational power struggles curtailing or making the program less effective was demonstrated in Nain. A vice-principal and teacher coordinator cited the time difference of one-half an hour between Labrador and Newfoundland island time as being a problem. He commented:

> Our classes are scheduled on Newfoundland time. When you have forty-minute periods and you are thirty minutes out of whack with what is going on the island, something is beginning or ending ten minutes early or late. The student I have here this year who goes on-line on Thursday has to come into the school at quarter to one while school for most other students doesn't start until quarter after one . . . . We don't get any cooperation from distance education . . . . I don't know if we're being inflexible or what?

When this situation was mentioned to another teacher coordinator on the coast of Labrador, the person was incredulous. It could not be conceived that one small school distance education centre would expect the distance education time schedule to be adjusted for one centre; rather, the person thought the centre should be flexible enough to accommodate its school schedule to that of distance education.

Further changes during the fall and winter which will likely have political ramifications include the proposed consolidation of all distance education instructors into one building in St. John's in the 1992-93 school year. The rationale for this move is to bring all the instructors into close proximity with each other to permit more sharing and exchange of ideas and ease of professional development. It is likely, however, that personnel at the small school sites will eventually object strongly to this move for at least two reasons.

Some students interviewed complained that they would like to see their instructors at least once to dispel the faceless aspect of the system. The two students, when asked about the importance of seeing the instructor at least once, responded:

> When we had Mr. ____, it seemed like we couldn't get to know him really well . . . . We never saw him but [now] we've met Mr. ____[a new teacher]; he has come out here a few times now . . . . I think it made a lot of difference. He was out to our graduation. We really got to know Mr. ___ and we hardly knew Mr. ____[the first teacher]: only as a teacher, . . . an on-line teacher.

The significant point here is that one of the reasons why the second teacher was able to get to know these students was because he was only a half-hour away by paved road while the first teacher was more than five hours away by road on the west coast of the province.

A second reason is that there has traditionally been a notion in rural Newfoundland (which may be real or imagined) that it is difficult to get equity of services in rural areas as opposed to larger urban centres such as in St. John's or Mount Pearl. The expression "nothing comes west of the overpass" (located on the outskirts of St. John's on the Trans Canada Highway) will take on deeper meaning when all distance education services become centralized in St. John's making it even more difficult for instructors to visit and get to know their students in small and remote schools most of which are located off the Avalon Peninsula.

Political pressures, therefore, continued to mount during the spring of 1992. The pressures appeared to be coming from a number of different sources. Conversion of distance education from pilot to permanent status coupled with public and school board pressure to expand the program to several more sites provided the major individual contribution. Transfer of all distance education instructors to St. John's will provide additional political pressure mainly from students and school personnel who feel it necessary that the instructors periodically visit the school sites. Local politics will likely increase in numbers and frequency as the total number of sites increases. All of these combined will likely result in a peak in the political pressures over-all.

Summary and Conclusions

Peaks and troughs in the three perspectives of the cultural, technical/organizational, and socio/political came at different times in the life of the distance education program during the period since inception (Figure 3). The peak in the cultural came just immediately before and during the early days of start-up in the fall of 1988. Cultural pressures relative to equalizing educational opportunity throughout the province had been constant for several decades but appeared to be at a peak just prior to and at the point of start-up. As the program got under way, this kind of pressure appeared to abate to reach a trough perhaps during the spring of 1992 just as the decision was made to extend the life and status of the program from pilot to permanence.

The peak in pressure from the technical/organizational perspective came late in the first year after start-up primarily with problems concerning equipment installation and use and instructor lack of inservice and preparation. Students and teacher coordinators adapted to the new technology, however, and the instructors (and others involved) soon became proficient with the on-the-job experience they were gaining. The trough in this area was likely reached at the beginning of the second year.

Socio/political pressure mounted during the winter and spring of 1992 to reach a peak near the end of the school term. Pressure mounted mainly because of the change in status of the program from pilot to permanent program; but, it also had to do with political pressures to extend distance education to more sites from parents and the general public, local pressures for various reasons and moves such as bringing all instructors together at one site in St. John's. All of these had to do with power struggles of one form or another by the various players involved. A trough in the cycle of political pressures occurred almost since start-up until the winter of 1992 when pressure began to build in this area.

The following table gives male and female enrollment figures for the five courses offered through distance education in the province during the 1992-93 school year (with total enrollments still incomplete):

Table 1

	Male	Female
Advanced Mathematics (First Year)	48 (42.9%)	64 (57.1%)
Advanced Mathematics (Second Year)	29 (39.2%)	45 (60.8%)
Advanced Mathematics (Third Year)	34 (43%)	45 (57%)
Physics (First Year)	41 (48.2%)	44 (51.8%)
French (Conversational)	8 (19%)	34 (81%)
	160 (40.8%)	232 (59.2%)

(Young, 1992b)

It is clear that there will be a substantial increase in the total number of students doing high school courses in Newfoundland and Labrador through distance education during the 1992-93 school year. It is also clear that the total number of female students enrolled in distance education in the province will be almost 20% higher than the total number of males doing high school courses by this means. This ratio appears to be slightly higher than the approximately 57% female to 43% male enrollment figures for Advanced Mathematics in the province generally.

Teacher coordinators and administrators interviewed listed several positive aspects of the distance education program including: the development of independent work and study habits; expansion of program opportunities in small schools; exposure of students and small school personnel to a completely new forms of communication; and, the raising of both the horizons of and the expectations for students in small communities. Participating students listed as advantages of the distance education program the following: good preparation for university since it promoted good work habits and independence; increased prestige among peers and within the school; gave easier access to and cooperation with instructors; development of close cooperation and comradeship among participating students.

Teacher coordinators and administrators also listed the following as problems with the distance education program: no (class) body with which students might identify; equipment problems; much time lost in faxing and copying; difficulties in selecting the "right" students; students intimidated by having to speak during teleconferencing and intimidated by the equipment; course difficulty and low marks in comparison with other courses; excessive time required for the distance education course having a negative impact on other courses; too much time, effort, and money devoted to a small number of students; and, the special attributes needed by instructors being difficult to find.

Participating students listed as disadvantages the following: the absence of a teacher in the classroom for assistance and keeping students on task; lost on-line time because of problems with other sites; heavy work load; difficulties in making contact with an instructor because he continues to talk during on-line time; shortage of on-line time; equipment problems; lost time in faxing; and, negative peer pressure.

A teacher coordinator at one school summed up the program in this way:

> I think the distance education program is a good program . . . . It offers students in rural areas courses they normally would not get because you cannot attract the teachers to these areas and if you do attract the teachers there is often not enough space opened in the time table to put these courses on. It's not perfect by any means but given my rate of four in four my first year and this year (of students successfully completing the course), . . . I think that's a pretty good batting average. If you have teachers in the classroom, there'd still be people failing.

Galvin and Bruce (1987) indicated that the future of distance education programs appears to depend upon certain administrative issues such as the resistance of teachers to the loss of the "best" students from regular classes and differences between schools in scheduling, achievement standards, and the extent of student preparation for advanced courses. Based on these parameters as measurement standards of success, the distance education program in the province of Newfoundland and Labrador is off to a good start.

References

Balsom, D. (1982). Applications of communication technology in adult education and community development programs by Memorial University Extension Service 1959-1982 (13-24). In Mandville, M. L. (Ed.), *"A man's reach should exceed his grasp": Distance education and teleconferencing at Memorial University*. St. John's, NF: Memorial University of Newfoundland.

Barker, B. O. (1987). *Interactive distance learning technologies for rural and small schools: A resource guide.* Eric Mini-Review. Las Cruces, NM: ERIC Clearinghouse on Rural Education and Small Schools.

Canadian Guidance and Counseling Foundation. (1991). CAMCRY Projects.

Corbett, H. D. and Rossman, G. B. (1989). *Three paths to implementing change: A research note.* Beyond Implementation Series. The Ontario Institute for Studies in Education – Curriculum Inquiry, 19, 2.

Deane, J. (1992). Small schools – big issues. *C.A.P. Journal, 2*(1), 33-34.

Distance Education and Learning Resources. (1991). *Distance education – The Newfoundland and Labrador project.* Department of Education, Division of Program Development, Government of Newfoundland and Labrador.

Fisher, R. D. and Warren, P. J. (1972). *Schools in Newfoundland and Labrador – A survey of existing facilities.* St. John's, NF: Department of Educational Administration, Memorial University of Newfoundland.

Galvin, P. F. and Bruce, R. (1987). *Technology and rural education: The case of audio-graphic telecommunications.* New York: Cornell University, Ithaca and N.Y. Department of Education.

Gilles, S. (1992). Board decision reversed. *C.A.P. Journal, 2* (1), 36.

Hansen, K. H. (1987). *Distance education and the small school: Policy issues.* Discussion Draft. Portland, OR: Northwest Regional Educational Lab. – Northwest Center for State Educational Policy Studies.

Hart, A. J. (1990). Small secondary schools: Making better use of distance education. *Rural Educator, 12* (1), 10-12.

Hobbs, D. (1985). *Bridging, linking, networking the gap: Uses of instructional technology in small rural schools.* Washington, DC: Department of Education.

House, E. R. (1981). Three perspectives on innovation. In R. Lehming and M. Kane (Eds.), *Improving schools: Using what we know.* Beverly Hills, CA: Sage.

House, A. M. (1982). Telecommunications in health and education. *Canadian Medical Association Journal. 124* (March), 667-668.

House, A. M. (1982). Teleconferencing at Memorial University (31-42). In Mandville, M. L. (Ed.), *"A man's reach should exceed his grasp": Distance education and teleconferencing at Memorial University,* St. John's, NF: Memorial University of Newfoundland.

Langton, G. (1992). Small school struggles for continuing existence. *C.A.P. Journal, 2* (1), 34-36.

McCormick, F. C. and McCormick, E. R. (1982). *A project on uses of technology in rural schools, final report.* St. Paul, MN: Educational Operations Concepts, Inc.

Moore, M. (1973). Towards a theory of independent learning and teaching. *Journal of Higher Education, 44*, 666-678.

Perlin, A. B. (Ed.). (1959). *The storm of Newfoundland.* St. John's, NF: The Newfoundland Publishing Services Ltd.

Rowe, F. W. (1964). *The development of education in Newfoundland.* Toronto, ON: Ryerson.

Royal Commission of Inquiry into the Delivery of Programs and Services in Primary, Elementary, Secondary Education. (1992). *Our children our future.* St. John's, NF: Government of Newfoundland and Labrador.

Small Schools Project. (1987). *Report of the small schools study project.* St. John's, NF: Province of Newfoundland and Labrador.

Starcher, D. (1982). Educational Television At Memorial University (25-30) In Mandville M. L. (Ed.), *"A man's reach should exceed his grasp": Distance education and teleconferencing at Memorial University.* St. John's, NF: Memorial University of Newfoundland.

Strasheim, L. A. (1989). *Proficiency-oriented foreign language in the small high school.* Eric Digest. Charleston, WV: ERIC Clearinghouse on Rural Education and Small Schools.

Swanson, A. D. (1988). Role of technology in the education reform of rural schools: implications for district consolidations and governance. *Journal of Rural and Small Schools, 3*(1), 2-7.

Task Force on Mathematics and Science Education. (1989). *Towards an achieving society - final report.* St. John's, NF: Province of Newfoundland and Labrador.

Task Force Report. (1979). *Improving the quality of education.* St. John's, NF: Province of Newfoundland and Labrador.

Tichy, N. M. (1980). Problem cycles in organizations and the management of change. In T. Kimberly and R. Miles (Eds.), *The organizational life cycle.* San Francisco: Jossey Bass.

Volkman, A. G. (1960). *Thoreau on man and nature.* Mount Vernon, NY: Peter Pauper Press.

Winders, R. (1988). *Information technology in the delivery of distance education and training.* Berrycroft, Soham Ely' Cambridge, EN: Peter Francis Publishers.

Withers, V. G. (1992). Speech delivered during interactive television telecommunications demonstration, March 25.

Young, D. (1990). *The distance education project: Using technology to improve educational opportunities in rural areas.* St. John's, NF: Province of Newfoundland and Labrador.

Young, D. (1992a). *The distance education pilot project: Using technology to improve educational opportunities in rural areas.* (unpublished).

Young, D. (1992b). Personal correspondence.

10

Engaging Students Through Experiential Programs

Bob Sharp

Analytical Context

This chapter provides descriptions of two Yukon experiential programs and outlines the processes followed in their development and implementation. The factors which gave rise to these changes may be characterized as originating from a cultural problem cycle closely followed by a technical problem cycle as defined by Tichy's model identifying conditions for change (Tichy, 1986). In both cases, the technical problem intermingled with the cultural cycle. This situation provided an optimal climate for change, consistent with the descriptions of change identified by Corbett and Rossman (Corbett and Rossman, 1989). They contend that effective change is undertaken when strategies to cope with technical, political, and cultural problem cycles intertwine as part of the organizational phenomena accompanying school change. This condition appears to be supported in the case to be presented. While the changes outlined in this chapter may have been triggered by a cultural problem cycle, technical and political problem cycles also played contributing roles.

A peak in the problems associated with the cultural cycle were felt by educational administrators, communities, and the political representatives of education, and were indicative of the process used in redefining the goals of Yukon education. This process specifically set out to encourage schools to undertake initiatives that would effectively lead to increased school retention. The stress generated by relatively high drop-out rates focused on the purpose and values of public schooling in the Yukon. The process of clarifying these values supported school and teacher efforts in coming to grips with stress in the technical problem cycle.

There was a concurrent peak in the technical problem cycle, manifested in teacher frustration with difficulties they faced in attempting to achieve emerging educational goals within the conventional school framework. The students had changed in their behaviors, goals, and attitudes. The composition of the student body presented realities which traditional schooling was not able to adequately deal with. The accompanying discord, combined with funding and organizational opportunities available to schools, supported this climate for change. This readiness for change was reflected in a wide range of questions students, parents, administrators, and teachers raised about the responsiveness of their schools and their effectiveness in addressing the needs and aspirations of the many students who were leaving the Yukon school system prematurely.

An examination of these two Yukon cases in terms of Tichy's analysis reveals some interesting insights. It may also be fruitful to consider the same three cycle topics, not as problem cycles but rather as cycles representing opportunity for change. Tichy's derivative of the three problem cycles are rooted in the core characteristics of organizations and are based in response to problems felt in each of the categories. Analysis of opportunity cycles may also prove to be a useful perspective for examining change. A focus on the problem/response process reinforces the focus on educational failures referred to by Corbet and Rossman which stem from trouble conditions. Examination of an opportunity cycle by it's very nature shifts the focus to the implementation process associated with an innovation, thus providing the context for positive analysis that Corbet and Rossman were seeking. An opportunity perspective recognizes the "pull" opportunity forces may exert on developmental processes accompanying change. Some of the inventive initiatives associated with these programs may be more accurately characterized as a recognition of opportunity for change, albeit the opportunities may arise out of stresses, rather than as direct responses to specific stresses. Periods of organizational stress may result in entrenchment. These are times when opportunity cycles are at a low ebb. Similarly, periods of low stress, that is, effective production, may also result in low opportunity for change. The changes identified in this chapter appear to be a response as much from opportunity as from responses to problem cycles. Changes taking place in the Yukon appear to have been driven by problems but the responses were often determined by opportunity. An examination of these initiatives from both stress pushed and opportunity pulled perspectives helps to support the analytical approach proposed by Corbett and Rosssman (1989) and provides a fruitful process for examining the Yukon changes that took place in this particular case.

Background

Northern educational jurisdictions have struggled to keep their students from leaving school before they graduate. The Yukon has also had to come to terms with high rates of student drop out (Sharp, 1985). Yukon educators have attempted to overcome this concern by making schooling a more meaningful experience for northern youth. Over the past 25 years, the Yukon Department of Education has engaged in a number of initiatives designed to increase student retention, some with a measure of success (Sharp, 1985). This chapter will trace the development of two initiatives, ACES (Achievement, Culture, Environment, and Service) and REM (Rural Experiential Model) that have contributed to the success of rural secondary schooling.

ACES was established to provide grade 10 students in Whitehorse with a wilderness based experiential program that developed self esteem and interpersonal relationships along with academic skills and knowledge. The success of this program set the stage for the development of the Rural Experiential Model (REM). This model was to provide an organizational arrangement that would permit offering experiential programs and extensive field experiences in small secondary schools. A history of the development of these programs may provide insights of value to other rural schools across Canada.

Establishing An Experiential Secondary Program

In early 1989, the Yukon Department of Education announced the "Return to Learning" commitments. These were a group of initiatives designed to provide increased ways of meeting the needs of "at risk" students. The programs developed under this commitment were intended to either bring these students back into school with success or to keep them from leaving school by engaging their interest and commitment. One of these initiatives was to provide a wilderness based educational experience.

The initial plan was to have identified "at risk" youths move out of school for a period of two to three months for a set of experiences in the "bush" that would provide a foundation for the development of both self esteem and bush skills. The Department of Education began more extensive planning for the wilderness program by striking a committee of four people who had considerable experience in working with at risk youth in wilderness settings. This committee reviewed the initial plan, and pointed out a number of potential pitfalls in it. They also outlined modifications to the

"Wilderness Model" so that it would meet some basic principles in a way that would also ensure ongoing school success. They reviewed a number of "wilderness" programs that had been offered in the Yukon over the past 15 years. A number of these Yukon initiatives have provided youth, particularly the "troubled adolescent," with an opportunity to develop useful skills, a sense of cultural identity and an improved self-esteem through experiential learning based on wilderness experiences. From these and a review of other centers, the committee identified the following three critical factors:

1. The program needs to provide "troubled" or "disenchanted" youth with educational experiences that contribute to their self esteem, interpersonal relationships, and clarification of their personal goals within highly motivating environments, consistent with existing school programs.

2. The wilderness experiences need to be linked to an educational structure that provides active experiential learning and subject integration. This needs to be supported through positive but demanding teacher-student relationships and the students desire to be in the program.

3. Successful wilderness programs have identified clear statements of philosophy which are reflected in their program themes. They have committed, people oriented staff. Where they have been school based, they involve the student in active learning rather than isolate the youth from the school.

Based upon these experiences and principles, the committee recommended a plan for a Yukon Wilderness program. In mid May, 1989, the Department of Education adopted the committee's recommendations, and detailed planning for the Wilderness component of the "Return to Learning" framework began. These plans identified a number of key principles rather than specific operational detail.

✎ Staffing

The program's staff needed:

a. a philosophical framework central to experiential education through wilderness experiences.

b. extensive wilderness experience and instruction in wilderness activities.

c. adolescent counseling skills combined with personal leadership qualities.

d. self motivation and possess a strong, well developed common sense.

e. possess skill and demonstrated experience in teaching combined with curriculum development, implementation, and evaluation skills.

f. the ability to provide instruction for both males and females.

g. the ability to provide instruction based on Yukon First Nations' traditions as well as upon western wilderness traditions.

h. demonstrated experience in dealing with youth in non-conventional settings.

✎ *Clientele*

The students needed:

a. to have chosen to participate in the program.

b. the belief that experiential learning based in wilderness activities will be a benefit.

c. to accept the different types of students the program will bring together and recognize the opportunity for personal development by all participants.

✎ *Content*

The content of the courses included in the program needed:

a. to reflect an experiential approach based in wilderness activities.

b. an ongoing link to conventional schooling so that some elements of the classroom are relevant to the wilderness experience and, conversely some elements of the wilderness experience are linked to parts of the regular classroom.

c. content based upon the environment in which one is located.

d. activities that may give the appearance of "risk" but are in fact safe but challenging.

e. the introduction and practice of traditional land-based skills which facilitates cultural understanding.

✎ *Location, Facilities, and Equipment*

The location, facilities, and equipment needed:

a. to be selected to support and further the goals and objectives of a wilderness program.

b. to be readily accessible to the clients of the program in terms of time and costs.

c. to permit the program to be carried out without becoming restrictive of focusing (the setting and facilities should not determine the program).

d. to be a safe and healthy environment.

✎ *Organizational Links*

The wilderness program needed to tie in with the organizational structure and scheduling of the school with a minimum of interference.

✎ *Evaluative Processes*

Evaluation of the wilderness program needed to be based on a philosophy of formative, ongoing appraisal which leads to change where change is deemed to result in program improvements. All actors involved in the wilderness experience were to play a role in the evaluative process.

With these principles as guidelines, ACES was developed and the program began in the fall of 1989. ACES (Achievement, Culture, Environment, and Service) was the name given to the Yukon wilderness program. The program provided youth with a grade 10 wilderness based experiential educational opportunity that served to develop self esteem, interpersonal relationships, and clarify personal goals. It was centered at F. H. Collins High School in Whitehorse following a school within a school model. A single teacher taught four subjects to one group of students for a semester at a time. This arrangement provided the teacher with considerable flexibility since the self contained class permitted scheduling outside the regular school timetables. Consistent contact with the school was achieved by integrating the four grade 10 courses (Socials 10, Physical Education 10, Environmental Studies 10 and Yukon Studies 10) with a number of experiential activities based in outdoor pursuits. Though termed wilderness, the program involved a balance between active and reflective components. There were complimentary, non-wilderness components including such things as in depth projects, reports based upon guest speakers, debate and discussion, trip planning, and so forth. ACES provided a measure of consistency with existing school curricula so that students earned course credit for subjects taken in non-conventional wilderness settings. The content of the courses and the course resources were designed to reflect a wide variety of

Yukon environments. The activities and resources developed for each course focused on cooperative learning through experiential activities.

ACES was co-educational and was developed for a wide spectrum of students with limitations only on their ability to take part in the physical and wilderness components of the program. Students chose to take part in the program. It was open to application from all grade 10 students and appealed to those who would benefit from an experiential based education in wilderness settings. Since the beginning of the program, approximately 20% of students in a grade 10 year chose to take part in ACES.

By maintaining a "positive peer" atmosphere, all students taking part in the program benefited from the mix of students. They made new friends, learned to cooperate and depend on each other and, for the at risk youth, found strengths in themselves. It was a program that would encourage success within the conventional school model. Space was reserved for some "at risk" students who were encouraged to take part by counselors. Students from rural schools could participate in the program and complete the alternate semester at F. H. Collins while living at the St. Elias Dorm or elsewhere in Whitehorse. Students from rural settings also took part in the program when the rural school was able to arrange the alternate semester of programming within their own school.

Equipment was selected to ensure safety in wilderness settings. The program provided outer clothing and equipment for an array of different outdoor activities. Students were responsible for providing good basic clothing, their own food, and cookwear for outings. Transportation was provided on a cost shared basis. Students were expected to share the costs of gas and other transportation expenses while the costs of vans, and so forth were covered by the program's budget.

The teacher of ACES received assistance in field activities from a number of support staff. The additional support staff provided specific expertise as required and was covered under program funding for the ACES program. This type of contractual arrangement was essential to permit safety and supervisory requirements of the various activities, some of which were of a relatively "high risk" nature. The ACES teacher demonstrated an understanding and acceptance of the philosophical framework central to experiential education in the wilderness environment. The teacher had extensive wilderness experience and instruction in wilderness activities, adolescent counseling skills, and personal leadership qualities. He also demonstrated experience in teaching, and curriculum development, implementation, and evaluation, an ability to provide wilderness instruction consistent with Yukon First Nations' traditions as well as Western traditions and had experience dealing with youth in nonconventional settings.

The Evaluation Process

Evaluation of ACES was seen as a vital component in the developmental process from the outset. A number of on-going evaluation activities have served a formative function leading to improvements in the program at the end of each semester. Evaluations provided both qualitative and quantitative information. They involved all the stakeholders in the program: students, teacher, school administration, parents, and the Department of Education. The evaluations focused on affirming positive features of the program and the development of alternatives to areas perceived as needing change. It addressed a wide range of topics to encompass the scope and complexity of the program. They included an analysis of the academic components of the program (courses, subject integration, and study activities), the field activities (selection of activities and sites, access and transportation, equipment selection, use, storage, and sharing, support personnel, and use of community resources) the growth and development of students (social, motivational, and behavioral), the teaching role (teacher load, departmental supports, school supports, safety and safety procedures/liability, communication with student, parents, school, Department, reporting) and other factors raised by stakeholders in the program.

Information was gathered as part of the evaluative process in a number of different ways:

1. Interviews with teacher, students, parents, and administrators.

2. Questionnaires distributed to teachers, students, parents, school committee, school administration, and department personnel.

3. Analysis of the daily journals and ongoing logs respecting ACES.

4. Analysis of long term student performance.

5. Assessment of student work across a wide range of activities.

How Has Aces Worked?

The program has evolved over time. Following each appraisal, the program has been adjusted to incorporate recommendations stemming from the evaluation. This included a forum in which parents and teachers met to discuss the program and to formulate recommendations for development and change.

The comparatively novel approach the ACES program used to address conventional academic subject matter raised questions about the students' performance. Questions were raised regarding the relative performance of students and whether the students were slipping in their academic performance because of the extent to which the courses were offered through experiential processes rather that through more traditional lecture processes. An analysis examined the students' scores in the subjects between their own grade 9 to 10 scores and between other students not in ACES, over the same two year period. These included marks students received in English, math, social, science, and PE. Social and PE were offered in the ACES setting while the others were offered in the conventional classroom setting in the alternative semester. The results show that students who participated in ACES had an average increase of 5% in each of these five courses compared to a decrease of approximately 3% for each of the students in the conventional programs of studies. It is also worth noting that the first semester students showed a greater increase in math, science, and English scores during their second semester following the ACES semester as compared to those who took ACES in the second semester.

In the first year of the program, 95% of the parents of students gave unsolicited statements of support for the program. They cited the growth in the maturity of their children, how they have accepted responsibility and have developed cooperative behavior at home and at school. The students have collectively cited their experiences as outstanding, "the most memorable of all in school." These indicators alone probably speak more strongly than the improved academic performance of the wilderness students.

All students enrolled in the program took part in an assessment that covered a wide range of topics and sought their views on the strengths and weaknesses of the program. These included assessments of:

☆ the educational, psychological, physical, emotional, and social rewards and challenges found in the program.

☆ how their experiences affected attitudes toward education, environment, and subject integration.

☆ the course work, home work, and use of instructional time, field activities, selection of activities, and the location of the activities.

☆ the transportation, selection, use, storage, and sharing of equipment, the support personnel, and use of community resource people.

☆ the safety and conduct of programs.

☆ the communications with student, parents, and school and the reporting and evaluation of their work.

☆ the relationships with the teacher and how these may have contributed or detracted from the development of a positive relationship.

☆ the types of field activities that were of the best value.

☆ other comments they may wish to make.

In general, student responses were both positive and constructive, indicating strengths to the program and providing substantiated recommendations where change was felt to be a value. The comments of these students characterized the benefits they felt ACES provided.

☆ *I think learning to work as a group was valuable. Knowing that not always you can be a loner, you need your friends help at sometime.*

☆ *That you didn't feel left out, there was someone to talk to all of the time.*

☆ *I felt the most beneficial aspect of the program was the fact that we were able to express ourselves freely and being given responsibilities and choices that we will most likely be faced with later in life. Also, I felt our closeness with the environment opened new doors for us.*

☆ *Hands on experiences.*

☆ *I think that the trips were the most beneficial part because on them we learned through experience about the world around us.*

☆ *Before this program, I didn't know how to canoe, I had never been in one, how to ski, how to survive in the outdoors. Now I do.*

☆ *Experiencing the many things we did, e.g., snow caving, snow profiles, trench foot, etc.*

☆ *I found the MacMilland trip hard, but when you worked at it and thought about what you were doing, I enjoyed it more. I would take the trip over again.*

☆ *The physical challenge and being away from the comforts of home. Being in situations where we had to examine and question our actions and our behavior.*

☆ *It showed me that different people have different skills and it made me realize that I'll try hard even though I think I'll have trouble next term.*

☆ *Made me re-examine how narrow my vision has been.*

☆ *Text books were interesting but really preferred learning through experiences.*

☆ *At the beginning I was somewhat fearful and doubting of myself but it seems now I have more courage and confidence and feel stronger as an individual.*

☆ *Enjoyed being able to contribute to the evaluation process.*

☆ *I think that when communication between student and teacher are good, then everybody's happy. We couldn't ask for a better person.*

☆ *I have been able to better recognize my own strengths and weaknesses. I can sort of recognize these qualities in others.*

☆ *I think they should make this a grade 11 program. Low numbers in the class make it easy. Extend the Juneau trip.*

The responses of parents showed a similar level of support across a similar range of questions and characterized their support for the program in the following comments:

☆ *We saw our son mature and felt the program to be excellent. He enjoyed what he was doing and also felt it was excellent.*

☆ *Academics were addressed in an integrated fashion that was conducive to the student absorbing and retaining information in a way seldom achieved with boring homework assignments.*

☆ *I feel the program matured my son.*

☆ *A different approach to a perfectly balanced subject matter. Strengths both academically and personally.*

☆ *She has put more independent effort into her studies and taken more responsibility for her studies than at any other time in her studies. She is thinking positively of completing her education and going on to some post secondary learning.*

☆ *Felt one important aspect of the program was social growth. Believe it had positive effects upon my son's behavior.*

☆ *Has caused him to enjoy school for the first time in his school career. Well suited to students who have not had much experience with reading, researching preparing, and presenting reports.*

☆ *Excellent opportunity for young people who may be confused as to their educational goals, to set their priorities and re-evaluate their goals.*

More than 90% of the parents that responded indicated, without reservation, that they would encourage their son/daughter to take part in the program again.

Based on these evaluative activities, the encouragement the Department of Education received to extend the program in grade offerings and the considerable supportive press coverage given to the program, the Minister of Education recommended two initiatives. The first was to extend the program to include a grade 11 ACES program and the second was to extend the principles underpinning the ACES model to rural secondary schools.

An Extension To Small Secondary School Settings

As the testimony above illustrates, the ACES program enjoyed an apparent success, however, the program was more accessible to students in Whitehorse than those in rural communities simply because of proximity and access. A number of measures which attempted to ensure that rural students had access to the program were only partially successful, particularly in overcoming the difficulties of students' leaving home for a semester. The Minister of Education, in a desire to see rural students be given a realistically comparable opportunity the ACES program, encouraged the Department of Education to inquire into methods a program similar to ACES could be provided to rural communities. This provided a quandary since one of the key elements of the apparent success ACES enjoyed was because students chose to be in the program. This represented only about 20% of the student population. Translated to rural settings, a similar ratio of participation would mean only 2 or 3 students would chose to participate in such a program. This was not enough to allow the program to function.

Clearly another approach was needed. A review of the essential elements that gave rise to the success of ACES were examined in respect to their transportability to rural communities along with a stock taking of the strengths small rural secondary schools enjoy. The keys to the ACES successes were seen as:

a. the experientially-based nature of the program;

b. the extensive field experiences and the relationships these experiences encourage among students and between students and teachers.

Small rural secondary schools too have their unique strengths. These include:

a. low student-teacher ratios;

b. staff become well acquainted with the students;

c. greater flexibility in scheduling and school time-tabling than the larger urban secondary schools;

d. closer, more personal relationships are developed with the community.

Given these conditions, a model was developed that appeared to contain the essential qualities of the ACES program while drawing upon the strengths of the small secondary school. This model was circulated to rural Yukon schools. They were given an opportunity to consider an innovative organizational arrangement for their schools that would, if accepted, be given extensive developmental support. The proposal, referred to as the Rural Experiential Model (REM), contained the following features:

A Proposal for a Rural Experiential Model (REM)

1. REM is a reorganization of school time. The model proposes that one secondary elective be offered in four time blocks, each a week long, distributed throughout the school year. This would not alter the instructional times for courses, but simply reorganize the way in which the time is allocated. This would mean that one less course would be offered during the regular school schedule, allowing the seven remaining courses to be given larger blocks of time.

2. Week long time blocks offer students a choice of options. All students would be required to select one elective for the full

year from those offered in the experiential context. These electives would typically be those that would benefit from intensive sessions of longer duration with the same group of students. These might include woodwork, construction, job shadowing, work experience, drama, art, practical arts, outdoor education, or selected academic programs – those courses that have substantial experiential components and would benefit from longer time blocks of instruction. These would then represent "option weeks" in which combined grade groupings may participate.

3. This approach would offer 100 hours of instructional time. The additional 20 hours allocated for standard secondary school courses could be picked up in 5 one hour classes used in preparation for each of the week long option sessions.

This model met most of the elements that underpin the success of the ACES program. REM provided a framework that could meet the following objectives:

1. An approach to school subjects that engages the student in an extensive array of experiential pursuits.

2. An instructional environment in which students need to work together, live together, and cooperate in order to achieve their goals.

3. Teachers who desired to extend the student's learning experiences beyond the bounds of the school and are willing to utilize experiential approaches in addressing conventional subjects.

4. The availability of equipment and people with expertise that will permit the safe delivery of experiential programs.

5. The time within the school system that will permit students to be away from school for blocks of days (i.e., 5-8 days at a time).

6. Program resources and curriculum guidelines that permit the program to function within the experiential context.

7. Unqualified support for the program from students, parents, teachers, administrators, the community, and the Department of Education.

Given the acceptance of the program, a number of steps were seen as essential in the process of implementing the REM. These were:

1. A school needed to "buy into" the outlined organizational structure.

2. The Department needed to work with the school to "fine tune" the proposal with more detailed analysis and a fuller outline of how this might work in specific settings.

3. The Department needed to provide the school with support along the following lines:

   a. The principal should be assisted in interpreting the model and putting such an organizational structure in place, including timetabling, allocation of staff, provision of information, and involvement on the part of the community.

   b. The school staff should be provided with support and time for planning and preparation for delivery of time block electives, including support to staff in terms of organizing and assembling and using the resources necessary to deliver time block courses.

   c. The community should be given information as to how this organizational arrangement may be useful in meeting a wider range of student needs, including information about student involvement, community involvement, and use of facilities both inside and out of the school.

4. Provide a general organizational framework. This might resemble four time blocks, each one week long per school year. A course offered in this time block would include a range of grades. For example, the construction program may include woodwork 9/10, construction 11 and construction 12 all within the same class.

5. Provide resources in a centralized format, including facilities that could be accessed during the "experiential weeks."

6. Prepare lists of appropriate resource people for community access along with necessary access funding.

7. Undertake the development of training activities and opportunities of on the job training with leaders/instructors.

Four rural schools asked Department personnel to visit their schools to discuss the model and explore implications such a model would have for their school. During these discussions, the school staff and administration realized that there was opportunity embodied within the model, however there was also additional work added to what was seen as an already hectic schedule. Following these discussions, two schools applied for a REM program in May

1991 and were given Departmental support for the program for the upcoming year. This support took the following forms:

1. Planning a project centered approach and addressing the curriculum content. It was necessary to ensure that the scope of the course of studies was addressed in the selection of projects and the process in which they were undertaken. Attitudes, skills, and knowledge were the basis of all curriculum. In this respect, the selection of the programs that would be offered in the time blocked scheme would be courses that place a larger focus on skill acquisition than specific content acquisition. Courses such as typing, math, or music which benefit from shorter periods of intense practice would not be taken in large time blocks. The content of math would "drive" the approach rather than the activities associated with project work.

2. Evaluation needed to be formative and ongoing. While some elements of more formalized testing may play a role, it was anticipated that the evaluative process would be ongoing and contribute directly to the learning. (i.e., a comment about a woodworking project would lead to direct improvement in the product while comments on ski technique would contribute to the skier's proficiency. Many of the strategies presently employed in courses such as PE would be used in the evaluative activities.

3. Scheduling with other groups needed to be considered in the process. While some opportunities may be made accessible through a time block schedule, others may be infringed upon. The details of scheduling and time-tabling needed to be prepared, simulated, redrafted, and re-worked a number of times in order to minimize conflicts.

4. Explaining to the community, parents, and others about the time block approach. This approach needed to be elaborated upon so that the principles were understood by all stakeholders.

5. Equipment and resources. There is a substantial pool of resources and equipment. Much of this is already available to many schools and would be made available on a wider basis.

Initial planning in each of the schools was addressed, and each school tailored the program to meet their own needs. In September, 1991, St. Elias Community School, a K-12 school of about 140 students and Watson Lake Secondary School, an 8-12 school of 125 students began their programs.

The St. Elias Community School began by offering four programs that covered multi-grade and multi-course credits in the areas of Outdoor Education, Cultural Studies, Art, and Woodwork/Industrial Education, all offered within the REM format. St. Elias Community School operated the program for grade seven to 12 students, and ran a seven course day on a weekly schedule. They offered Science, Social Studies, Math, English, Physical Education, French, and an option. At four different times in the school year, for a week at a time, groups were to be taking a REM option. Using administration time to cover for the release of teachers who teach across the elementary grades, the secondary staff were able to staff the week long time blocks. The scheme held some initial difficulties in the preparation time since the principal was uncertain about the staffing the school would be getting in the next year. This was seen to be a determinant of the courses that could be offered. There was also a need to resolve the problem of payment for a half-time teacher who would be working an additional two weeks. In the REM evaluation, the school and the Department of Education were to work in partnership, conducting formative analysis as the program unfolded. Support for the preparation time was seen as best involving release time and collaborative planning time for teachers as well as providing resources designed to support the hands-on process central to each of the schemes. The school felt that student attendance may pose a difficulty during these intense weeks since an absence represented a significant percentage of the course time missed.

Watson Lake Secondary School began by offering six programs that covered multi-grade and multi-course credit in fields of Outdoor Ed, Cultural Studies, Art/ Theater/ Drama productions, Journalism/Yearbook program and a Clothing and Textiles program. Watson Lake Secondary School operated the program for all the school, running a seven course day on a weekly schedule. They offered Science, Social Studies, Math, English, Physical Education, French, and an option. At four different times in the school year, for a week at a time, groups take the same REM option. Using administration time to cover for difficult students, students who were ill, and to accommodate the unexpected, teachers were able to staff the week long time blocks, with two programs being team taught. An evaluation of the REM program was to be conducted in a similar fashion to that used in the St. Elias Community School.

How Has Rem Worked Thus Far?

As with the ACES program, evaluation of the REM programs were seen as a vital component in the developmental process from the outset. A number of on-going evaluation activities were established to serve a formative function. Evaluations were to provide both qualitative and quantitative information and involved all the stakeholders in the program: students, teacher, school administration, and the Department of Education.

Surveys were provided to students, teachers, and school administrators following the first session and discussions were held with school staff to identify adaptations and affirm strengths in preparation for the next sessions. These evaluation surveys addressed a wide range of topics and arrangements that encompass the scope and complexity of the REM programs.

Information from the surveys has been analyzed in a number of different ways:

1. Interviews with teachers, students, and administrators.

2. Questionnaires distributed to teachers, students, and school administration.

3. Teacher assessment of student work across the courses offered.

The comparatively novel approach of the REM programs raised opportunities for community involvement and suggested other areas requiring assessment. A number of community residents took part in the week long sessions and each of these individuals were asked to participate in the program's evaluation.

Following the responses of the students, school staff, and community participants, the REM programs have received an overwhelming vote of support. While the program option is a change and the "Hawthorne Effect" may no doubt be present, many of the specific comments made by the students and teachers indicate the process offers more than a simple change.

Teachers who taught a component of the REM program in both schools were asked to analyze their programs, identify the principal strengths the organizational strategy held, and recommend ways in which problems and/or gaps could be overcome. Each responded to a survey that attempted to make the evaluative process less demanding of their time without biasing their responses.

Teachers were asked to provide some overview comments, analyze the resources available to their program, discuss the strengths and shortcomings of the organizational structure, and comment on the degree to which this approach affected academic, social, and personal growth of the students. Students were also asked to take part in an evaluation of the REM model.

Each of the teachers indicated that the program provided real benefits to the regular schedule of events. They all indicated the program should be carried on and most recommended an extension of this model to other types of classes and to other schools.

A number of summary comments sum up their views:

☆ *The entire week allowed for working cooperatively with students to be sustained without me having to switch to "English Teacher" mode. I loved it!!*

☆ *Do it again*

☆ *Offer this in all schools*

☆ *A worthy option to traditional time tabling which offers a much needed variety to the school.*

Teachers in both schools are eagerly looking forward to the next REM session since they have considerably greater preparation time and a better understanding of what to expect than they had from the first session. The first session was offered in the last part of September. While this schedule caused some difficulties, three teachers commented that the early start had contributed to the establishment of positive student/teacher relationships that would see them through the school term. Teachers also indicated that the support they received is essential to the success of the program.

☆ *Support is crucial, organizing substitute teachers or re-allocating staff to cover is vital to maintain PR and teacher support.*

☆ *The REM included many community members. It was a high profile activity which many community members were aware of. It had a positive effect.*

☆ *Department of Education provided encouraging support, enthusiasm, and funding.*

Students also provided feedback that endorsed the REM approach. They were asked to fill out a survey, with Likert response scales, that addressed their feelings about the REM course they took, the content covered, the cooperation required of them and others, how well they spent their time, and invited comments for improvement and identifying the strengths of the REM approach. The survey provided nine questions, each with a 1 to 5 Likert scale and a place for comments and two general comment areas at the end of the survey. Students consistently scored all facets of the program at the high range of the response scales, which indicated that each of the factors surveyed was seen as contributing to the success of their week's activity. Their responses were both positive and constructive, indicating strengths to the program and providing substantiated recommendations where change was felt to be a value.

☆ *It was a relaxed atmosphere but I don't believe we could do it with math or science. We learned something in a relaxed atmosphere.*

☆ *Being out of class and being outside was great.*

☆ *I was able to finish my project in the week.*

The REM process is still undergoing development as is the ACES program with an extension to a grade 11 program this year. It may be too early to make conclusive statements about the success of these particular approaches, yet the early indicators are very positive. As one of the teachers put it: *I think we should stick to the plan and keep flying.*

It is a delight to hear this view expressed in rural schools. It demonstrates small secondary schools have some special opportunities that are realized when their relative size is used to their advantage.

11

OUR STUDENTS, OUR FUTURE

A STUDY ON THE IMPLEMENTATION OF WHOLE LANGUAGE IN THE DEHCHO, NORTHWEST TERRITORIES

Bryce Knudson

Efforts to improve school systems and school effectiveness have been necessarily preoccupied with the initiation and implementation of change. At no time in this writer's experience is this statement more true than in the Northwest Territories where the education process attempts to reflect the unique nature of its peoples' past – their traditions, history, and values. In the evolution towards self determination, the process is molded to provide an appropriate response in preparing its children and young people for the future.

The territorial Minister of Education presented a plan to guide all educational activities within the school system (Kakfwi, 1991):

> [A] holistic approach to learning [is needed] – one which is balanced and acknowledges the importance of addressing all student needs – physical, social, emotional and spiritual, as well as intellectual; and one which is integrated and acknowledges that learning does not occur in isolation. It supports the importance of the learning process – a process which provides students with the skills to enable them to function effectively as confident, responsible members of this constantly changing society . . . . [T]he future of the N.W.T. depends on its children. By working together, we can ensure that our children are well prepared for that future (p. 1).

We live in a world of constant change, the impact of which is becoming greater with the furor of modern technology. Consequently, those involved in education must contend with a great deal of change themselves. They have to assist students to learn new skills and parents to acquire new attitudes which will allow them to adjust more easily to our ever changing world.

In the school setting the principal is responsible for the organization and operation of the school. In northern, rural, sparsely populated areas, this responsibility is notably more visible by the community. Accordingly, the role of principal as change facilitator is crucial, as indicated in the study undertaken by Newton and Wright (1987) and as this author has indicated elsewhere (Knudson, 1990). The principal must be aware of the factors in the school and community which facilitate and prevent change. Goals related to the change must be clear, as only then can decisions about what to retain and what to modify be made.

School administrators play a crucial role in causing a school to be more or less innovative. Fullan and Newton (1988) referred to the principal as the "central causal agent of change" (p. 419). Michael Fullan (1985) further submitted that "educational change is at once simple and complex and therein lies its fascination" (p. 391). Since the 1950s the significance of the role of the principal concerning change initiatives in the school setting have been recognized in the literature on educational change. To illustrate further, Demeter (cited in Carlson et al., 1951), contended that:

> Building principals are key figures in the [change] process. Where they are both aware of and sympathetic to an innovation, it tends to prosper. Where they are ignorant of its existence, or apathetic if not hostile, it tends to remain outside the blood stream of the school (p. 61).

Fullan (1982) submitted that principals' actions and views of their role relative to educational change may, in part, be determined by their locus of control, the degree to which they feel controlled by outside forces.

Bell (1979) suggested that the principal plays the most influential role in the school; however, this influence is not effective if the change is mandated or imposed. Consequently, the distinction between purely directive and facilitative leadership is crucial. It is difficult, if not impossible, for the principal to direct or mandate change that is not wanted by the staff or that he/she does not actively endorse. Evidence is very strong on the role played by the principal in the implementation and continuance of any change proposal. Bell (1979) argued that principals function best as "gatekeepers" giving signals about whether new behaviors will be rewarded or not, setting the school climate by giving cues about how important different parts of the school program and operation are. Newton and Wright (1987) substantiated this notion and maintained that:

the administrator must act on a 'feel for leadership' that includes knowledge of the context, the innovation, reflection on the implications, interaction with the principle actors, and the development of plans that build on the specifics of the situation (p. 365).

Schools face many pressures for change because planning for change in education is not only necessary and desirable but inevitable. Since the change process has been successful in the two schools selected for the study to be reported here, it is hoped that valuable knowledge will be gained on implementation plans that involve local school and community factors.

Researchers and innovators have provided valuable insights on planned change in recent years, as displayed in Table 1, which summarizes the four main categories of factors affecting implementation (Fullan, 1985, p. 73).

Factors Affecting Implementation

✎ *A. Characteristics of the Change*

1. Need and relevance of the change

2. Clarity

3. Complexity

4. Quality and practicality of program (materials etc.)

✎ *B. Characteristics at the School District Level*

5. The history of innovative attempts

6. The adoption process

7. Central administrative support and involvement

8. Staff development (in-service) and participation

9. Time-line and information system (evaluation)

10. Board and community characteristics

✎ *C. Characteristics at the School Level*

11. The principal

12. Teacher-teacher relations

13. Teacher characteristics and orientations

✎ D. Characteristics External to the Local System

14. Role of government

15. External assistance[1]

Corbett and Rossman (1989) contended that the principal, as the key figure in the change process, must be involved in the innovation from three perspectives: technical, political, and cultural. The technical perspective refers to how work is done and interprets implementation problems as the result of systematic planning failure. Barriers to implementation can be described as low quality innovations, unavailability of important resources such as the provision of adequate staff time and information, and the lack of opportunity to discuss and adapt the innovation.

The political perspective focuses attention on the interplay of divergent interests among participants in the change process. It reflects the use of power and authority to bring about change.

The cultural perspective emphasizes socially shared and transmitted definitions of what is and what ought to be and the symbolic meanings practitioners, students, and the community give to change efforts (Corbett and Rossman, p. 165). Ingrained sets of values, beliefs, and norms are reflected in the differences of those involved. Research has shown that for lasting change to occur, that is, for acceptance and enduring adherence to new practices, accompanying support and grounding in the school's culture is necessary (p. 185).

The willingness and ability of the school administrator are critical factors to meaningful, effective, and successful change. It was not all that long ago that innovators seemed to look for methods of bypassing the principal in attempts to have changes implemented directly in the classroom. However, it was soon discovered through work of such researchers as Corbett and Rossman and Fullan that if the principal does not actively support an innovation, it will not likely do well. The evidence is very strong both in the change research and this author's experience that the principal plays a decisive role in the implementation and continuance of any change proposal.

---

1   From *The Meaning of Educational Change* (p. 56) by M.G. Fullan, 1982, Toronto: O.l.S.E. Press. Copyright 1982 by the Ontario Institute for Studies in Education.

The focus of this chapter will be the role of the principal in implementing change. A study was conducted to investigate the implementation of whole language in two small northern rural schools. The four factors presented in Table 1 provided a conceptual framework for the study.

Study Background

✎ *School Sites in Context*

On April 1, 1990 the communities in the Dehcho region of the southwestern Northwest Territories accepted the challenge to manage and direct the educational affairs of the eight schools in the division by forming a Divisional Board of Education. The Board office is located in the community of Fort Simpson, in the building originally constructed as a residence for students from the Dehcho district. The division is comprised of eight communities ranging in school size from six students and one teacher to 275 students and a staff of eighteen with four classroom assistants.

The two principals selected for this study were asked to present descriptions regarding their role perceptions as administrators of their respective schools as well as strategies they employed in the implementation of whole language. Furthermore, they were asked to reflect and comment upon their use of the technical, political, and cultural framework in the implementation process and what their experiences suggested about appropriate strategies for implementing change successfully. The principals were selected by the author for various reasons including their leadership styles and their commitment to holistic education. In addition, they are both competent, experienced administrators of two of the larger schools in the division. Each has been given a fictitious name for purposes of this study and to provide them with some anonymity.

Whole language implementation is strongly encouraged by the Department of Education and has been mandated by the Divisional Board of Education to be fully implemented by the fall of 1992. This process articulates a vision for education in the Northwest Territories, whereby students will acquire the knowledge, skills, and attitudes they will need to be responsible, confident members of a rapidly changing, diverse society.

Helen is principal of a school of 100 students, grades K-9, with a staff of six (including herself) and three support staff. She teaches full time, except where she can juggle the time-table thereby providing a little much needed administration time. The following nar-

ration by Helen describes her experiences in the implementation process of whole language.

First Case Illustration Narrated by Helen

In the spring of 1989 I was interested in a change from my position as Methods and Resources teacher in Fort Simpson and was looking for a new challenge. I had been teaching in the N.W.T. for twelve years and had taught at all levels from K-10 and in many subject areas.

I had a strong interest in literacy and had spent many years teaching language arts and had evolved into a competent language teacher. My work with special needs children further strengthened my holistic belief in language learning. As well, I felt I had the ability to run a school and therefore decided to apply for the principal/teacher position in Fort Liard. Fort Liard is a small Slavey Indian community of approximately 450 people on the banks of two rivers: the Liard River and the smaller Petitot or Black River. The Echo Dene School had approximately 79 students when I arrived in 1989 and has increased to 92, not including approximately eight school age students who do not attend regularly.

✎ *Teaching Language Arts.*

The Department of Education was attempting to prepare boards, superintendents and teachers for the implementation of "Whole Language" by the 1992 school year and with my background and interest I wanted to become involved in this implementation. Since I had implemented mainstreaming in the school in Fort Simpson under very adverse and trying conditions, I felt I could manage the strains and stresses of this Whole Language implementation, especially since I, as principal would have the authority to do so.

My years of teaching experience, courses I had taken, reading and work with other educators led to a strong belief in a holistic approach to literacy. I was looking forward to this new challenge and set out, once I had this position, to implement Whole Language at Echo Dene School. The principal at this time was a very traditional language teacher and so was the staff who had been teaching using Basal reading series, which had always been used. All the staff but one was leaving and I set out, on a visit to Fort Liard to speak to this teacher and assess the materials available at the school.

✎ *The Story Of Whole Language.*

This particular teacher was completing his first year of teaching and was quite apprehensive, but enthusiastic. His instruction in university was based on a holistic approach, but once actually teaching he followed the school program and taught using a Basal reader, phonics, and spelling books. Because he didn't feel very confident about this he asked if he could follow the Basal program the following year and ease into a holistic approach.

I felt this was the best approach as it is virtually impossible to expect someone to teach something well that they are unsure of. So the plan with this particular teacher was to allow him to use the Basal series, and with my help, ease into a Whole Language system. I had two more staff members coming to our school and since I was involved in hiring I set out to look for people with holistic experience. I was looking for primary and intermediate teachers and hired two individuals who were quite holistically oriented.

With three of the teachers, including myself, holistically oriented and one quite interested I set out to get the school "ready." I canceled the requisitions for the Basal series, except for the one intermediate class, and set out to purchase books with the money allocated for Language Arts materials. The Superintendent of our region was enthusiastic about implementing Whole Language and had arranged for a course on Whole Language to take place in the early fall of the next school year. I had already taken this course, but set out to get the staff enrolled. All were enthusiastic and I arranged Professional Development funding for them, as well as had them enrolled in the university through which this course was offered. The course was to take place in the Government Centre in Fort Simpson for one week in September. The schools were closed for this week and I was to remain in Fort Liard for a week of much needed "administration time." I was principal of the school, but I was also a full-time teacher responsible for the junior high program. My load was very full but I felt confident and enthusiastic.

The next step was to develop a library, which is essential for any school. Echo Dene School had been completed in the winter of 1988 and was not large enough. The designated library had to be used as a classroom and therefore the school went without a library. My project for this year was to set up a library. The Community Education Council had extra funding which they needed to use and they were very supportive of the development of a library. This was an almost overwhelming task, but one which all the staff felt strongly about. Now the problem of where, what to order, how to set it up, when do we have the time, who does what and so on, needed to be dealt with.

I started ordering books and throughout the year, once I had staff input on the types of books they needed for their curriculum and interests, ordered whenever there was money available. New shelves were built locally and the library started to take shape. Without going on endlessly about the library I'll briefly summarize it's development. The outer office area which is approximately 8m x 4m was designated the library. A small office just off this area was the library workroom and reference area. A color-coded system was to be used as the Dewey Decimal system was far too expensive in terms of time and money. Categories were set (Fiction, Science, Social Studies, Sports, etc.) and Work Bees were begun. The staff had numerous evening sessions and some community members got involved. It was a lot of work but by February of 1990 the library was usable. We continue to work on the library and have a few regular volunteers who help us. Extra money always goes into the library and it has become a small but very important focal point of our school.

The next school year saw an increase in staff and I now was to teach half-time and look after the special needs program the other half, as Methods and Resource teacher. My administrative duties were to be fit in somehow. Part of my morning was to teach language arts to the junior high class and with consultation with the staff I decided to become the librarian for an hour each morning with regular library periods for each class. I felt that if we were to encourage reading and attempt to have children become literate, a proper library program was necessary. By placing importance on the library, especially from the school administration, I felt it would show where I and the staff as a whole, felt the impetus.

As the educational leader of the school I know I had to be resource person for the whole language program. It takes time to teach people to develop a holistic philosophy and requires a lot of work on their part. A Professional Development day was spent instructing the staff in theme development and I was fortunate with my staff - not only were they hard working, but eager to learn and willing to try new things. Before the Christmas vacation of that first year of Whole Language implementation, one of the intermediate teachers was abandoning his Basal reader and the university training in whole language came back to him quickly.

The other teachers were quite comfortable and were busy developing themes and integrating other subject areas into their language arts program. Now the language arts program cannot be singled out as an isolated program, as it is integrated with science, social studies, health and the other subject areas. I believe my proactive approach was important in the implementation of Whole Language.

It was necessary for me to lead by teaching language arts in a holistic manner, in-servicing staff, taking on the library project and establishing myself as the librarian. My time was at a premium but by taking on these projects it demonstrated where I felt the need and importance lay.

Since that first year, we have had staff changes and various other new projects, but the library remains a focal point of our school and whole language is going strong. This next school year, my third as principal, there will be more staff turnover, as well as another addition to our staff. We are getting more students in school & attendance is getting better which warrants more staff — teachers, special needs assistants and counselors.

Why? — I know it has something to do with the school as a whole — but I like to think it has something to do with the way the school is run. During my Principal Certification courses I learned about leadership and the importance of the principal in setting the mood and tone of the school. I would like to think I have done a competent job of developing a good school. By laying emphasis on Whole Language I have set the tone for a literate school; this has already become evident. Teachers talk about how much their students are reading, and in the case of the intermediate teacher who was here during the "Basal period," he is surprised and pleased at the changes in the students' reading and writing abilities, interest, and enthusiasm. Parents comment positively on the amount their children read and encourage this. More parents are buying books for their children and our annual Book Fair is always a huge success. At our Awards ceremonies we give books instead of certificates, to promote the importance of reading and to give students something they will actually use over and over again.

Next year I will turn the librarianship over to one of our classroom assistants, as I have teaching responsibilities at the junior High level. I believe the way has been paved and the library will continue to flourish. We have had more courses on whole language and my staff members are well on their way with a holistic philosophy.

Perspectives On Innovation: Implementation Of Change With The Whole Language Program

✎ *Technical Changes.*

It was set out very clearly to all staff that we were going to work toward making Echo Dene School a *literary* [italics added] place. I made it clear that I expected all staff to work toward that goal and took many opportunities during staff meetings, as well as individual meetings, to encourage teachers to work towards this. I gave them many suggestions in the form of (a) articles (which were sometimes discussed at a staff meeting), (b) in-service, (c) courses, (d) resource books and materials, (e) library, (f) librarian, to name several of the ways I provided encouragement. As stated previously I allowed teachers to become familiar with the whole language philosophy by leaning on their basal program, using teacher's guides, and resource material but I made it very clear that we were headed for a school wide holistic approach and I expected them to get *on-stream* [italics added]. They had the choice of materials and I had asked them for suggestions for books, kits, and other materials that they felt comfortable with. With the intermediate teacher I allowed him to start off with the basal program used previously, but also ordered a whole language reading kit which he felt would help him. He has since even abandoned this kit and all the books in the kit have been incorporated into the library and the guides put on the shelf with all the other Resource materials. He was allowed to experiment and experience without undo pressure until he felt confident. I made sure teachers could come to me with concerns and I tried to give positive feedback about what I saw in their classrooms.

✎ *Political change.*

I had worked in schools where I felt very isolated from the administration and had been allowed (basically no one ever really checked on what I was doing) – to do what I wanted in my language arts program, especially after I had proven I knew what I was doing. I wasn't comfortable with this isolation because I didn't feel it was a school or team approach. There were so many factions doing different things. I felt there needed to be some goal or comprehensive plan for the development of literacy. As Principal of a school I would be able to develop the programs the way I felt they should develop, of course keeping in mind departmental policy. In this case I was fortunate that Whole Language was being promoted and becoming policy. This opportunity seemed perfect for me and I set about developing a strategy to implement a change in Language Arts instruction. This strategy has already been outlined in the first section.

✎ *Cultural Change.*

The staff members knew from the onset that they were to teach a whole language program. They knew this was a major concern of mine and that I would be working with them to make sure a holistic philosophy was being developed. I believe there was some pressure to live up to my expectations and as professionals they wanted to do the best they could. I believe there was guidance for them whenever they needed or wanted it and that they were motivated to offer a good program for their students and to be successful as educators. Because we had a small staff there was much sharing of ideas and materials, and people felt they could work together. I tried to foster a team approach and even though they knew I was the principal and could and would make decisions, I did ask for staff input and consensus in as many matters as possible. The teachers I have had under my supervision during my tenure as principal have been enthusiastic, hard working individuals who have endeavored to work to my expectations as well as their own. I attempted to show by example that Whole Language can work. The types of things I did in my class and in the school as a whole, stressed language literacy and this mood prevailed and was adopted by the staff. Peer pressure and influence still works among adults as I observed in our school. Teachers enjoy feeling that they are an important part of the whole, and will work harder if it is part of a team approach and toward a common goal. We have attempted school-wide themes which means staff and students have to work together to build the theme. Even though it is quite demanding and needs much planning, the resulting satisfaction is felt by all. I truly believe that this implementation would not have worked so well if it hadn't been implemented by the principal. By becoming involved and proactive I was able to ensure that it was being implemented by all staff. Teacher evaluation stressed this as well and was documented. It could have died a quiet death [italics added] like so many other programs left in isolation, but did not because of the on going implementation by the principal.

Donna administrates a school of 130 students, grades K-9, with a staff of eleven (including herself) and four support staff. She teaches half time as a methods and resource teacher.

Second Case Illustration Narrated by Donna

The community of Fort Providence on the banks of the Mackenzie River began as an outpost camp for fur traders. The Slavey Indians from the outlying areas visited the camp a few times a year to sell their furs and buy supplies. The Catholic Church set up a Mission school in 1932 in Fort Providence and the families began to leave their children in the residence so they could attend school while their parents continued to lead a traditional life. Other children from communities farther up the Mackenzie River were also brought to Providence at the beginning of the school year and stayed in the residence until the school year ended. Eventually a settlement started to develop and families began to build permanent dwellings on the riverbank. A road was constructed in the 1950s and Fort Providence became accessible from Yellowknife to the north and Edmonton to the south. In 1956, a day school for kindergarten to grade six was built at the site of the present school. Students could now live at home with their families and attend school. As the years progressed, additional grades were added and the school presently offers kindergarten to grade nine.

In August of 1981, I arrived in Fort Providence as one of a staff of ten teachers with almost one hundred seventy students on register. Attendance was extremely poor and parental interest and involvement was almost non-existent. Over the next four years, enrollment slowly declined and attendance dropped to sixty percent. At the present time enrollment is one hundred thirty eight students with eight teachers on staff for the 1991-92 school year. Since the day school opened, the student population of the school has been predominantly Slavey with a small population of Metis and non-native children.

My tenure as principal began in August of 1985. During the 1985-86 school year, a pilot project was started in our school to improve attendance and to get the children into the school on a regular basis. With the help of a support staff member, now referred to as a School Community Counselor, our attendance was brought up to eighty percent and students who had only been a name on a register page in the past were in school. Of course this caused other problems to become evident. Most of the students were below grade level and little support from the home was only compounding the problem.

✎ *Teaching Language Arts.*

Upon my arrival at Elizabeth Ward School, I found the teachers using the Nelson Basal Reading Series. The students progressed through each reader and were required to complete the workbook and studybook pages as outlined in the teachers' guides. However, most of the students were not experiencing much success with the use of the Basal reading program. The students progressed to about the grade three level in the readers and then reached an almost unsurpassable point. Many older students were seen in classes with the grade three or four readers trying to complete the workbooks so they could move to the next reader.

Other schools in the Territories were also trying to deal with this problem and during the fall of 1981 the Department of Education offered a three day workshop dealing with the Language Development Approach. One staff member from each school was introduced to the approach by Jim McDirmiad and Strini Reddy. The trained staff member was expected to share his or her knowledge with the rest of the school staff. The teachers were encouraged to promote the four strands of communication-listening, speaking, reading, and writing using stories and activities. The use of the Basal series as a program was discouraged although the readers could be used as anthologies.

Many teachers at Elizabeth Ward School that year tried to use the approach but were very discouraged. The little bit of in-service they did receive did not prepare them to run a program without a teacher's guide. Using the language development approach, the teacher was controlling the vocabulary and also the grammar learning that was taking place. They found it took a great deal of planning time and they felt unsure of what skills they were to teach and when to teach them. Within a very short period of time, the teachers returned to the Nelson Reading Series with a fervor.

✎ *The Story of Whole Language.*

For the next five years, the Nelson program was used in regular classes while I, as Special Needs teacher, pulled some students from the regular class and used my own version of the Language Development approach. In May of 1987, a Whole Language course was offered by the University of Victoria for Special Needs teachers, then referred to as Methods and Resource teachers. I was now principal and the Method & Resource teacher opted to take this course. Upon her return from the course, the methods and resource teacher started to talk to me and to other staff members about the approach.

In the 1987-88 school year, the staff agreed to start the transition to whole language. However, a definition of the approach was never really discussed and confusion reigned. Myself and other long term staff members thought whole language was a new term for language development and went into the transition with this approach as our goal. Two days of professional development were designated to whole language and we viewed a video of a workshop given by Strini Reddy. I then presented a workshop on the primary science curriculum which had been written using the language development approach.

At the Edmonton Teachers' Conference in February, the staff was encouraged to attend a full day session given by Orin Cochrane from the Winnipeg based C.E.L. (Child-centered, Experience-based, Learning) group. His presentation emphasized the importance of reading to students and having a wide variety of books available for them to read. Although this didn't quite fit into my definition of whole language, I began to discuss with staff the amount of oral reading they were doing in their classrooms and also their use of books as reading material for students. I was not surprised to find that primary teachers were reading books at least once a day and always had books available for students to read or look at in their spare time. The junior and intermediate teachers rarely read anything to their students except basal reader stories and the only time their students had free reading was during the fifteen minutes designated to USSR (Uninterrupted Sustained Silent Reading) time. At these levels, the teachers had concerns, with my insistence that the students be given time to read on their own, since the books they were capable of reading and understanding were primary books. At the time, I sympathized with them and did not push the matter. However, we agreed to spend a number of evenings organizing the books in the library. We decided to purchase books instead of Basal reading material for the next school year, as well.

Every year our school has a staff turnover of two or three teachers and this always causes problems in continuity. In May of 1988, I saw it as an opportunity to hire three teachers who had some experience with whole language and who could help the rest of us on staff make the transition. I was successful in acquiring a grade one teacher who had just completed her teacher training with numerous courses in whole language, and an intermediate teacher from the Northwest Territories who had been involved in writing the new Junior High Language Arts Curriculum. Although I was starting maternity leave in August of 1988, I decided I was going to use my staff to my advantage and timetabled the intermediate teacher to teach the junior class language arts as well. When I returned to my position in January of 1989, I saw that change had begun. The grade one class was excited about books and were eagerly reading anything they could find. They were buddy reading with one of the junior classes and this had caused other teachers to pair their classes and meet at least once a week for a reading session. The grade ones were encouraged to write daily and their progression through developmental spelling was becoming evident. The junior and intermediate classes were allowed to read primary books to practice for buddy reading sessions and they were enjoying all the stories that had never before been read to them. They were also beginning to read other books during free reading time. It was evident that more books were needed to meet the demands the students were placing on our very small and fairly outdated library. We were also finding it impossible to deal with the care of the library since we were not fortunate enough to have a librarian and it was becoming too much work after school for a staff member. As a staff, we decided to purchase a large number of books and start to build classroom libraries. The task of ordering books was given to the two staff members who were using whole language and like their students, had developed a love of books.

A goal was set by our superintendent to have whole language implemented in all the schools in our region by September of 1992. In order to provide training for teachers, the regional office organized a Whole Language course from the University of Victoria to be taught in Fort Simpson in September of 1989 and 1990. The grade two teacher and I attended the course and it finally became clear to me what whole language was. I realized that the terms language development and whole language were not interchangeable and that I had two excellent whole language teachers on my staff!

Once-back into the school, I began bombarding my staff with professional articles on whole language. I used part of our staff meetings to discuss the articles and to share the successes of the two whole language classrooms. After visiting other classrooms, I met with each teacher to discuss the positive changes I was beginning to see. We set up times for me to teach their classes while they visited one of the whole language classrooms. During the winter, we spent- one evening a week viewing the tapes made by Norma Mickelson for a whole language course offered on Knowledge Network. After the viewing, we would informally discuss the information in the tapes and relate it to what was happening in our school and which of the items we might be able to try.

As teachers started to become more informed and began to use the approach, other concerns became apparent that had to be dealt with at both a school and regional level. The report cards that were presently being used by the region were not appropriate for a teacher using the whole language approach. Evaluation and grading became a big concern for staff and administration. In order to alleviate some of these concerns, the regional office invited teachers to aid in the development of a more appropriate regional report card and held a working session for a small group of staff dealing with the new Language Arts curriculum due for release in the fall of 1990. The working group compiled a package of evaluation forms available on the market to help teachers keep anecdotal comments on students. A full day session dealing with evaluation was offered to all teaching staff in the region at the regional conference in September, 1990.

Another area of concern was educating the parents. Our parents were accustomed to their children bringing home readers and workbooks and to having report cards with letter grades. The parents of the primary students were soon sold on the approach after being invited to their children's grade one class and seeing the children reading and writing and thoroughly enjoying coming to school. A parents' night was organized for September of 1990 and a large group of parents showed up to view an unedited video of their children at work in the classroom. As the tape ran, I provided the commentary explaining the approach and the differences they were seeing in the classroom. After the video, the parents visited their children's classes, looked at the work they had been doing and talked to the classroom teacher about the planned program for the year.

In order to help the parent and also the teacher to see the progress made by each student, I require all teachers to keep a file of student work that is dated, as well as a writing file for each student. During parent teacher interviews, or when a concern about a student arises, these files are readily available to refresh a teacher's memory or to show to a parent. Once the teachers began using the approach and saw the successes they were having with their students, it was not hard to keep them motivated and trying new ideas. Buddy reading has now become buddy writing and has produced some interesting pieces of work. We hold three Book Fairs annually to help parents buy books at a reasonable price for their children and also to obtain the free books offered by the book fair companies for our library. We have also held a reading assembly which kicked off a school-wide challenge to read one thousand books in a month. Whenever the opportunity arises to enter a writing contest, I encourage all staff to have all of their students enter; we have been quite successful at bringing recognition to Fort Providence, even at the national level.

Not all teachers are at the same point with whole language. When the board office offered Part One and Part Two of the Whole Language course in the fall of 1990, I was the only member of my staff that took Part Two and one other teacher took Part One. However, I was able to send our native language instructor, our language technician, and another native teacher to a whole language course offered in another community by the University of Saskatchewan. Some teachers are using the approach quite well without any training and I continue to encourage the others. During the 1990-91 school year, we were visited by many teachers from the region who wanted to view our classes and observe our teachers using the whole language approach. The visits have been a big motivator for the staff who have not minded being watched and enjoy sharing their successes and failures with other teachers from the region.

Even though we have come a long way from the basal reading series, we still have a long way to go until we reach the point where our students are fully literate when they leave our school after grade nine. As I mentioned earlier, it became evident to me after taking the whole language course that I was not really aware of the definition of whole language. I realize now that as a staff we have not discussed or put on paper a definition of whole language for our school. We have placed a great deal of emphasis on the reading side of whole language and must start to balance this out with more emphasis in writing and speaking. At one of the first staff meetings in the new school year, we, as a staff, must develop a definition to ensure that we all understand what we mean when we say Whole Language.

Although three new staff members have been hired for the 1991-92 school year, I plan to continue the process and begin to integrate language throughout the curriculum. We have begun to develop books in Slavey, the students' native language, to allow the native language instructor to use the approach. It will continue to be an ongoing process to fully implement whole language into our school and from the success we are seeing, it will be beneficial to our students.

✎ *Summary*

Although the implementation of whole language was mandated by the Department of Education, the process at Elizabeth Ward School came from the grass roots level. The teachers who were hired and had been using the approach were able to interest the rest of the staff and me in learning about the approach. Once I became clear about what whole language was, I became an advocate and continually bombarded the other staff members with information as well as shared the successes of other teachers. The Board office has been extremely supportive and has helped the implementation process to keep moving along.

If I have the opportunity to implement another new teaching approach while in an administrative position, I will make sure I understand and have all the information available before I start to push the approach with the staff. I realize now I could have caused the staff to become discouraged and to oppose the approach because of my confusion. However, I had the proper mind set, the process became quite easy, and proceeded very quickly.

During implementation of the whole language approach, I have been extremely lenient with staff, allowing them to decide whether they will attend courses. In the future, I will insure the staff members are aware that I feel they need more training and will do everything possible to get them into courses. I am sure we would be farther along in the implementation process if we all had the same background.

The entire process has been a learning experience for me and I can now look back and see both the successes and failures. The process will continue and the approach will constantly be modified throughout the years. We are definitely seeing success in our students' reading abilities and that makes the process worthwhile.

Case Analysis

As agents of change in the implementation of whole language, principals Helen and Donna assumed leadership roles. It should be noted that in both instances, the initiatives for change were "top-down." In other words, the pressure to innovate originated at the Department level, the superintendent's office, and the principal's office.

✎ *The Technical Style*

Teachers in both schools were continually led through sequences of activities that involved receiving information on new practices. They were encouraged to try them out and were permitted to make judgments about how well the new practices fit their particular classrooms and teaching styles. Both principals concurred that practice increased the likelihood of commitment. Therefore, uncommitted or slack time was critical to promote teacher skill development and to enable trial, experimentation, and practice. Commitment to the innovation was reached as a consequence of, and not before, adoption.

The planning teams in each school consisted of the teaching staff and principal. The principals attempted to provide adequate resources externally or rearrange or reassign those presently existing within the school. The planning meetings initially were instigated by both principals; they attended these meetings and provided necessary encouragement and technical assistance. Teachers were given exposure to experts wherever possible, whether internal or external, and were encouraged to pursue training, collaboration, and mentorship in whole language practices.

Through numerous visits to the schools, the author was impressed with the comradeship and positive school climate that existed both in the schools and within the classrooms. Time in staff meetings was impressively and professionally spent. The principals, although in control, were treated as team members and discussion took place freely and openly. Principals were sought for advice and collaboration. With their hectic teaching schedule and lack of "slack time," the author feels that the administrator's presence was a positive incentive for change. It should also be noted that the administrator's presence at meetings encouraged teachers both during and after the meetings.

Another vital factor for successful implementation is effective timely communication both within the school and between the school and external agencies. This was accomplished by frequent planning and staff meetings as well as individual consultations. Any external relevant information was quickly and efficiently dispersed among staff members. Consequently, successful change initiatives occurred based on a solid foundation of information, research, and expertise readily available and accessible to teacher implementers.

✎ The Political Style

The political path reflects the use of authority (the right to make a particular decision), and power to bring about change. Power is the ability to influence behavior or to get others to behave in ways that, in the absence of the influence attempt, they ordinarily would not (Schlechty, 1976). The principals referred to in this study used this position to boost the project without overtly using negative pressure or persuasion. Incentives, in the form of encouragement, recognition, and positive performance appraisals were used extensively. Rules and procedures were altered if the principals felt the necessity and new practices were built into existing guidelines and strategies. As disclosed in the case illustrations, when teachers were not likely to change on their own, measures such as these provided additional stimuli. Once reluctant teachers felt the inevitability of having to attempt the innovation, the teachers shifted to the technical path of implementation.

It should also be noted that the principals often delegated tasks and responsibilities for certain aspects of the whole language innovation. This delegation of responsibility to the teachers provided incentives in the form of recognition and encouragement for other team members to compete in a positive way. This accentuates research devoted to analyzing the principal's role in effective schools whereby principals routinely delegate much of the routine school manager tasks and concentrate on being the instructional leader.

✎ The Cultural Style

The cultural style is somewhat different from the technical and political. In Wilson's (1971) words, it is "shared knowledge of what is and what ought to be" (p. 90). Both principals commented that observable changes in the traditional cultural norms occurred when teachers accepted the innovation. Both cases illustrated that the greater the discrepancy in beliefs created by the innovation, the more likely the teacher's route to implementation would move through a cultural path.

The climate of change was deliberately and earnestly fostered in both schools first by the principals, then by administration and planning team members. The principals' unique positions within the school permitted them the opportunities to build culture and foster a climate of change. Encouragement and assistance were provided to teachers and students; rituals and ceremonies were performed to support the new vision of the school. Of obvious significance is that the principal in either case would not assign or expect more of her teachers than she would do herself or was not actively involved in. It became very evident during site visits through the school year that the group of teachers and principal, in both schools, became a powerful, highly visible informal group closely affiliated with the new vision of the school, extremely supportive of the principal, and willing to work very hard in support of the new vision for the school. Consequently, with the inevitable staff turnover, new members would be encouraged and feel compelled both socially and professionally to join the ranks.

Conclusion

In this study a number of issues that are involved in planning for educational change, with specific reference to the role of principal, have been identified. The principal's role as change agent is extremely important in a rural northern setting. Constraints are imposed by lack of resources, both financial and material, lack of expertise, and even neglect. Isolation and lack of planning time make any implementation process difficult. The principal must be in the front lines and play the dominant role as change agent for successful changes to occur.

Educational change is a fact of life in our schools. Moreover, to be effective, change must be carefully and adequately planned. Planning does not automatically guarantee success. However, schools that do engage in good planning increase their chances of success. Therefore, the planning process is extremely important to school administrators who are contemplating change.

Based on a review of the literature, the findings from this study, and experience the author has gained in the field, the following conclusions are offered concerning the principal's role in planning for educational change:

1. The principal must plan thoroughly and appropriately in order for effective change to take place. Chances of successful change are limited if planning is inadequate or lacking.

2. The principal must clearly define the need for change and he/she must have a vision of what ought to be. This need and the vision has to be supported by those who will be affected by the change.

3. The principal must display a positive, supportive, and innovative attitude towards the change taking place.

4. The principal must make provisions for those affected by the change to be involved in the decision making that leads to the change.

5. The principal must ensure that adequate communication takes place regarding the change process. All of the processes involved with change must be adequately publicized to everyone affected and must be understood by all who are involved.

6. The principal must not be afraid to make decisions. If the group cannot solve the problem or does not wish to solve it, the principal should provide the necessary leadership.

7. The principal must constantly monitor and evaluate the change. The evaluative information collected should always relate to the purpose or objective of the change.

It is apparent that the processes of educational planning and change are very complex notions. There is seldom an orderly movement from research, to planning, to change, to development. Both process and product are important. The nature of the process used will influence the form and content of the plans for change. Beeby (1967) contended:

> If the educational administrator is to take his rightful place in planning, he must be prepared to learn the rules of the game as other professions understand it, while still stoutly defending, whenever they be threatened, the values that seem to him proper to education (p. 36).

It is noteworthy that the study of educational change since 1970 has progressed from documenting failure to analysis of success and is presently focused upon the management of change (Fullan, as cited in Gambell and Newton, 1989). Consequently, this chapter has focused on the success of whole language implementation in the two schools selected for the study.

Change is occurring within our society at a phenomenal rate. If it were not for change, the principal's task would be relatively easy. Planning would be without problems, because tomorrow would be no different from today. If planning and change were not a significant part of the principal's responsibilities, and modifications to adapt to educational change were not implemented, his/her effectiveness as school manager would be reduced. The survival of the school would be in jeopardy.

The education system is complicated, and the interrelationships that exist within it even more complicated. It cannot be wrong for those involved in education to reflect on past changes and to contemplate future ones, with the intent of making things better than they now are. Consequently, the ability to plan for change is imperative if our schools are to keep pace with our rapidly evolving technological society.

Woody Allen, who is very successful and has worked diligently at his career, gave us a quote that will not work well for school administrators. He stated: "Being a success is 80% luck and 20% just showing up." Not in our case Woody, thank you very much.

References

Beeby, C. E. (1967). *Planning & the educational administrator.* UNESCO: International Institute for Educational Planning.

Bell, W. E. (1979). Diagnosing a school's readiness for change. *What to look for when starting an innovation.* Santa Clara Country, CA.: Central California Facilitator Project.

Carlson, R. D., Gallaber, A. Jr., Miles, M. P., Pellegrin, R. J., & Rogers, E. M. (1965). *Change processes in the public schools.* Eugene. OR: University of Oregon.

Corbett, H. D. & Rossman, G. B. (1989). Beyond implementation series. Three paths to implementing change: A research note. *Curriculum Inquiry, 19* (2), 163-190.

Fullan, M. G. (1982). *The meaning of educational change.* Toronto: O.I.S.E. Press.

Fullan, M. G. (1985). Charge processes & strategies at the local level. *The Elementary School Journal, 85* (3), 391-420.

Fullan, M. G. & Newton, E. E. (1988). School principals & change processes in the secondary school. *Canadian Journal of Education, 13* (3), 404-422.

Cambell, T. J. & Newton, E. E. (1989). Implementing whole language. *Journal of Educational Administration & Foundations, 4* (2), 40-52.

Kakfwi, S. (1991). *Our students, our future: An educational framework* (March, 1991). Yellowknife, NT: Northwest Territories Education.

Knudson, B. W. (1990). *A study of the principal's role in planning for increased parental involvement.* Unpublished master's thesis, University of Saskatchewan, Saskatoon, SK.

Newton, E. E. and Wright, R. (1987). Forces affecting change in small rural schools. *School Organization, 7* (3), 357-366.

Schlechty, P. (1976). *Teaching and social behavior.* Boston: Allyn & Bacon, 1976.

Wilson, E. K. (1971). *Sociology: Rules and relationships*. Homewood, IL: Dorsey Press.

12

The Effect Of Teacher Supply And

Demand On Rural Education

Keith C. Sullivan and Murray Sandell

Introduction

There was a time when school systems plodded along in the comfortable assurance that demographic change would occur slowly enough to give them time to react. That time, however has passed. Startling changes are occurring very rapidly (Weldon, Hurwitz and Menacker, 1989, 29).

Canada is now starting to examine a recurring problem with its school systems, that is, a shortage of well qualified new teachers. Until the 1960s systems were coping with increasing student enrollments, coupled with new expectations for better educated teachers which lead to large demands for university educated teachers. However, from the mid 1970s to late 1980s provinces were coping with declining school enrollments and a stable teaching force, causing the demand for new teachers to drop sharply (Burstall, 1980 & Jackson, 1977). For example, in the period of time from 1972-1980, partly because of a strong supply of teachers, it was possible to reduce median class size from 27 to 24 students and the percent of part-time teachers more than doubled from 2.4 to 6.0 percent. Mainly because of declining enrollments and declining needs to replace teachers, the percentage of full-time teachers under 30 years of age dropped from 44 to 23 percent (Canadian Teachers Federation, 1981). By 1985 most provinces had large numbers of teachers in mid-career with an average teacher age of 40 years (Canadian Teachers Federation, 1985) leaving few vacant teaching positions at the end of each year.

In the early 1990s, concern is being raised in some parts of Canada about the possibility of another shortage of teachers, this time being motivated by a small growth in the number of students in certain areas and an aging teaching force with early retirement plans, combining to produce the loss of many teachers. The loss of teachers can be positive if enough additional well trained teachers are available to replace those leaving. For years educators have been concerned about the lack of young teachers in the system.

There seem to be two important questions for rural areas in teacher supply and demand issues. First, will there be enough well qualified teachers to fill the positions and, second, will the transition stages include large movements of teachers from rural to urban areas? In the past, new teachers found most jobs in rural areas when more experienced teachers move to fill jobs in urban areas (Sullivan, 1971). Although little attention is paid to rural vs. urban concerns in teacher supply and demand studies, if history repeats itself on this issue, we will have to ask if teachers educated in urban universities are well prepared to teach in rural areas (Murphy, 1984; Williams, 1985; Williams and Cross, 1987). On the other hand, some evidence indicates that for the first time, more migration in the general population is from urban to rural areas (Naisbett, 1992), which might also effect teacher migration.

This chapter will address two issues. The first, the need for teachers in Canada, will include the analysis of recent teacher supply and demand studies. The second, how the movement of teachers will effect rural schools, is addressed by a series of interviews of teachers in rural areas.

The State of the Study of Teacher Supply and Demand

This chapter will address the state of teacher supply and demand in Canada and present evidence from rural teachers in Nova Scotia with respect to how they will react if positions become available in urban areas.

Teacher supply and demand studies are best classified as needs assessments where the actual and the preferred states are compared. Kay Adams (1983, p. 55) used the term "need sensing to refer to the broad array of strategies a complex organization uses to collect information for charting its future."

Studies of predicting supply and demand are difficult because both the actual and preferred states are guesses based on predicting from the past. The quality of the guesses depends on the accuracy with which researchers measure the past and predict the future actual and preferred states. The difficulties are with the unpredictabilities of human behavior and the fragmentation of demand and supply trends (Grissmer and Kirby, 1987).

U.S. States have been involved in teacher demand and supply studies more than Canadian provinces because American school systems have been experiencing a shortage of teachers, especially in mathematics and science, since the late seventies. Even so, Grissmer and Kirby (1987, p. xvi) concluded that in the U.S.

"Current forecasts of teacher attrition are weak compared to forecasts on enrollment and pupil/teacher ratios, mainly because of inadequate and unanalyzed data." Some states have this data, but nationally it does not exist. They suggest that research should be supported to develop improved attrition forecasts for use in teacher supply and demand models, and data on the returning teachers from those who have temporarily left the system as it is an important supply component.

In Canada, Statistics Canada and the Canadian Teacher Federation work together to project enrollments and teacher forecasts for the country and by Province. But a recent study in the Maritimes found that most school systems in that area do not find these enrollment projections accurate and produce their own enrollment forecasts by Province. Projections for teacher supply were generally not done (Samson, Sullivan and Uhl, 1991).

Other than the obvious problem of not having enough teachers for the classrooms, one of the main reasons for being aware of the need for teachers is so teacher education is not governed by a chronic shortfall of teachers which leads to lowering the standards. The late 1970s was the first time in many years that teacher education programs and policies were not driven by a severe shortage of teachers (Albert Fiorino, 1978).

Arguing "for or against the existence of teacher shortages is a glass-half-full, glass-half-empty type of argument. A more appropriate question . . . is where are the 'imbalances' in the supply and demand for teachers . . . and how may these imbalances become balanced?" (The Maryland State Board of Education, 1987, p. 5).

A Model for Studying Teacher Supply and Demand

There are numerous models for determining teacher supply and demand. One teacher education analytical model used in Canada, the Flexor Model, consists of school teacher and teacher education modules (Hansen Group, 1978). A simulation model for Oregon's educator labor market used a Markov chain (Baugh and Stone, 1980). Other studies (Berry, 1984) have used qualitative research study techniques to examine the market patterns of initial career choice, position availability, recruitment and selection, turnover, and mobility.

In 1988, the Centre for Educational Statistics (1988, p. 3) used econometric methods to forecast the number of public school teachers in the U.S. "as a function of per capita income, revenue receipts per state sources per capita, and elementary enrollment."

A study by the Connecticut State Department of Education (1988, p. 5), used a teacher shortage index containing three components, teacher qualification, the application rate for each position type, the potential pool of teachers, to more accurately identify five areas of teacher shortage, which was required by state statutes.

The model for this chapter came from a Nova Scotia Study (Samson, Sullivan and Uhl, 1991), with 13 variables measuring teacher supply and 8 variables measuring teacher demand. The conceptual framework, as shown in Figure 1, was drawn from work completed by the Rand Corporation (Haggstrom et al., 1988, Grissmer, 1987), the Maryland State Board for Higher Education (1987), and the researchers' experience as teachers, professors, and administrators in American and Canadian school systems and universities.

FIGURE 1

TEACHER SUPPLY AND DEMAND CONCEPTUAL FRAMEWORK FOR STUDY

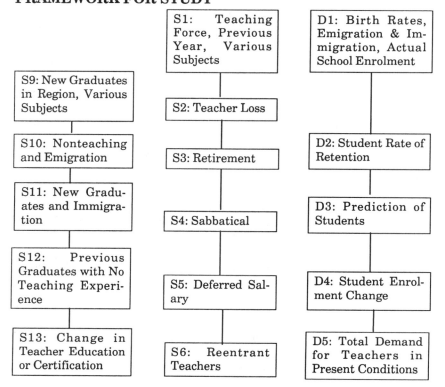

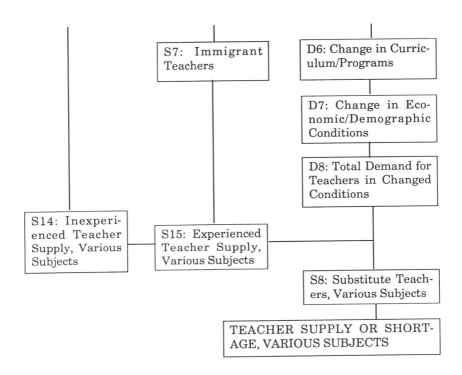

Canadian Studies of Teacher Supply and Demand

Four provincial studies, one regional study of three provinces, and one national study of teacher supply and demand have been published in Canada since 1988. This section briefly reviews the results of these studies.

✎ *British Columbia*

As part of "The Report of the Royal Commission on Education, 1988: *A Legacy for Learners*," from British Columbia, an analysis of teacher supply and demand for British Columbia was completed. The analysis and conclusions were mainly documented in the publication "The On-site Personnel Who Facilitate Learning: Commissioned Papers: Volume 4" (Tuinman and Brayne, 1988).

It was concluded that this B.C. study was a broad look at teacher supply of inexperienced teachers, experienced teachers, and the total demand for teachers and, therefore, the need for teachers in B.C. for the next ten years. It lacked precision in levels and specific qualifications of teachers being supplied and required.

However, the B.C study concluded that over the next ten years, public school enrollment should increase by 65 000 students. By applying the 17.71 student:teacher ratio, 3600 additional teachers will be needed. Another 26 000 will leave the system for numerous reasons over this time period. The estimated 8500 unemployed teachers in the province would pick up the opening teaching positions until 1990-91, but after that the projected shortage of teachers by 1993-94 will be around 2500 teachers. From *A Legacy for Learners: The Summary of Findings 1988* (Province of British Columbia, p. 38), the Commission recommended that the provincial government provide the three universities with the resources to develop, in a coordinated fashion through a tri-university committee, the numbers and kinds of teachers needed in the next decade.

✎ *Ontario*

In 1989, a study was published entitled *Perspectives on Teacher Supply and Demand in Ontario, 1988-2008* (Smith, 1989). The study used the calculations and projections for Teaching Force and Actual School Enrollments from Statistics Canada as used in the Canadian Teachers' Federation (1989) publication *Projections of Elementary and Secondary Enrollment and the Teaching Force in Canada 1987-88 to 2006-07,* which will be discussed later.

The study concluded that by the mid-1990s teacher retirements alone will equal the number of teacher graduates in Ontario, with the number of retirements staying high until approximately 2008 when there will likely be a sharp downswing. The total number of teacher positions will also have an increase because of small increases in student numbers, Kindergarten expansion and more teacher preparation time. The study draws on the CTF study reviewed below to conclude that approximately 1000 new teaching positions a year will be needed for the next ten years in addition to the replacement positions. The increases will not be uniform across the province as some systems will actually be decreasing while others will be experiencing major increases.

Supply teachers have been picking up the vacant positions available in the recent past, but this supply appears to be mainly exhausted. The most severe shortages will be in mathematics, sciences, technological studies, and French. At the same time that large numbers of teachers are retiring, so will there be a large number of professors retiring, possibly as high as one half of the Education faculty by 1993. Without increasing the number of graduates from Ontario universities, the shortage could be as high as 2500 teachers a year by the mid-1990s. However, it should be kept in mind that in the late 1960s, Ontario universities produced more then 13 000 teachers, while in 1989 they graduated just under 5000 teachers, leaving a great deal of room for expansion.

✎ Manitoba

In December 1991, the report entitled *Teacher Supply and Demand for the Public Schools of Manitoba (1989 -2000)* (Manitoba Teacher Supply and Demand Task Force) was released. It used calculations of ten year (provincial) and five year (regional) projections of provincial teacher demand, teacher acquisitions, and required beginning teachers, and surveys of Manitoba school superintendents regarding teacher supply and demand.

The task force concluded that even though student populations will slowly decline, a strong demand for teachers will continue in the province over the projection period to the year 2000, creating a strong need for new teachers. For example, in 1989-90, 47% of the 1063 teachers hired were first year teachers who were newly certified in the previous year. However, the study did not predict the supply and demand relationship. The task force wrote that "Whether the future demand will transform into a shortage, an adequate supply, or a surplus of teachers still remains to be seen" (p. 49).

This study was the most concerned with the supply of teachers in remote rural areas, concluding that northern Manitoba would have a teacher withdrawal rate that was much higher than both greater Winnipeg and rural Manitoba. They recommended that rural and northern school boards be provided with additional funding to attract and retain qualified teachers and that the province and universities work together (with additional funding) to provide students in teacher education programs with experiences in rural and northern environments.

✎ Maritimes

The *Study of Teacher Supply and Demand for the Canadian Maritime Provinces to the Year 2003-2004*, (Samson, Sullivan & Uhl, 1991) used the conceptual framework in Figure 1.

Taking the teaching force as a whole, there will be an oversupply of teachers in the Maritime Provinces to the year 2000-01. The largest surplus of teachers will occur both in the Anglophone schools (280 teachers) and in the Francophone schools (85 teachers) in 1992-93. Shortages will first appear in the Anglophone schools in 2000-01 (77 teachers) and increase consistently until reaching 284 teachers by the year 2003. In the Francophone schools, shortages will begin in 2001-02 (16 teachers) and reach 56 teachers by the year 2002-03. There will be a slight decline in the shortage, to 46 teachers, in 2003-04.

Isolating the elementary and the junior high levels, the demands for Anglophone teachers will surpass the supply in almost every year between 1991-92 and 2003-04 . By the year 2003-04, the elementary schools will need 221 teachers, the junior high, 219 teachers. Conversely, at the high school level, there will be a surplus of 345 teachers in 1991-92 which will decrease to reach a low of 156 by the year 2003-04. However, the grand totals revealed that overall, if the notion that a teacher can teach at any level and any subject is held (which is how teacher certification is generally handled in the Maritimes), teacher shortages are not expected to begin in the Maritime Provinces until the year 2001-02 when the shortage of 77 teachers will increase every year to 284 teachers by the year 2003-04.

An overall surplus of French teachers for the senior high level is projected in the Maritime Provinces for the entire study period. The surplus ranges from a high of 53 teachers in 1993-94 to a low of 43 teachers in 1999-2000. It is clear that the teacher training institutions have reacted to the shortage of French teachers as evidenced by the increase in the number of teachers being trained in this area, 56 teachers in 1986-87, 108 in 1990-91, and 149 by 1993-94.

In 1988-89, it was estimated that there were 4515 substitutes with teacher training on the list of substitute teachers in the Maritime Provinces' Anglophone school system. Of the 4515 potential teachers, this study concluded that approximately 79% would teach full-time and 11% would teach at least 50% of the time if jobs were available. Moreover, 30% would relocate in the Maritime Provinces if a teaching position were offered to them. The responses of the sample of substitute teachers that were surveyed indicated that if the pool of substitute teachers remains at the 1988-89 level in the Maritime Provinces, to the year 2003-2004, teacher shortages can be avoided. There may however be isolated areas within the region that will continue to have recruiting problems, but there should not be a general shortage.

The results for Francophone teachers in the Maritimes indicates that the total demand (all levels) for Francophone teachers is not expected to exceed the supply until 2001-02. Further, as was the case for the Anglophone schools, teacher shortages are projected in all areas for the entire study period at the junior high level. Similarly, at the elementary level, a general shortage will also prevail during most of the study period with the exception of the category of regular teachers which will have a small surplus between 1995 and 1998 and in 2000-01. Conversely, a surplus of teachers is anticipated at the senior high level during this entire period. In the case of Francophone schools, it is expected that surplus teachers from the senior high level will fill many of the positions available at the junior high and elementary levels.

There were an estimated 435 teachers in the pool of Francophone substitute teachers in the Maritime Provinces in 1988-89. Of these substitutes, about 73% teachers would go to work full-time and 18% are willing to work at least 50% of the time. Approximately 17% or 74 would be willing to relocate in the Maritime Provinces. It is evident that substitute teachers could play an important role in filling the need for teachers should shortages occur.

✎ *Newfoundland*

The Government of Newfoundland and Labrador published a teacher supply and demand study in January, 1990 entitled *Toward 2000; Trends Report 2: Elementary-Secondary Projections*. As the title indicates, this was a second report on issues effecting teacher supply and demand in Newfoundland, the first being published in 1986 dealing "specifically with demographic trends and the resultant impacts upon the educational system" (Press, 1990, p. 1).

To the year 2000, Newfoundland school systems will continue to experience a decline in the number of students because of the decline in fertility, decline in the number of females of childbearing age and little change in the overall migration to the Province. The teaching force needed will also decline and although a large number of teachers will retire, the province will continue to produce a surplus of teachers, although the study did not conclude how large the surplus would be. Demand for French teachers will remain strong, but demand for most subject/specialty areas and for classroom teaching will decrease. Most supply of teachers will come from teachers already in the workforce.

✎ *Canada*

The Canadian Teachers Federation (1989) completed a Canada wide study entitled *Projections of Elementary and Secondary*

Enrollment and the Teaching Force in Canada 1987-88 to 2006-07. This study, with respect to supply, was only concerned with the present teaching force at the macro level of elementary and secondary and not with function levels. None of the other supply variables listed in Figure 1, such as retirement, were analyzed. The researchers completing the Maritime study referred to in this chapter found that local school districts and the provincial departments did not find the CTF predictions to be similar to their own predictions and they did not rely on them.

However, the results of the CTF study predicted that between 1991-92 and 2001-2002, the number of elementary students will increase by 1.03%, the number of secondary students will increase by 8.98%, while new elementary teaching positions will increase by 2.96% and new secondary teaching positions will increase by 9.80%.

Summary of Teacher Supply and Demand Studies

Enrollments in British Columbia and Ontario are predicted to increase, with the Maritimes remaining stable and Manitoba and Newfoundland decreasing. Retirements over the next eight to ten years will make many teacher positions available and when coupled with increasing enrollments (Ontario and BC.), teacher demand will outstrip supply.

The one Canadian study available did not seem to be reliable and three of the ten provinces have not released recent studies. However, with the available research evidence, the main conclusion is that Canada can supply enough teachers for the foreseeable future, but the supply seems to be relatively close to the demand and will need to be monitored closely.

One of the largest concerns with a possible shortage of teachers is that teacher education not be governed by an intense need for teachers, leading to a sharp reduction in the qualifications required to enter the profession. Ontario has already been required to hire personnel for the classrooms, that do not hold any degree. Another concern, which is mentioned in the Manitoba study and dealt with in depth in the next section, is that the need for teachers may not be felt equally in rural and urban areas.

A Rural Perspective

As mentioned earlier in this chapter, in the last forty years, when teachers were in short supply, the need for teachers was not uniformly spread between rural and urban areas, with the former always paying a price with their teachers leaving for positions in the more populated areas. What will happen this time when the predicted need for teachers becomes a reality?

There is some indication that old familiar trends may be changing. John Naisbett (1992), the author of *Megatrends*, believes that the general population movement from rural to urban areas that has been the pattern for decades, has recently been reversed in the United States. Will the same happen to teachers? Will they want to stay in the rural areas and even move from urban to rural areas when the opportunity arises?

To assist with providing answers to these questions, interviews were held with a variety of teachers from rural areas in one school system in Nova Scotia. The methodology and the results are presented in the following sections.

Discussions with Nova Scotia Rural Teachers About Supply and Demand

✎ *The Participants*

Eleven educators were interviewed for the information in this chapter. Participants were asked five open-ended, semi-structured questions. Each interview, conducted in the participant's school, was fifteen to twenty minutes in duration.

Six teachers, representing three categories of experience, (Early Career [1-10 Years], Mid-Career [11 to 20 years], and Later Career [21+ Years]), were interviewed from "Greenfield Rural High School," (all school and teacher names have been changed to assure anonymity).

Greenfield Rural High School is a rural high school located in central Nova Scotia. Ninety-nine percent of the 850 grade 7-12 students travel to school by bus. Because Greenfield Rural High School is located only 45 minutes from metro Halifax/Dartmouth, some staff members commute daily from the city, but the vast majority live in the area.

Green Bay Elementary School, with a student population of 200 students, is one of Greenfield's feeder schools and is located approximately twenty miles from Greenfield Rural High School, in an even more rural area. The principal and three teachers representing each of the categories were interviewed. A second principal of another rural elementary school on the opposite side of the district with 200 students, was interviewed to provide a second administrative perspective.

The following is a list of the career stages and professional responsibilities of the interviewees.

Irene	Late Career	Junior High Math
Ernie	Late Career	Junior High Science
Phil	Early Career	Junior High Phys Ed
Florence	Early Career	Jr/Sr High Family Studies
Carol	Mid-Career	Jr. High Eng/Soc. Studies
Graham	Mid-Career	Jr. High Eng/Soc. Studies
Karen	Mid-Career	Elementary, Grade 4
Doug	Late Career	Elementary, Grade 6
Angus	Late Career	Elementary Principal
Harold	Mid-Career	Elementary Principal
Sandra	Early Career	Elementary, Grade Primary

✎ *Retirement Factors Other than Age and Experience*

Teachers were asked, **"What factors (other than experience and age) determine whether or not teachers in rural areas retire?"**

Most teachers felt that rural teachers would be influenced by the same variables as those in urban areas. Some felt the lower cost of living in the rural area might be an incentive to retire earlier. The factors included job satisfaction – feeling appreciated and able to make a contribution, personal commitments and family concerns, sufficient talent and money to pursue other occupations, attractive salary incentives, and RRSPs. Several mentioned burn-out as a powerful factor.

As Phil, an early career teacher stated, the factors determining retirement include:

savings accumulated, job satisfaction and feeling appreciated, salary incentives, and RRSPs. All the money in the world isn't worth it if you don't enjoy it.

Graham, a 12 year mid-career teacher stated:

I sense a level of frustration at that point (in their careers). People calculate how much an hour they'd make. Is it worth it? There is more concern with the retirement benefits. The government is aware of this and offers 'the golden parachute.'

Doug, a prospective retiree stated his considerations before retiring, in the form of rhetorical questions:

> Do I have other interests outside my job – something I wish to do with my life? Is there any reason I can't do with a reduced salary?

✎ *Are Rural Teachers Anxious to Retire?*

A second question asked was, **"Are more or less rural teachers jumping at the opportunity to retire? Why or why not? What will you do?"**

All teachers interviewed sensed that teachers today are anxious to retire as soon as possible. Florence, an early career term teacher with less than a year's experience responded:

> I don't know. It seems to me a lot feel the need to get out when they sense a lot more stress but that is just a guess.

Phil remarked:

> I wasn't around ten years ago, but I think so. (More teachers are jumping at retirement) I seem to hear it more now. Few, once they reach that point, stay on. That's partly financial. They'd work for less money if they stayed on, but I think that retirements are good all around for the system.

Graham concurred that more teachers in general are seizing the opportunity to retire, but that there are no differences between rural and urban teachers. He reported further:

> It's rare today to find someone who will teach after they hit that magic number. A lot of teachers are frustrated with the cutbacks in educational spending. More is expected from less, therefore many teachers take the first door out.

Many teachers interviewed pointed to "burnout" as causing teachers to retire as soon as feasible. Those whose retirement was imminent were emphatic. As Ernie exclaimed:

> absolutely! (teachers are quickly seizing the opportunity to retire) The pressure of the job today, the monotony, the grind, being tied to one place. Retirement does not mean I am discontent with my job, I'm just tired!

Another prospective retiree, Irene, expressed her disillusionment even more directly.

> [For] teachers who have been in the system so long, with the current lack of discipline and low morale, school is no longer

a nice place to be. They want to get out. Financially speaking, one more year would be the intelligent thing to do, but one more year and I'd be in the NS (Mental Hospital). I'm from the old school. It isn't working for us. It may be for some of the younger teachers. I don't want to be part of it any more.

It was interesting that even younger, less experienced teachers indicated that they would either not teach all their career or would retire as soon as they were able to do so. Phil verbalized the following:

I think I would retire when I could. I don't know if I'll be a teacher for 30 years or retire earlier; so many things could happen.

Carol, an early career teacher explained:

Personally, I think I would retire (at the first opportunity) and start a whole other career related to teaching – maybe teaching teachers. Also, I like to write.

Florence remarked:

Probably (I would retire when I could). I don't know for sure what the future holds. I'd probably take time off for family, perhaps job sharing.

Doug, a later career elementary teacher with 28 years experience reported:

I think more teachers are looking forward to retirement now than a few years ago. There are a lot more pressures, discipline has never been worse and then there's the attitude of parents.

This teacher described other pressures.

Every spring I wonder how many teachers are going? How large my class will be? Will I have split classes? What support will be there?

When the question was personalized, he responded:

I'm ready now (to retire). I'd go sooner if I could get a pension, as I'm all set up and have lots to keep me busy.

Karen, another mid-career elementary teacher agreed that more teachers are talking retirement as soon as they can, but suggested this may be a short lived phenomenon. She stated:

A lot of these teachers (talking prompt retirement) are in a group who entered the profession with a low license, then put in a lot of extra work to upgrade. Now they are ready to relax, retire, and enjoy life.

With respect to her own situation, she reported:

Teaching is stressful even in the best of times. I'm not sure I'd like to stay in education any longer than I'd have to. It depends on how things go in the next ten years.

Angus, an elementary principal close to retirement, summarized the view point of most experienced teachers:

Twenty years ago more teachers stayed until the age of 70-75; you wouldn't hear of a 55 year old retiring. In those days I would stay on another 10 years.

It would appear that younger teachers are, at the very least, keeping their options open. It seems reasonable to predict that as the stresses and frustrations in teaching increase more and more teachers will consider or seek creative options such as job sharing, sabbaticals, deferred salary plans, study leaves, and early retirements. Only one of the 11 people interviewed indicated a reluctance to retire as soon as possible, which for most teachers in Nova Scotia is usually around the age of 55 years.

✎ *The Movement from Rural to Urban Areas*

A third question the interviewees were asked was, **"With numerous opportunities for employment, would there be a major shift of teachers from the rural areas to the urban areas? Why? Why not? What are the factors involved?"**

None of the teachers interviewed predicted a major shift of teachers to urban areas should positions become available. Graham, who presently lives and also has taught in an urban area, expressed the feeling of most teachers interviewed:

I think in general it would result in a marginal shift of teachers. Living in an urban area, I might at some point shift to an urban centre, however, having taught in the city, I would be wary of moving. I wouldn't want to leave behind the children and the respect you get from them unless the 'grass were just as green.' The longer you serve with a district, the more likely you are to stay. Other factors inhibiting such a shift include seniority, retirement packages, and long term service awards, which after 10 years start to build up.

He added:

I can't see myself living in the city forever. I grew up in a rural area.

Carol echoed this dilemma:

I'm torn. I grew up in the country. Now I live in the city. Rural students are more friendly and respectful. On the other hand, if I moved I would be closer to home.

This teacher suggested that if offered a position in an urban centre, she might take a year's leave just for the revitalization this experience would provide.

Florence, also living in an urban area, made this revealing comment about the topic:

Once my husband finishes school, he would probably like (us) to move to the rural area.

Several teachers implied that the inability to transfer seniority was a major inhibitor to a major shift of teachers from rural to urban areas.

Irene, a teacher who has always resided in the rural community asserted:

I wouldn't be caught dead living in the city – the hectic lifestyle, the traffic. If I had to do that every day! I need the wide open spaces and the privacy. If you grow up in the country, it's pretty hard to adjust to the city.

Sandra, an early career teacher commented:

It seems to me that those who taught both in the rural and urban areas would really prefer the rural.

She added:

Teachers who now live in the city and commute would likely make the move closer to home unless they feel strongly in favor of their current placement. People do get comfortable where they are. But I don't see a major shift.

Several elementary teachers suggested that teacher age and marital status would be a factor. Karen explained:

I think job openings might encourage younger teachers to move to the urban areas. When I was younger, I enjoyed the city. Now I enjoy the country and the less hectic life style. I see the reverse shift with some older and middle aged teachers moving to the country as positions open. I think it would balance out.

Harold, a mid-career elementary principal concluded:

Younger teachers might shift to the urban areas due to the social and cultural opportunities.

Teachers did not perceive the potential shift of rural teachers to urban areas to be a serious problem. Clearly, even the teachers residing in the urban areas were cautious about the prospect of shifting. Should they make this move, they were inclined to do it on a trial basis. At the same time, they often pined for life in the country. It would appear that with the increased stresses on the teaching profession, urban teachers may desire a position in the less stressful rural schools. Therefore, it does not seem likely that there will be a major shift of rural teachers to the urban centers.

Most interviewees believed that the quality and quantity of substitute teachers will decline as the better teachers are absorbed by the new job openings. Some felt this phenomenon would level off shortly. Some felt that standards for substitutes might have to be lowered to accommodate the totally inexperienced graduates or older out of touch retired teachers. Both would require support systems.

With respect to the economy, teachers felt that if the economy declined then jobs would be lost through attrition causing more stress to be placed on existing teachers. Most felt that the recession hits equally hard in rural and urban areas. A few believed that the lower cost of living and relative higher status might attract workers to the rural community. The more children, the greater the need for teachers. A few teachers were upbeat, suggesting that if the economy picks up, with education as a priority, and improved teacher/pupil ratios, there would be a significant need for teachers. While the economy is the ultimate culprit, it is the educational funding by the government and then in turn, the decisions by school boards with respect to staffing allotment, that determines teacher demand.

Most teachers had difficulty perceiving curriculum changes having a major impact on teacher supply and demand. They all agreed that there would be no difference between the rural and urban provincially mandated curriculum, although several felt rural schools were behind their urban counterparts in such things as computer training.

Teachers acknowledged that as technology rapidly changes, teachers equipped to teach it will be needed. This seems to suggest retraining or hiring specialists. New courses planned in the Public

School Program, such as Fine Arts and Physically Active Life Styles will also require retraining or specialists. These increased expectations and pressures may impact on the willingness of prospective teachers to enter the profession.

In an interview with Harold, a mid-career elementary school principal, the distinction between a rural and an isolated rural school became apparent. Harold explained:

> I work in a rural, isolated school. Access to many features is unavailable, such as health care, libraries, and cultural experiences. They don't even have access to the basic necessities. Most of the clientele must plan a day to do errands such as grocery shopping in the town (20 miles away).

Harold emphasized the impact this had on staffing:

> Not everyone wants this. We have to find the balance between finding the best person for the job and a person willing to accept it. As soon as they get permanent status, many of them transfer. I have to live with the fact of a transient staff – most stay three years.

On the positive side, this resulted in a young, energetic staff, with fresh and stimulating ideas. On the negative side, there was a lack of consistency and long term commitment.

It would appear that the isolated community appears to represent what is often portrayed as the stereotypical "rural" community. In other words, while teachers do not anticipate a major shift from rural teaching positions to the urban openings, this shift in fact will continue to take place from the isolated to the less isolated area as opportunities arise.

Conclusions

There is support for the need for more teachers than the supply will provide in the next ten years in British Columbia, Alberta, Ontario, and possibly Manitoba. The Maritimes will have a strong need for teachers but the present supply will meet demand, while Newfoundland will have a significant surplus of teachers. Retirements and general attrition will open up more jobs than in the last ten years. However, across the country supply should be able to meet demand, although many teachers will have to travel to other provinces.

The evidence from Nova Scotia teachers indicates that a large migration of teachers will not occur from rural to urban areas. A change in life styles will hold teachers in the rural areas more than in the past. However, as indicated in the interviews and the Manitoba study, the most remote areas will continue to lose many teachers when they have the opportunities to move to less remote areas, but not necessarily to urban areas. School boards and teacher education institutions should be supported and encouraged to deal with this potential problem.

References

Adams, Kay. (1983). Needs sensing: The yeast for r & d organizations. *Educational Evaluation and Policy Analysis*, Spring, 55-60.

Baugh, William, and Stone, Joe. (1980). *Simulation of teacher demand, demographics, and mobility: A preliminary report*. Oregon University, Eugene, Centre for Educational Policy and Management. Dec., 12p, ED197491.

Berry, Barnett. (1984). *A case study of the teacher labor market in the southeast. Miss Dove is alive and well*. Occasional Papers in Educational Policy Analysis, Paper No. 413, Southeastern Regional Council for Educational Improvement, Research Triangle Park, N.C.: Nov., ED251967.

Burstall, Clare. (1980). Falling rolls: A Canadian response. *Educational Research*, p. 3-13, Nov.

Canadian Teachers' Federation. (1985). *Dynamics of an aging teaching profession: Report of a seminar*. Ottawa, Ontario. October 20-22.

Canadian Teachers' Federation. (1981). *Key characteristics of teachers in public elementary and secondary schools, 1972-73 to 1979-80*. Statistics Canada, Ottawa, March.

Canadian Teachers' Federation. (1989). *Projection of elementary and secondary enrollment and the teaching force in Canada 1987-88 to 2006-07*. Ottawa, Ontario, January.

Centre for Education Statistics. (1988). *Targeted forecast, April 1988*. Washington, D.C.: 4p, April, ED293840.

Connecticut State Dept. of Education. (1988). *Fall hiring report: Certified professional staff vacancies as of September 1, 1987*. Hartford, 29p, ED299255.

Fiorino, Albert. (1978). *Teacher education in Ontario; A history, 1843-1976*. Commission on Declining School Enrollments in Ontario, Apr., 187p, Publications Centre, Ministry of Government Services, Toronto, ED197470.

Grissmer, David, and Kirby, Sheila. (1987). *Teacher attrition: The uphill climb to staff the nation's schools*. Rand Corporation, Santa Monica, California: Aug. ED291735.

Haggstrom, Gus, et al. (1988). *Assessing teacher supply and demand*. Rand Corporation, Santa Monica, California: May, 106p. ED299224.

Hansen Group. (1978). *The future for teacher education in Ontario. Simulation experiments to examine the impact of environmental factors and policy decisions on Ontario teacher education institutions 1978-2002*. Mississauga, Ontario: 64p, Sept., ED197462.

Jackson, Robert. (1977). *Declining enrollments and teacher assignments*. Atlantic Institute of Education.

Manitoba Teacher Supply and Demand Task Force. (1991). *Teacher supply and demand for the public schools of Manitoba: 1989-2000*. Manitoba Education, Ministry of Education and Training, Dec., 106p.

Maryland State Dept. of Education. (1986). *Teacher supply and demand in Maryland (1986-1989)*. Baltimore. 83p. ED275689.

Murphy, Peter. (1984). Rural schools in British Columbia. *Rural Educator*, Fall, p6-8.

Naisbett, John. (1992). *The 1990s: Front row seat to change*. Keynote Address at Business Communications Update Conference, Maritime Telephone and Telegraph, Halifax, May 26.

Press, (1990). *Toward 2000; Trends report 2: Elementary, secondary projections*. Government of Newfoundland and Labrador.

Province of British Columbia. (1988). *A legacy for learners: The summary of findings*. Government of British Columbia.

Samson, Réal, Sullivan, Keith, and Uhl, Norman. (1991). *A study of teacher supply and demand for the Canadian maritime provinces to the year 2003-4*, Maritime Provinces Education Foundation (Council of Maritime Premiers), March, pp. 1-388.

Smith, L. (1989). *Perspectives on teacher supply and demand in Ontario, 1988-2008*. Government of Ontario.

Sullivan, Keith. (1971). *Predictors of teacher mobility and turnover in Alberta*. Unpublished Master's Thesis, University of Alberta. 1-121.

Tuinman and Brayne. (1988). *The on-site personnel who facilitate learning: Commissioned papers*. Vol.4. Government of British Columbia.

Weldon, Ward, Hurwitz, Emanuel, and Menacker, Julius. (1989). Enrollment projections: Techniques and financial implications. *School Business Affairs*. Oct. Pp. 28-31.

Williams, Peter. (1979). *Planning teacher demand and supply. Fundamentals of educational planning*. United Nations Educational, Scientific and Cultural Organization, Paris: 103p, ED213107.

Williams, Richard and Cross, William. (1985). *Early field experience: A recipe for rural teacher retention*. Paper presented at the annual National Rural and Small Schools Conference, Bellingham, WA: Oct. 9-12, 12p, ED284700.

Williams, Richard and Cross, William. (1987). Preparing rural teachers in Canada. *Rural Educator*, p. 22-25, Fall.

13

The New Brunswick Centre for

Educational Administration

Kenneth Cameron and Rod Campbell

This chapter is about the conception, growth, development, and sustaining of a Centre for Educational Administration in a small Canadian province, New Brunswick. It is not a traditional research study. It relies largely on anecdotal data and reflections of the authors, who had a clear stake in the success of the Centre. This chapter, then, seeks to examine the actions of the key players in the development of a Centre for Educational Administration and to the extent that the authors were among the players, it is necessarily a subjective account.

As is often the case, to present a clear account of any educational innovation, context is important. What apparently works for New Brunswick may be more a factor of local circumstances and idiosyncratic behavior, rather than some broader generalized conception. Readers will determine to what extent, if any, the political and economic circumstances of New Brunswick are comparable to their educational settings. At the outset, it is important to understand something of the demographics which impinge on public education in New Brunswick. The Province has a total population of approximately 750 000 people, more than 250 000 of whom are French-speaking Acadians. The population is distributed in small communities near the sea and along three major river valleys. Fewer than one third of the population live in communities of more than 50 000 people. The Province's economy is dominated by primary industries – forestry, mining, fishing, and agriculture – and is home to two of Canada's outstanding entrepreneurial families, the Irvings of Saint John and the McCains of Florenceville. New Brunswick remains Canada's only officially bilingual province and the school system operates with one political head, the Minister of Education who directs the Department of Education which has Anglophone and Francophone branches – each with a Deputy Minister of Education. Apart from the very broadest policy issues and an equitable funding model, the two branches share little – essentially operating as two Departments.

Currently the Anglophone section has approximately 90 000 pupils with 5200 teachers and principals. The Francophone system has 31 000 pupils and 2200 teachers and principals. Anglophone teachers are organized into the New Brunswick Teachers' Association; the Francophone teachers have the Association des enseignants Francophones de Nouveau Brunswick. The two groups combine resources to create the N.B.T.F./F.E.N.B. which is the bargaining agent for all teachers in the Province. In keeping with the linguistic character of the Province, the N.B.T.F./F.E.N.B. is a bilingual organization. Since 1967, all salary and working conditions are negotiated provincially between the N.B.T.F. and the Provincial Government. All teachers, regardless of their communities, are paid according to their level of education and experience. School Boards have no taxing authority except by a rarely used local referendum for specific projects, and are limited largely to implementing a centrally prescribed curriculum with the financial resources provided by the Provincial Government.

The New Brunswick Context

These are the basic facts about New Brunswick that have a bearing on the development of the New Brunswick Centre for Educational Administration. Beyond these, closer observations of the political, economic, and educational climate in which the Centre was conceived will be offered. These circumstances help to explain why the Centre began as it did and also explain how it was slowly transformed into a significant element of the total Anglophone school system.

The N.B.C.E.A. emerged in 1984 in the most unlikely of conditions. The Province's education system was in the throes of the first radical reforms since the centralization of all government services that was completed in 1967. The reforms were viewed by most teachers and some trustees with considerable suspicion and hostility. The Conservative Government led by Premier Richard B. Hatfield was elected in 1982 for the fourth time since 1970, but with the slimmest of majority. The Government which had harmonized relations between the two linguistic communities by creating the Official Languages Act and a dual system of education was being criticized largely for its economic policies. The failed Bricklin Sports car venture became the touchstone for all the economic critics and the prospects for a fifth electoral victory were hardly sanguine.

To respond to the apparent disenchantment reflected in securing only a bare majority in the election of 1982, Hatfield created the Office of Government Reform. It's announced purpose was to streamline government services and to find a new road to economic recovery. The office was directed by two Cabinet Ministers, now Senators, Brenda Robertson and Jean Maurice Simard, and was to look carefully at the high cost departments: Health, Social Services, and Education. The various reviews undertaken led to significant cutbacks in funding to the three big spenders and led to sharp and heated exchanges between the New Brunswick Teachers' Association and the Office of Government Reform. Indeed the N.B.T.A. often referred to the Office of Government Reform as O.G.R.e. (N.B.T.A. News, March, 1985).

In an article entitled "Punching at Clouds – Seeking the Elusive OGRe," N.B.T.A. President, Bert Hanratty, set the tone which persisted throughout the period. To cite briefly, his remarks reveal much. He wrote:

> The much-heralded 'report' given to the consultees five minutes before the Premier's [Hatfield] entrance turned out to be a collection of notes, press releases, and speeches which stimulated far more questions than they answered. In extremely vague terms, longer on rhetoric and nostrums than on clear directives, we were told that the government is committed to improving New Brunswick's educational system and that we are invited to match that commitment (Hanratty, 1985).

These opening salvos were not the only shots directed toward the Government. Hanratty went on in the same article:

> Indeed we have more than reservations; we are completely opposed to many of the directions hinted at by the Premier. . . . We have to oppose the return to the sort of high school where everyone fits the mold or gets out (Hanratty, 1985).

Nor did it end with these remarks. The N.B.T.F. was about to enter into a new round of collective bargaining. In his speech to the Annual General Meeting of the N.B.T.F., Co-President, Bert Hanratty once more drew the battle lines with the Government. In searching for some silver lining in the climate of confrontation, he argued:

> We've come through some very difficult times whose negative features I've outlined and we've come through them united and toughened by the very adversity we've faced together. I

wouldn't try to claim credit for the phenomenon . . . . The major credit has to go to the elemental fortitude and defiant spirit of our members – they have soldiered on through some of our bleakest days (*N.B.T.A. News*, June, 1985).

Small doubt that the speech was intended to stir the troops (to extend Hanratty's metaphor) to action and indeed action resulted. An ongoing battle raged over the next two years between the Government and the Teachers' Association. The upshot of this confrontational relationship was that the N.B.T.A. also ran head-long into conflicts with the Department of Education and School Trustees.

In a very uncharacteristic fashion, the N.B.T.A. began address-ing the Department of Education simply as the bureaucratic arm of the politicians. Previously, despite disputes between the N.B.T.A. and the Department, there had been general goodwill and acceptance of mutual goals in education. An editorial in the N.B.T.A. News illustrates the dismal level to which relations had been reduced. The editorial headline read "High School Reorgani-zation: the quintessential con." The editorial alluded to the Deputy Minister in the same context as the popular movie "The Sting" and while the politicians were still clearly the villains, Department officials were being cast as supporting players.

Well Teachers beware! the 'sting' is on again. Only this time the politicians are trying their darndest to create an illusion of reform while dismembering the high school education system. The deception is coached in the seductive language of persuasion. All students will learn generic skills, gain new self-confidence and acquire the common attitudes important to our way of life. The removal of the program tracks will eliminate the stigma attached to level three courses. With no tracks students can hardly fall on the wrong side. What a brilliantly simple solution to something as complex as attitudes, values and mores . . . . The subtle deception that's being perpetrated here must be exposed. Parents need to know about the con game. If the politicians truly believe this is genuine reform, they have mastered the ultimate trickery of even fooling themselves (N.B.T.A. News, March, 1986).

Again the politicians are in the fore-front but the directions for education emerging from Government Policy were the work of Department officials and this perception reduced the communica-tions between N.B.T.A. officials and Senior Management of the Department. It wasn't that they discontinued relations altogether but that meetings simply took the form of posturing and the reiteration of each side's stance on specific issues. Moreover, the number of interactions among officials was reduced and "like the greatest virtue and worst dogs, the fiercest hatred is silent" (Anonymous, cited in Potter, 1988).

The economic climate in New Brunswick was equally as dismal as the political climate. Indeed, the politicians of the day were faced with increasing public demands for resources in the face of declining revenues and rising deficits. Since 1967, the government of New Brunswick had maintained central control of financing education. For the purpose of this chapter, it is one other indication of conflict among the central organizations in New Brunswick, primarily the N.B.T.A. and the N.B. Department of Education. Each spring, the ritual of budget watching and budget analysis unfolded. The tensions occasioned by this process were heightened when Brenda Robertson of the Office of Government Reform announced:

> We are planning to improve this system through the introduction of a number of measures aimed at achieving economies of scale in service delivery (Clarke in *N.B.T.A. News*, October, 1983).

Prompted by this announcement, Gerald Clarke, Faculty of Education, University of New Brunswick, reported on the creation of an Education Coalition to address the issues of budget restraint with respect to education. Clarke reported that twenty-one organizations had met ranging from the Canadian Association for the Mentally Retarded, (now the Association for Community Living) to the N.B. Federation of Home and Schools and the University of New Brunswick Alumni. While the specific issue for the Coalition was the introduction of a public kindergarten system, the broader issue was education budgets. Citing N.B.T.A. President, Pam Bacon, Clarke reported "Provincial spending devoted to elementary and secondary education has constantly decreased from 24.9% of the total Ordinary Account spending in 1971 to 16.5% in the estimates for 1983-84" (Clarke, 1983).

With the Provincial government the sole revenue collector, the funding for education had to compete with all government priorities and as the conflict persisted about broad government policy directions, the underlying political motivation was the discrepancy between revenue and expenditures. In a letter to the editor, John Baxter, Minister of Finance, described the Government's dilemma:

First of all, not only education but almost every department of Government has seen its share of expenditures decline. This is because the debt service costs have been growing much faster than total expenditures. The recession and very high interest rates for a period of years were part of the cause . . . Unless the deficit can be eliminated and the borrowing reduced, almost every department of Government will continue to see its share of spending reduced until the rate of increase in debt service is again at or lower than the overall rate in government spending (*N.B.T.A. News*, October 1985).

The program of financial restraint was manifested in a spring rite of layoff notices for teachers. In each of the years from 1983 to 1985, more than 200 teachers received layoff notices. The reduced levels of Government revenues were clearly exacerbated by the recession which began in 1981. The decline in student numbers gave Government a reason, understandable to the general public, as to why education costs should decline. Again to cite Finance Minister Baxter:

In the early 1970s it cost about $100 million for 175 000 students while today [1985] the costs are over $430 million for only 140 000 students (N.B.T.A. News, 1985).

Financial restraint was the watchword for the period from 1984-87. It led to a deterioration of relationships among the teachers, trustees, and Department of Education officials.

While the conflict between teachers and the Government, or teachers and the Department has been chronicled, it is less easy to find direct evidence of deterioration of relationships between teachers and trustees, or trustees and the Department, or indeed trustees and the Government. Partly, this is explained by the role of trustees in New Brunswick. With the Government holding all revenues centrally, the role of trustees is significantly reduced. Moreover, some trustees were elected in civil elections while others were appointed by the Government. Each year the trustees from the School Boards would put forward a budget to the Department of Education for approval. The Department of Education was charged with the responsibility of disbursing, in an equitable fashion, funds provided in the budget for education by the provincial government. School boards would argue and wrangle over details in the budget and would want to be sure that other boards were receiving no more than their fair share, but ultimately these wrangles were tantamount to shadow-boxing. The bottom line was the Department could do little to secure more revenue than the politicians were prepared to give and trustees could do little to get more than their share prescribed by a education funding formula. In short, the debates were brief because neither trustees nor the Department had much room for decision making around budgets.

In a similar vein, teachers through the N.B.T.A. bargained provincially with the government "Treasury Board." Trustees had representatives on the Government's negotiating team but these representatives were powerless when it came to cost items in collective bargaining. In virtually every round of collective bargaining, including one that wasn't resolved until a teacher's strike (June, 1981), the final solution was achieved by the direct involvement of the Premier or other Cabinet Ministers. Trustees were reduced to being cheerleaders on the sidelines. The behavior of School Boards in relation to the Department of Education and the Government became one of debating details rather than addressing broader issues. While trustees may have believed education was underfunded, they saw their role as using judiciously what was given to them rather than mounting major efforts to secure more.

However, at the Board level, there was potential for conflict between teachers and Trustees. Even though salary and working conditions were established provincially, School Boards hired, fired, promoted, demoted, and laid-off teachers. With several hundred layoff notices issued annually, the potential for conflict was great. Superintendents, the Boards' senior administrators were the first level of grievance under the Collective Agreement between the NBTF and the Treasury Board. The Trustees were the second level. (NBTF/Treasury Board Agreement, 1984). There were some bitter grievances heard including a number with respect to hiring, transfers, or demoting practices, one of which went to the Supreme Court of Canada before a final resolution was made. (Donald Dickson, griever and NBTF Bargaining Agent, Appellants and Her Majesty in right of the Province of New Brunswick as represented by Treasury Board, 1979.) Suffice it to say that relations between teachers and trustees were strained at best. Some Boards did endeavor to carry on regular liaison with the local teachers representatives; but others chose to assert what little authority they had through powers prescribed in the New Brunswick Schools Act.

The level of acrimony between and among the stakeholders in education militated against collaborative undertakings. For more than a decade, there had been an annual meeting involving teachers, trustees, and the Department of Education. This was abandoned at the time because the Department felt they would simply be one more forum for the N.B.T.A., Trustees, or other interest groups to express their displeasure with the restraint policies. It was under these inauspicious circumstances that the Centre for Educational Administration was born as a collaborative venture of the various contending groups. That any innovation was undertaken in this environment is surprising; that it developed requires considerable explanation. Regardless, the period marks the conception of the Centre and the first phase of three that unfolded over the next eight years.

Phase One – 1984-87

The development of the New Brunswick Centre for Educational Administration can be conceptualized in the context of Kurt Lewin's description of the process of organizational change. In his classic explanation, Lewin (Lippett, 1958) described successful organizational change as passing three consecutive phases. The first of these he referred to as "unfreezing" the existing structures and procedures. The second phase he described as "moving" toward new practices and the third phase he envisaged a "refreezing" of the new practices into the organizational structure. Given the cool, if not freezing climate of relations among the stakeholders in education, Lewin's analogy seems appropriate. There was certainly a need to thaw some of the rigid and hardened positions.

In part, the "unfreezing" began by the initiative of the Deputy Minister of Education, Harvey Malmberg, who although held guilty by the N.B.T.A. of complicity with the Government's restraint program, wanted to have a productive dialogue among teachers, trustees, and Department officials. The earlier mechanism of an annual forum was abandoned because of the persistence of public posturing by all of the stakeholders. Another mechanism needed to be found, if the school system was to make even modest advances within the framework of Government restraint. Malmberg approached two professors of Educational Administration at the University of New Brunswick, Dr. Ken Cameron and Dr. Larry Bezeau. He put forward the idea that a Centre for Educational Administration at U.N.B. could be central to realizing some ambitious goals in education. The upshot of the meeting was that Cameron and Bezeau agreed to be co-directors of a centre which would be supported by a ten thousand dollar start up grant from the New Brunswick Department of Education. Given the fiscal restraint across the system already described, it was a courageous undertaking for a senior bureaucrat under siege. Cameron brought to the Centre twenty years of public school experience, many of which were as a Junior High School Principal. Bezeau was a recently arrived professor at U.N.B. in Educational Administration whose field was the Economics of Education. The co-directors were motivated in large part by what they saw as a need to counteract the adversarial relations then existing among the various stakeholders in public education. It seemed to them that a university-based centre might provide an arms length forum where these groups could collaborate, addressing issues of common concern in a non-confrontational atmosphere.

At the outset the Co-directors took on the centre as a kind of "hobby farm." They worked on its development as time permitted from their normal research and teaching duties at U.N.B. The Co-directors took the initial step in forming an Advisory Board by inviting representatives from the Department of Education, the Superintendents' Association, the School Trustees' Association, the District Supervisors' Association, and the Principals' and Vice-Principals' Council of the N.B.T.A. That all parties agreed to participate was the first indication that the "unfreezing" had begun. N.B.C.E.A. was not a player in the adversarial relations and was perceived as Cameron and Bezeau had hoped.

The first major activity of the Centre was a series of annual conferences dealing with issues such as superintendent and school board relations, staff renewal, and the educational reform proposals of the Office of Government Reform. The last of these conferences, in keeping with the Center's role as an honest broker, was entitled, "Reform Fallout: An Objective Look at the Organization of Public Education in New Brunswick." The organizers wrote in their promotion of the event.

> We hope to stand back from the detailed day-to-day interaction among school boards and the Department of Education and take a careful, analytical look at what is happening. We will do this in the light of the recent initiatives of the Office of Government Reform and in the broader context of what is happening in Canadian education. . . . Those who attend the second annual conference . . . will understand that the opportunity that this provides for interacting with a variety of other persons who share a common interest in the quality of education in New Brunswick (*NB Educational Administrator*, January, 1986).

In reporting the event, the organizers reiterated N.B.C.E.A.'s purpose:

... to provide a forum for the exchange of ideas on educational matters. In the normal course of events, principals, trustees, teachers, Department of Education personnel, superintendents, district office staff and others rarely have the opportunity to meet on neutral ground to discuss issues of common concern. These conferences provide a unique opportunity for an exchange among all those concerned with policy-making and the management of public education in New Brunswick (*NB Educational Administrator*, June, 1986).

Phase one also saw the development of a quarterly newsletter for the Centre. The first issue was published in 1985 using the grant from the Department of Education. The New Brunswick Teachers' Association agreed to publish the newsletter and distribute it to principals and vice-principals throughout the Province. The School Trustees' Association agreed to distribute the newsletters to Superintendents and Trustees. This cooperation in the face of many difficulties augured well for N.B.C.E.A. It was acting as an honest broker in education and was increasingly being asked for input on issues. For example, the Co-directors were invited by various stakeholders to participate in professional development programs in those first two years.

Concurrently with the recognition of N.B.C.E.A.'s role in education came a shift in Government policy. The context was changing, as the Hatfield Government, now 17 years old, began the countdown towards an inevitable election. In April 1987, the editor of *N.B.T.A. News* described new initiatives emerging from the Department of Education, particularly those supporting teacher growth.

The outburst of curriculum and professional development activity at the Department of Education is encouraging. There has been nothing like it in the past decade. . . . [I]t's a harbinger of better days for education (Campbell, 1987).

The changing climate offered an opportunity to N.B.C.E.A. to move from its hobby farm operation where it acted as an honest broker to assuming greater initiatives. The undertaking of an annual conference and the publication of a newsletter stretched the scarce resources of the Centre, but this began to change in the winter of 1987. Marven Betts, a recently retired Superintendent in New Brunswick, volunteered his services to spearhead an exploration of how the N.B.C.E.A. might advance its role in professional development. He wrote a proposal to bring together various stakeholders in education to look at creating a leadership assessment process. Betts brought together in February 1987 representatives from the University of New Brunswick, Department of Education, School Trustees' Association, school superintendents, school principals and the New Brunswick Teachers' Association to hear Gene Burdenuk, Assistant-Director of the University of Western Ontario's Education Leadership Centre, speak about its Leadership Assessment Project.

The Department of Education provided additional funding to allow N.B.C.E.A. to study other Centres in Canada and the United States. A Task Force was established by the N.B.C.E.A. to pursue this investigation. Ultimately, the Task-Force recommended that the N.B.C.E.A. enlarge its mandate to become actively involved in leadership development. Marven Betts, who spear-headed the work of the task force wrote:

> There is increasing agreement that principals are the key to quality schools. Studies tell us over and over that the principal is the single most important person in setting a tone, implementing a program, or changing the direction of a school. Despite the critical importance of school leadership, school boards invest very little in the selection and training of their school principals. Most boards continue to rely in their selection on certification, teaching reputation and a personable manner. Many candidates meet these requirements but they often lack a strong sense of purpose, decisiveness, educational values, sensitivity and stress tolerance; attributes generally considered to be essential to quality leadership. It is a rare district where leadership potential is identified and future school leaders are selected because they have been found to possess fundamental conceptual and human skills upon which leadership competencies can be built (Betts, 1987).

Betts put forward to the school trustees of the Province a challenge to alter fundamentally their approach to preparing teachers to become vice-principals and principals. He challenged the Department of Education to support leadership development in a more tangible fashion beyond the modest grant offered to N.B.C.E.A. He challenged the New Brunswick Teachers' Association to support leadership development for a significant portion of its members. In this last effort, Betts received the support of

N.B.T.A. Deputy Executive Director, Dawson Murray, who was a member of the Task Force that visited various centres in Ontario. Indeed, Murray carried the proposal to the N.B.T.A. governing bodies and successfully secured the N.B.T.A. support including a three year commitment for funding.

By the fall of 1987, N.B.C.E.A. had the direct financial support of the N.B. Department of Education, the New Brunswick School Trustees' Association and the New Brunswick Teachers' Association. The N.B.C.E.A. was able to hire Marven Betts on a part-time basis during the fall of 1987 and the winter of 1988 to launch its first major professional development activities.

Phase Two – 1987-91

Phase One relied on the volunteer efforts of the Co-Directors, Professors Bezeau and Cameron. The shift from a hobby farm operation to employing a co-ordinator parallels Lewin's second phase of organizational change, "moving." Having helped in the "unfreezing" of some adversarial structures, N.B.C.E.A. could begin to help the system move forward in a modest way. There were many expectations when Marven Betts became the first employee of the Centre in the fall of 1987. Betts, who was well known as a Superintendent of Schools in New Brunswick, had the reputation as being an innovator particularly with respect to advancing the school system through professional development programs. An office for the Centre was established within the Faculty of Education at U.N.B., part-time secretarial assistance was arranged, a small professional library was created and the planning of in-service programs for potential and practicing school administrators began.

New Brunswick had already a significant professional development program for teachers. The N.B.T.F. had negotiated up to 13 days for professional development, parent teacher conferences, and so forth, within the framework of 195 day school year. School superintendents made use of five of these days for Professional Development, the N.B.T.A. had 19 Subject Councils that met three days a year and the New Brunswick Department of Education organized a wide range of in-service sessions related to the introduction of new programs. For school trustees, there were annual and regional meetings which had a small professional development component; for the most part the trustees got to listen to lectures from someone.

Professional development for Principals and Vice-Principals was limited largely to one of the N.B.T.A. Councils; the Principals' and Vice-Principals' council conducted a one day workshop each fall and two days in the spring. The quality of the programs varied significantly from year to year, depending largely on the volunteers among the members of the Council who organized the events. Principals also attended national or international conferences occasionally at their own initiative; only a few participated as part of an overall professional development initiative within districts. Preparation of vice-principals or teachers was reduced to paper qualifications and success in an interview. New Brunswick has a Principals' Certificate which can only be earned after an initial degree through Graduate Studies in Educational Administration.

While there was a lot of Professional Development activity, it was determined largely by each of the stakeholders. The N.B.T.A. and its Councils guarded jealously the three days of their conferences. School Superintendents guarded their local days and the Department of Education carved out its area of curriculum implementation. The trick for N.B.C.E.A. was to find an area which didn't crowd some other group's turf. In the winter of 1988, Betts, on behalf of the N.B.C.E.A. invited Bruce Joyce and Beverly Showers to present their findings about School-based Staff Development. More than two hundred principals, school trustees, Department of Education officials, and District Office staff attended. It marked a departure from the earlier N.B.C.E.A. conferences, in that it was not a dialogue conducted at arms length for the educational stakeholders; instead it was a professional development event that offered direction to school districts and schools. Joyce and Showers' emphasis on the importance of school leadership served to inform the stakeholders of new directions which the N.B.C.E.A. would attempt to promote.

Betts expanded this "moving phase" in the area of professional development by undertaking two other programs which were to become linchpins of the operation. Consistent with the case for strong leadership at the school level made by Joyce and Showers, these programs focused on the development and support of administrators at this level in the system.

The Center's Task Force recommended that one of the linchpins of its leadership development program should be leadership assessment through the process created by the National Association of Secondary School Principals in the U.S.A. The process was consistent with assessment centres used by military and business communities to identify and develop potential leaders. The Educational Leadership Centre at the University of Western Ontario was already established and the N.B.C.E.A. decided to become a satellite of Western's Educational Leadership Assessment Centre (E.L.A.C.) to gain official status with N.A.S.S.P. Throughout the negotiations to establish N.B.C.E.A.'s assessment capacity, Gene Burdenuk, Director of E.L.A.C. was enormously supportive and offered sagacious advice.

There were serious impediments to overcome. The N.B.C.E.A., in the beginning of 1988, had no affiliation with N.A.S.S.P., no trained assessors, no trained assessment centre directors, and certainly no participants. However, by November, 1988, affiliation with E.L.A.C. was formalized and an initial group of 28 principals, superintendents, assistant superintendents, university professors, and teacher association staff were trained as assessors.

The N.B.C.E.A. was attracted to the N.A.S.S.P. process by the broad range of opportunities it offered for leadership development. Foremost, of course, were the growth opportunities available to participants preparing for principalships. To date, the N.B.C.E.A. has conducted nine assessment centres attended by approximately 80 teachers and vice-principals. Equally as important is the professional development for the assessors. The N.A.S.S.P. Assessor training and the experience of serving as an assessor provide significant professional development for practicing administrators. Principals, who comprise the majority of our assessors, also got the opportunity to work closely with Superintendents, Department of Education officials, N.B.T.A. staff, school supervisors, and university professors, all of whom are included in our 75 member assessor team.

Growing out of the Assessment Process, the N.B.C.E.A. was assisted by Gene Burdenuk and Roslyn Moorhead of E.L.A.C. in the creation of a follow-up program for participants at Assessment Centres. Called "Skills for Excellence in Educational Administration," it is led by four principals who have worked on the program.

A second linchpin of N.B.C.E.A.'s entry into professional development was initiated in the winter of 1988. Betts had investigated the I/D/E/A Program (Institute for the Development of Educational Activities) originally developed through a Kellogg Foundation Grant. I/D/E/A provides a structure within which practicing administrators, assisted by a facilitator, may come together to collaborate in the planning and implementation of improvements in their schools. N.B.C.E.A. financed the training of ten facilitators from New Brunswick. Similar to the model employed for assessor training, the Centre drew from superintendents, district supervisors, N.B.T.A. staff, and principals. All of the facilitators had working groups within a year of completing their training. Of the original ten groups, nine remain operational and most of these no longer require an N.B.C.E.A. facilitator. They have become autonomous, self-sustaining professional development support groups. The Centre is currently drawing upon the resources of the I/D/E/A facilitators in creating a new program for principals who want an I/D/E/A support group experience.

A third major initiative launched in 1988 was N.B.C.E.A.'s Educational Leadership Academy. The Center's position on the Academy is that it had to follow some basic tenets embedded in the Assessment Process and I/D/E/A. That is, it should not be a one shot professional development activity with no follow-up or support from the Centre. There were enough of those limited experiences available elsewhere. The theme for the Academy is generated through the input of the N.B.T.A. Principals' and Vice-Principals' In-Service Committee. The theme for the Academy changes from year to year and there have been slight adjustments in its format. At its inception, the Academy was to be an intensive, extended professional development program for a small group of school administrators. In its inaugural in 1988, the Academy had three parts: An introductory session on "Situational Leadership" in the spring, a four day session on "Building a Positive School Climate" during the summer, and a one day follow-up session in the fall to discuss the extent of implementation of the ideas generated at the Academy. To date, more than 100 principals and vice-principals have participated in the Academies.

These projects were launched in the face of much uncertainty over continuity in personnel and sustained funding for the centre. In the spring of 1988, Marven Betts left the Centre to become the Executive-Director of the New Brunswick School Trustees' Association. He had coordinated the introduction of the assessment process I/D/E/A and the Leadership Academies. His personal efforts had increased the visibility of the Center's work to School Boards and individual trustees throughout the Province. Now, the Centre would operate for the better part of a year without a coordinator and facing a future which was, at best, uncertain.

Because the N.B.C.E.A. was beginning to establish a broader reputation in the education community, it was able to draw upon its' network to secure a replacement for Marven Betts. The New

Brunswick Teachers' Association was persuaded to allow its Director of Communications and Research, Rod Campbell, to be seconded to N.B.C.E.A. for a period of 18 months on a half-time basis beginning in January, 1989. Campbell had already been involved in the professional development activities of the Centre. Along with Jim MacKay, a staff development officer with the Nova Scotia Teachers' Union, he had conducted the first of the Educational Leadership Academies. As well, he was in the first group of administrators to be trained as assessors. But more importantly Campbell brought first hand knowledge of teachers and principals in the school system. The existing network to school boards and superintendents was extended through his appointment. Campbell also brought substantial experience in creating professional development programs. He had been the Director of Professional Development of the N.B.T.A. and subsequently the Director of Research and Communication. He knew administrators and teachers who could both direct ánd benefit from N.B.C.E.A.'s undertakings.

With Campbell's appointment the Center's personnel problem was resolved temporarily, but the funding problem remained. The N.B.C.E.A. existed through annual grants from the New Brunswick Department of Education, New Brunswick Trustees' Association, and New Brunswick Teachers' Association. Each spring, the Centre would approach the funding agencies, point to the efforts of the previous year, outline plans for the next year, and hope. To supplement these grants, the N.B.C.E.A. was encouraged by its Advisory Committee to charge fees for its events to cover the operating costs and some of the overhead costs. This decision led to the Centre realizing sufficient revenue to move from part-time secretarial assistance to a full-time secretary beginning in October, 1989.

The need for financial stability to permit long term planning consumed much of the Executive Director's time apart from his professional development activities. One false start which intermittently took time from other efforts was the attempt to expand the Centre to serve the Atlantic Region and in entrepreneurial parlance to expand the potential client base. A proposal was put to the Atlantic Canada Opportunities Agency, a Federal institution primarily designed to serve the business community, but ostensibly interested in education which would improve the region's competitiveness. In keeping with that notion, N.B.C.E.A. sought and received the support of the four Anglophone teachers' organizations in the region (New Brunswick Teachers' Association, Nova Scotia Teachers' Union, Prince Edward Island Teachers' Federation, and Newfoundland Teachers' Association) to advance a proposal for an Atlantic Centre for Education Administration. The proposal argued that one approach to alter significantly the public school system in the region was through the identification, development, and placement of a new type of school leader. N.B.C.E.A. proposed:

> to develop entrepreneurial school leaders who will understand the important links between public school education and regional growth. We want the next generation of students to be educated in school environments which build confidence in the region – which forge links to business and industry and teach risk-taking (A.C.O.A. Proposal, 1989).

The exercise was a great source of frustration. At the outset it seemed possible to overcome the Federal Government's reluctance to become directly involved in provincial education matters. A.C.O.A. had to be convinced that the Centre would not be just an arm of the four Provincial Departments of Education and the direct involvement of teachers' organizations seemed to answer that concern. The mandate of A.C.O.A. itself was uncertain, although a significant grant had already been made to Mt. Allison University and Université de Moncton to study entrepreneurial attitudes of public school students (P.E.P., 1988). Nevertheless, after more than 18 months of discussions, proposals, and revisions, it was clear no support would be forthcoming. For the N.B.C.E.A., it was an object lesson that convinced the Advisory Board to move forward slowly at a pace to meet the needs of its existing clientele, rather than trying to leap forward with substantial government support.

The final months of the Center's second or "moving" phase of the development saw a rapid expansion in services. N.B.C.E.A. began to look for opportunities to develop leaders, not only for the administration of schools, but also leaders in Board offices, among school trustees, and more directly among classroom teachers. This extension took the Center's leadership initiative beyond school administration to curriculum and instruction areas.

In the spring of 1990, N.B.C.E.A. responded to a request from several school districts to organize a conference to promote Cooperative Learning, being popularized by David and Roger Johnson at the University of Minnesota and Robert Slavin at Johns Hopkins University. N.B.C.E.A. brought Edye Johnson-Holubec, a sister to David and Roger Johnson and Dr. William Zangwell, an associate of Robert Slavin, to offer keynote addresses at a major provincial conference. In addition, N.B.C.E.A. identified key teachers who were already using Cooperative Learning in their schools to be concurrent session leaders at the conference.

To encourage school based staff development, and to underline the belief in collaborative leadership, the conference actively promoted the efforts of principals and teachers to build school support teams. Trustees were encouraged to attend so that Boards might lend support to the efforts of teachers and principals within schools. The conference set another direction for the Centre and, since 1990, nine supervisors, teachers, and administrators have been funded by the N.B.C.E.A. to take advanced training in Cooperative Learning. N.B.C.E.A. is able to offer Johnson and Johnson's "Brown Book Training" and offer training in Johns Hopkins materials, including T.G.T. (Teams Games Tournaments). These leaders are not confined to leadership in educational administration, but are significant members of an ever-expanding cadre of leaders developed by N.B.C.E.A. to serve the overall education system.

Finally, in Phase Two, the Centre put together a series of two-day seminars, which it entitled: Leaders Educational Administration Development Seminars (LEADS). Topics included: Situational Leadership, Team-Building through Myers-Briggs, Discipline for Tomorrow's Schools, and School Based Staff Development. These programs were designed specifically to meet the needs of principals and vice-principals.

Phase Three: 1991 – 92

The third phase of the Centre's development was characterized by a move to full time staff, long term planning, and secure funding. Lewin described the third phase of change as "refreezing," so that the new ideas introduced in the "moving" stage could be consolidated and entrenched into the operation of the organization. Phase Three of N.B.C.E.A.'s brief history has some of these characteristics. Phase Three could be dated from July, 1991, but was preceded by several months of discussions and negotiations. The uncertainties of Phase Two had been forestalled but not resolved. The New Brunswick Teachers' Association had already extended Rod Campbell's secondment by one year and by the winter of 1991, a decision had to be taken concerning his return to the N.B.T.A. The forbearance of the N.B.T.A. had been stretched to the limit. Negotiations intensified with the Department of

Education to provide some ongoing support to the Centre, so programs would be consolidated. N.B.C.E.A. had the solid support of the Deputy Minister of Education, Earle Wood, who had been involved with the N.B.C.E.A. Task Force in Phase One. In May, 1991, the Minister of Education for the Province of New Brunswick, the Honorable Shirley Dysart, and U.N.B. President, Robin Armstrong signed a six year agreement that would ensure the Center's future over a longer term. At the same time, the Department of Education made it clear that it expected the Centre to generate sufficient revenue to cover its operational costs beyond the single professional position. At the end of the six year period, U.N.B. Faculty of Education will assume sole responsibility for the position. Given this arrangement, Rod Campbell resigned from the N.B.T.A. and in July, 1991, became a full-time employee of the University of New Brunswick as Executive Director for N.B.C.E.A.

Even with the firm financial support from the Department of Education and U.N.B., the Centre continues to rely heavily on the support, participation, and guidance of the stakeholders, particularly the N.B.T.A. which still provides a sustaining grant and the N.B.S.T.A. which contracts many of its professional services from the Centre.

Lewin observed that organizations which successfully integrated new ideas into their structures did so by consolidating the ideas initiated in the "moving" stage. What has N.B.C.E.A. done to consolidate its rapid expansion? The Centre continues to offer 3-4 Assessment Centres, annually assessing 36-42 potential school leaders and involving 54-65 trained Assessors in that process. The Centre will be inviting up to ten districts to create I/D/E/A Principal and Vice-Principal Support Groups. The summer of 1992 will see the sixth Annual Educational Leadership Academy, which we offer on the Mt. Allison University campus. The LEADS program will be expanded to include two new programs: Initiating a Peer Coaching Program and Conflict Resolution Strategies for Principals. A series of workshops on teaching School Trustees group facilitation skills will be expanded to include a broader range of leadership development skills. Leadership training for teachers will be expanded. To date nearly 600 teachers in New Brunswick have received Brown Book Training. In the past year, the N.B.C.E.A. has also undertaken cooperative education training programs in Prince Edward Island, Nova Scotia, and a joint New Brunswick-Maine session through a chapter of Phi Delta Kappa.

During the past two years, N.B.C.E.A. has worked very closely with the B.E.S.T. Consortium of School Districts in New Brunswick (Building Effective Schools Together). In conjunction with B.E.S.T., the Centre has organized a major program on "Invitational Education" developed by William Purkey in North Carolina and John Novak at Brock University. In the Fall of 1991, forty school teams were assembled to develop the program. Trustees and District Office Personnel from each of the English School Districts also attended. The N.B.C.E.A., N.B. Department of Education, and the Federal Department of Employment and Immigration supported the initiative as part of its strategy for dealing with "at risk" pupils. Follow-up seminars were conducted for all of the schools involved to assist in implementing the ideas.

B.E.S.T. offered N.B.C.E.A. a significant grant to meet individual requests of school districts. The Centre was able to second Jim Jackson, a former superintendent and staff developer, to prepare a pilot program for District Leadership Development. Jackson drew on the literature of effective administrators to prepare a program he named "Leadership 2000, Plus." It is designed to prepare teachers and incumbent Vice-Principals to become principals. He also developed a sister program called "Pedagogy 2000" which offers leadership development to teachers who want to improve instructional skills in preparation to becoming Department Heads or Subject Co-ordinators. Both programs have been piloted; the Leadership 2000 Plus in three districts and the Pedagogy 2000 in one district. The B.E.S.T. consortium is reviewing these programs for broader implementation for 1992-93 school year. If accepted, N.B.C.E.A. will broaden the concept of teams to the district level and have an extended leadership development program throughout the Province.

Finally, the Centre has embarked on its first school-community project. It is offering in New Brunswick the Lions-Quest Canada program called "Skills for Growing." This elementary school program involves Lions Clubs in supporting schools drug education programs. The Skills for Growing program can only be offered in districts where teachers receive an intensive in-service session over three full days. N.B.C.E.A., again with the support of the Federal Government, trained two principals and two teachers to be leaders in this program. In 1992, two "Skills for Growing" workshops were conducted using the Center's leaders.

Conclusions and Speculations

The N.B.C.E.A. has accepted Larry Lezotte's tenets about schools. Lezotte believes schools are either advancing or falling behind. None are in a steady state. The N.B.C.E.A. has enjoyed several successful years, but it is clear that its professional development mandate requires forward thinking and continued moving. There are several new prospects emerging. One of the most promising has to do with moving programs to other provinces in the region. The Nova Scotia Teachers' Union has forged a partnership with the N.B.C.E.A. to offer programs in Nova Scotia for principals and vice-principals. The partnership provides the N.S.T.U. with a representative on the N.B.C.E.A. Advisory Board and N.B.C.E.A. will provide workshop and seminar leaders for the themes that the N.S.T.U. wants to pursue. The N.S.T.U. will do the required promotion for the events and assume responsibility for registration of participants and on-site arrangements. Two events have already been conducted, one on Team-Building and a second on conflict resolution.

Also in Nova Scotia, N.B.C.E.A. has discussed cooperating with a consortium of school districts which wants to undertake an assessment process and leadership development program. Several meetings have occurred, including the N.B.C.E.A. Executive Director addressing the Nova Scotia School Superintendents' Association Annual Meeting. These discussions have not reached a conclusion, but the prospect is bright for some form of collaborative work.

The last portent of the future also envisages a larger role for the Centre in the Maritime Provinces; indeed it is a partial resurrection of the A.C.O.A. proposal. N.B.C.E.A. was invited to submit a proposal to the Maritime Provinces Educational Foundation, the education arm of the Council of Maritime Premiers. M.P.E.F. has the mandate to undertake projects or programs of inter-provincial cooperation. For example, the M.P.E.F. undertook the development and publication of a Maritime Studies textbook which is now used in all three provinces. In a current review of its programs, an area the M.P.E.F. wanted studied was the degree to which there could be cooperation in the development of leadership for schools and school systems. Among the thirteen recommendations of an M.P.E.F. "Report on Maritime Cooperation on Education/Grades Primary to Twelve" was the following:

> During this time of intense change in our region, sound
> administrative leadership is essential at the school district,

provincial and regional levels. It is recommended that M.P.E.F. undertake discussions with M.P.H.E.C. (Maritime Provinces Higher Education Commission), [with] the objective of developing a Centre for educational/administrative leadership in the region.

N.B.C.E.A. prepared a brief for M.P.E.F. in April, 1992. The brief argued the need for leadership development in the region. In part, the paper argued:

There is an enormous need for new thinking about school leadership. The societal demands are legion. In the past, principals of schools were expected to manage scarce resources well – ensure the prescribed curriculum was taught and that discipline and order were maintained. These are still expected, but if schools are to be proactive – if schools are to prepare students to cope with change, if schools are to be in the vanguard of societal change – the management paradigm must be discarded for entrepreneurial school leaders. As one management consultant described it, risk-taking leaders are needed: those who believe they are entrepreneurial, those who believe in themselves, those who attempt to do more than what's expected, and those who seek situations with added responsibilities (White, 1988). The need for leaders is clear, the path to finding potential leaders and preparing potential leaders is rough and winding (Brief to M.P.E.F., 1992).

The brief proposed the creation of a Maritime Centre for Educational Administration. The goals of the Centre would be to:

1. Develop and implement a process to assess potential school leaders for the anticipated needs of tomorrow's schools

2. Develop a cadre of Senior Administration to take advanced training and subsequently offer training in a wide variety of leadership development programs.

3. Offer Summer Educational Leadership Academies that will challenge leaders to be more entrepreneurial in their outlook.

4. Offer consulting services and training programs to schools, districts, and departments on Educational Leadership.

5. Conduct educational leadership research that will assist in policy development for school boards and Departments of Education.

6. Publish a quarterly newsletter for all schools in the region on current research and issues in educational administration (Brief to M.P.E.F., 1992).

The N.B.C.E.A. has achieved some of these goals within New Brunswick. It remains to be seen whether these modest successes can be extended to a larger region. In the Fall of 1992, the M.P.E.F. will make a decision on regional co-operation in leadership and development.

Regardless of the outcome of these discussions, the N.B.C.E.A. is slowly consolidating the work undertaken in Phase Two. In its relatively short life, it has provided professional development opportunities to several hundred principals, teachers, trustees, and other public school administrators. In a province comprising only 5200 Anglophone teachers, N.B.C.E.A. has a significant cadre of leaders who assume professional development activities on its behalf. These include the 75 N.A.S.S.P. accredited assessors, five principals training for Skills for Excellence, four trained in Situational Leadership, one trainer for Myers-Briggs Team Building, one for School Discipline, five for Johnson and Johnson Cooperative Learning, four for Johns Hopkins Cooperative Learning, ten I/D/E/A Facilitators, four Skills for Growing instructors, three Peer Coaching trainers, two Conflict Management Trainers, and six Invitational Educational Facilitators.

This list of trained leaders is one indication that N.B.C.E.A. has had some impact in rural New Brunswick. From its beginnings, it began to "unfreeze" the attitudes of adversarial relations and took on the role of an honest broker in legitimate educational debate. When it assumed a professional development focus, a new "moving" stage emerged. Currently N.B.C.E.A. is endeavoring to "refreeze" the attitudes of cooperation and collaboration towards professional development. If this phase is successful, N.B.C.E.A. will survive to play a role.

References

Letter from Hon. John Baxter, cited in Jack MacKinnon. (1985, October). The budget proposal: Back to the drawing board. *NBTA News*, Vol. XXVIII, No. 3.

Betts, Marven. (1987). Leadership assessment and development process. *N.B. Educational Administrator*, April, No. 7.

Bezeau, Lawrence. (1986). Research abstract: Level and inequality of per pupil expenditure as a function on finance centralization. *N.B. Educational Administrator*, January. No. 2.

Cameron, Kenneth. (1986). NBCEA conference '86. *N.B. Educational Administrator*, June, No. 4.

Campbell, Rod. (1986). High school reorganization: Trekking bravely toward oblivion. *NBTA News*, March, Vol. XXVIII, No. 20.

Campbell, Rod. (1986). High school reorganization: The quintessential cow. *NBTA News*, March. Vol. XXVIII, No. 20.

Campbell, Rod. (1987). Professional development on the upswing. *NBTA News*, April, Vol. XXIX, No. 10.

Clarke, Gerald M. (1983). Education at risk. *NBTA News*, October. Vol. XXVI, No. 3.

Brief to M.P.E.F. (1992). Proposal for a Maritime Centre for educational administration. April.

Hanratty, Bert. (1985). Punching at clouds: Seeking the elusive OGRe. *NBTA News*, March. Vol. XXVII, No. 10.

Hanratty, Bert. (1985). Calling all education advocates. *NBTA News*, June. Vol. XXVII, No. 13.

Lippett, Ronald, Watson, Jeanne, and Westley, Bruce. (1958). *The dynamics of planned change*. New York: Harcourt & Brace & Co. Reference to Lewin, Kurt (p. 129).

Potter, Peter. (1988). All about success. New Canaan, CT: William Mulvey.

Projet Entrepreneurship Project (PEP). (1988). A project of ACOA conducted by Universite de Moncton and Mt. Allison University. October.

NBCEA, NBTA, NSTU, NTA, PEITF. (1989). Proposal to the Atlantic Canada Opportunities Agency. Atlantic Centre for Educational Administration. (1986, January). *N.B. Administrator*, No. 2.

14

Summary

Understanding Change in Education in Rural and Remote Regions of Canada
Doug Knight

Change is not what it used to be, argues Charles Handy (Handy, 1989: 4). Change is discontinuous and requires upside-down thinking. To understand change better, we need new paradigms, new ways of conceptualizing what it is (Pressman and Wildavsky, 1984). We need to be able to think differently about change so that we may learn how to influence change, how to bring about change, and how to learn from change. The stories recounted in the previous chapters are excellent examples of changes that have taken place in education in rural and remote regions of Canada. They provide a variety of illustrations of what can be done, and descriptions of how it was done.

Rural education, and education in remote areas of our country, is changing and being changed. Rural educators are responding to economic, political, social, cultural, technological, and environmental pressures similar to those occurring anywhere, and everywhere. At the same time many rural educators are also pushing to change schools, to make schooling better for our students. As Earle Newton has suggested in the first chapter, hopefully this book has provided the reader with rich descriptions and careful analysis of a variety of change endeavors that will provoke further reflections and insights.

The survival of rural and remote schools is dependent on provincial policies and local practices. It is dependent on the quality of the schooling experience for students: the relevance and purposefulness of the programs (provincial curriculum), and the adequacy of delivery (local practice). It is not enough to keep a school open if it is not providing quality education, particularly one that meets the needs of rural communities. The future of rural and remote areas depends on the availability of individuals, and communities of learners, who have the knowledge, skills, and attitudes to be productive and self-supporting. There is much that is changing in education in rural and remote regions of Canada, as the preceding chapters in this book attest to, that provide optimism to those who wish to ensure the viability of small, rural, and remote schools. There is much to celebrate about the many successes that are occurring. And there is much yet to study. The purpose of this concluding chapter is to (1) synthesize what has been learned about the process of change from the preceding reports, and (2) provide a few reflections on some educational issues in rural and remote areas of Canada that have been raised by the many authors that have contributed to this book.

A Synthesis

Each of the preceding chapters has provided a perspective on education in rural and remote regions of Canada that suggests that much is currently being done to redress many of the issues that have plagued us in the past. There is an optimism that much can be done to bring about real and lasting change.

There are many examples to suggest that "you *can* do that here": Knudson described how a "whole language" approach was being successfully implemented in two schools in the Northwest Territories. Sharp provided two examples of "stay-in-school" programs in the Yukon that are well adapted to local circumstances. Cameron and Campbell outlined the evolution of a province-wide (and potentially Maritime-wide) professional development centre for administrators that has been built through the collaboration of key educational stakeholders. Weibe and Murphy described the participation of parents in collaborative school management, a mode of school governance that requires principals and teachers to be highly sensitive to community values, and to be a positive force in the development of the community. On a similar topic, Gulka and Knudson reported on the implementation of a policy to promote meaningful parent involvement in rural schools. Bosetti and Gee in Alberta, and Downer and Downer in Newfoundland described two successful developments of unique distance learning programs, each adapted to the local context. King told a compelling story of a native community (the "ihtowin"), the world of the Aboriginal child, and the need to ensure that formal schooling experiences are as one with the life of the community. Isherwood and Sorenson shared their involvement in the progressive devolution of educational governance to local communities in the North. And Marshall related how a shared services arrangement between a number of small, isolated Boards in northwestern Ontario, developed over a period of time, was helping to provide much needed financial, educational, and student oriented services. Garland, however, made us acutely aware of how fragile change can be, and how political forces may impede the best of intentions. There is much to be learned from these stories about how change takes place, and about the types of changes that are occurring in rural and remote regions of this country.

Findings on the Process of Change

✎ *A conceptual framework*

Many of the authors referred to the change frameworks provided by Tichy (1980), House (1981), and Corbett and Rossman (1989). It was demonstrated in many of the chapters that a combination of political, cultural, and technical perspectives provided a more complete view of the change process. Each of these factors, or perspectives, helped in the identification of pertinent elements that were at play through the initiation, implementation, and institutionalization (where this stage was reached) of the innovations. Several of the authors suggested that it was also necessary to keep in mind, as Corbett and Rossman (1989:166) have suggested, the interactions and inter-relationships of all the dimensions. As change efforts were described chronologically, various factors were perceived to ebb and flow in their utility to account for what was happening at any given time. In several of the studies the need for change was triggered by technical problems, followed by political responses, and resulted in changes to the organizational culture. In at least one instance a change in the organization was triggered by political forces, which challenged the existing culture. As House (1981) and Corbett and Rossman (1989) have also suggested, we need to examine the innovation or change, the innovation in context, and the context itself to better understand what is happening.

For those readers interested in moving from description (here's how it happened) to prescription (here's how to do it), the transposition is daunting, if not complex. We are only beginning to understand how change occurs, and less is known about how to facilitate change. There is a growing belief that bringing about change is not an instrumental activity but an exploratory one (Pressman and Wildavsky, 1984; Knight, 1991). It is not so much an activity of following the right steps, but rather one of constantly exploring what steps are the best ones to take, and analyzing the consequences. The process of change, if it is not to be left to happenstance, requires that there is vision (Newton and Newton, 1992). Handy (1989) has suggested that it is a process of questioning, theorizing, testing, and reflecting. Handy goes on to explain that change, or rather organizational learning, requires people who can take responsibility for their actions, have a clear view of where they are going, want to get there, and believe that they can. They must also have a "negative capability," or be able to live with uncertainty and mistakes. And they must be able to reframe their image of the world, or see things from different perspectives. Schon's work on the Reflective Practitioner (1983, 1987) and Senge's work on Learning Organizations (1990) also provide some helpful perspectives on the nature of change, and the process of learning and exploring.

✎ *The findings*

From the "cases" reported in the previous chapters there has emerged a number of common findings about the change process. Although the innovations, and the context for their implementation were quite diverse, there were conceptual similarities. Some of these findings help to confirm what other studies of change have already suggested, but there are findings that provide new insights as well.

1. A finding common to many of the studies was that the change being implemented was a response to an identified and generally agreed upon need. Whether it was a distance education program responding to a need for more diversified course offerings taught by qualified instructors, a need to ensure the continued viability of small schools (and their local communities), and a need to redress program inequities across the province (Bosetti and Gee, Downer and Downer), or a shared services arrangement that permitted small Boards to provide financial, educational, and student services in a cost effective manner (Marshall), or a need for programs that would help to resolve a high drop-out rate amongst students in remote communities (Sharpe), in each case it was obvious that doing things differently was preferred to keeping things the same by those involved. In each case the change was either initiated from the "top" or came about through some type of mutual agreement between school staff, central office staff, politicians (trustees), and the community. Where a need is strongly identified amongst the stakeholders, and the resolution is perceived as reasonable, the source of the initiation for change does not appear to be a critical issue. Marshall suggested that successful change occurs where there is an identified need, a desirable resolution, brought about in an

appropriate manner that is politically acceptable and technically feasible. Rather a tall order in most situations!

2. As Fullan (1982) has previously stated, change was found to be an adaptive learning process (Isherwood and Sorenson, Bosetti and Gee, Knudson, Marshall) that was enhanced by the participants ability and willingness to solve problems. The change process required on-going monitoring, evaluation, and a positive problem solving attitude by those directly involved to ensure successful continuation.

3. Another finding from these studies was that in most circumstances the innovation being implemented required modifications, over a period of time, in order for it to continue to address the identified problem. The original concept may have stayed intact, but specific strategies were altered to meet emerging conditions. Bosetti and Gee found that it was essential for the participants to maintain a problem solving attitude as the distance learning program was in the midst of its own development. What was offered to the participants was a concept, some financial resources, and some technical and political support. What was required was personnel that were willing to take risks, and wanting to make the program succeed. Cameron and Campbell described a project that evolved over a period of several years, and continues to evolve as new needs and opportunities are determined. Marshall spoke of problems in the provision of shared services between several jurisdictions that were dynamic, and thus needing constant attention and vigilance. Incremental successes, however, ensured that changes, and support, continued for the program. Isherwood and Sorenson were involved with an "adaptive learning process" in which planned changes occurred slowly as the participants rose to the challenges, and developed the skills and attitudes necessary to continue. In all of these studies there was a high degree of flexibility amongst the participants which ensured adaptations to procedures and strategies. The original concepts, in a broad form, were maintained.

4. It was also found that a willingness amongst the participants to cooperate with each other was important. Isherwood and Sorenson found that the participants, under the guidance of firm leadership, were willing to cooperate despite the existence of divergent views. They were able to reach beyond themselves to resolve what were considered intractable prob-

lems. Knudson described the use of cooperative decision making and the need for good communication in the implementation of a curricular innovation. Marshall spoke of the willingness of several Boards to share in the control of an administrative unit, a potentially threatening position to the autonomy of each Board. The individuals involved in each case were able to grasp a broader view, to "see the big picture," and were willing to work together to resolve a problem. A certain level of maturity amongst the participants enhances the success of any change endeavor.

5. A significant finding is that in every case the innovation, program, project – the change being implemented – was perceived by the participants to be a workable resolution to the problem. Not only was a need identified, but so too was a solution that had a strong intuitive appeal for the participants. These solutions were politically acceptable, technically feasible, and did not stretch the beliefs and attitudes of the participants beyond their tolerance levels. There was anxiety and uncertainty, but not enough to scuttle the process. Several of the authors suggested that in some cases adjustments to belief systems needed to occur but that given time and an appropriate supportive climate, these changes would occur (e.g., Marshall, Sharpe, Gulka, and Knudson). What appears to be essential is a soundly based idea that has appeal, and a flexible process that permits the participants to add their own details and make their own adjustments to the concept.

6. In one form or another leadership was a key ingredient to successful change. Isherwood and Sorenson referred to "strong" leadership that was required to pursue a sometimes difficult process of the devolution of governance to local Boards. Knudson suggested that leadership capable of being decisive when appropriate was necessary for successful change to occur. Gulka and Knudson found that the school principal was the key to the implementation of increased parental involvement in schools. It was the principal who had to support and pursue the idea. As well, the Board and central office administration had to offer active support by supplying consultative assistance, training for parents, and financial support for transportation. The New Brunswick Centre for Educational Administration was initiated and sustained by several leaders: two Deputy Ministers, two University professors, a retired superintendent, and a staff Director from

the Provincial Teacher's Association. Each of these leaders was committed to the concept, and provided opportunities for key stakeholders to play a role in its evolution. Individuals in positions of authority helped the change efforts by providing support (financial and/or moral) and by pressing to see that action was taken. Leadership, whether characterized as initiative, persistence, persuasiveness, commitment, decisiveness, boldness, vision, or symbolic behavior, plays an important part in any change effort.

These studies and reports of successful innovations from across Canada provide us with many interesting observations of the process of change. In summary, it was found that change:

✔ is facilitated when there is an identified and generally agreed upon need or problem; it did not matter that the innovation was "top-down" as long as the change was perceived by the participants as a reasonable response to a real problem;

✔ requires an ability and a willingness on the part of the participants to solve problems and to see the "big picture;"

✔ is enhanced by flexibility: the process should support adaptations and modifications to the innovation;

✔ is a process of adaptive learning: the participants are open-minded, and constantly seek to resolve problems;

✔ occurs more readily when the participants are willing to be cooperative;

✔ is more readily accepted when the problem resolution is perceived as soundly-based, feasible, and manageable;

✔ requires leadership of some form, be it initiative, persistence, commitment, decisiveness, or the ability to promote participatory management;

✔ is context sensitive, that is, local circumstances of a political, cultural, and technical nature affect the change process in idiosyncratic ways, and thus require a sensitivity to these types of issues, and to be addressed as they arise.

Some of these findings support what is already suspected about change, but others challenge our conventional wisdom. One significant point is the issue of where change should be originated: from the bottom up or the top down. The findings from these studies suggest that this is not the issue as most of the innovations were top-down, but everyone accepted the innovation as a reasonable resolution to an agreed upon problem. Where the initiative comes from appears not to be the issue if the participants acknowledge first that some form of change is required. It is not an issue of authority or power, but one of need. This notion certainly requires further study.

Issues

One of the ongoing dilemmas in rural education is that much of what is done in schools is to enable students to leave for jobs in the cities (Hass, 1991). Rural educators work hard to provide their students with the knowledge, skills, and attitudes that will permit them to compete in a global economy, and to give them all the advantages (and as few of the disadvantages) that students in urban areas have. The outcome is often that rural students turn to the cities for work for it is there that they can utilize what they have learned. The good news is that rural schools can provide students with a quality education; the bad news is that much of this course-of-action is counter-productive to the viability of rural life, and that rural depopulation contributes to the increasing difficulty in achieving success (see Hathaway, 1990).

In 1935 the Minister of Education in the Province of Alberta published a report on rural education, "What Is and What Might Be in Rural Education in Alberta." To some extent this report could be reissued in 1993 with few changes but the date. Many of the issues addressed in 1935 remain much the same over these past 58 years, and the solutions in some cases are no less elusive. There are still concerns about meeting the educational needs of rural communities particularly at the high school level, about the un-equal distribution of wealth and the resultant anomalies in financing school systems, about school closures, declining enrolments, and efficiencies of size in administrative units. Great strides have been made, however, to ensure more uniform working conditions for teachers (it would be rare that a Board would be in arrears for a teacher's salary as some were in 1935), to provide greater access to students to diversified programs, to retain students in school longer, and to provide a better distribution of resources.

But many of the issues still remain, perhaps in part because many of the demographic trends have not changed, and perhaps because our attitudes and values have not changed significantly. The population of rural areas in Canada continues to decline in proportion to the growth of urban areas. Small schools continue to be closed. School system consolidation is still sought and deemed desirable by centralized governments. Funding for education in general, and for low wealth areas in particular remains the bane of governments. And the challenge of delivering top quality programs where student and staff numbers are low continues to engage rural educators.

As if these long-standing problems were not enough to deal with, the authors in the preceding chapters have raised many additional issues. Perhaps the broadest of these issues is the need to examine where rural education is going, and to develop a vision for what it might be. How well do we understand what effect current educational policies and practices are having on rural education and rural communities? To what extent is the curriculum "urbanized?" What impact does our current education system have on rural students and on rural communities and families? Does the education system promote rural life and support rural communities? Does it provide students with the knowledge, skills, and attitudes that permit them to find or create gainful employment in rural areas? What role can, and should the education system play in rural and remote areas? To what extent is education in rural/remote areas different from education in urban areas? What might a vision for rural education be like? Whose needs and values should it address?

An issue that is related to that of vision is one of standardization. There prevails, at least to some extent, in public education across Canada an inclination to standardize education whether it is through the delivery of programs and the structure of educational organizations or through the outcomes that are desired. Rural schools are more like urban schools than they are different (Nachtigal, 1982). A perspective often prevails that there is "one best way to do things," and that this way is the "city way." Is standardization of schools and school systems, policies, and practices, desirable? Is there a balance between standardization and diversity? What should be standardized and what should be left to individual schools, systems, and communities to determine? Are there goals for schooling in rural areas that are not shared by urban systems? Are there (provincial) government policies that are not applicable to rural or remote areas as they do not address real rural problems, or if they do, they do so in a way that makes the solution unworkable? Can standards for rural schools be different than standards for urban schools? If there is strength in diversity, as many farmers and ecologists will attest, why then are schools more alike than different? There is a growing realization that quality schools exist in many forms.

Hass (1991:435) described the world view or Old Story that predominates education in North America, one that is standardized and centrally controlled, and contrasted that with a new paradigm, or New Story that

> sees raising up children as the job shared among parents, the school, and the community, a holistic approach to creating the next generation of Americans. The curriculum under the New Story would be flexible and adapting, more focused on problem solving and discovering strategies than on memorizing facts. It would allow for mutual causality and mutual influence, with teachers and students, parents and administrators all having a say in the process of education. Learning, under the New Story, would be shared and the contributions and perspectives of all would be welcome.

If one were to visit an elementary classroom in Delia, Alberta, Rae/Edzo, NWT, Lawrence Station, New Brunswick, or London, Ontario there would be significant similarities in the schooling provided to students. But there would be many differences in the communities, in the local values and beliefs, in the culture. There is much evidence in the preceding chapters to support the notion that context makes a difference in what happens, and how it happens. Cecil King in Chapter 2 describes eloquently the need to respect and appreciate the uniqueness of culture and community. The issue remains: what should be standardized and what should be diverse?

Embedded in this issue of standardization is the issue of control and autonomy. Who should have control over what? Will those that hold the power now be willing to share? The Northwest Territories is moving towards decentralized government (Isherwood and Sorenson, chapter 3). In most provinces there are local school boards with some control over finances and local policy. There is tremendous diversity across Canada, however, in the degree to which local schools and Boards are autonomous. How much local autonomy, and thus diversity, is desirable? For example, sometimes local majorities need to be protected from their own bigotry and prejudices. There are balances between individual rights and group rights. If collective wisdom transcends individual wisdom, then it stands to reason that the larger the group the wiser its decisions may be. But there are many issues that are best decided locally. There are many goals of education, many different philosophies that are equally desirable. There are many geographical differences that translate into different program needs. Should local School Boards and schools have greater control over the types of programs provided than they currently do? Should they have more control over the financial resources available as well?

Marshall (chapter 4) raised the issue of the need in some rural areas to share services. Weibe and Murphy (chapter 6) and Gulka and Knudson (chapter 7) wrote about parent participation in rural schools. What other partnerships are desirable? Most rural schools have close ties with their local communities. In what ways might they be closer? To what extent do students learn in the community, outside of the schools? Could schools and communities become "learning communities" or a "Community Education Jurisdiction" for example (Staples, 1990)? What types of school and business partnerships are there, and could there be in rural areas? Partnerships and shared services can generate both financial, social, and educational benefits.

This book is about optimism for our students in rural and remote schools. It contains the stories of educators from across Canada who are able to share successful ventures. It contains a perspective about change, a framework for thinking about change, that may help some to translate visions into realities. Yes, you can do that here!

References

Alberta Department of Education. (1935). *What is and what might be in rural education*. Edmonton, Alberta.

Corbett, H. D. and Rossman, G. B. (1989). Three paths to implementing change: A research note. *Curriculum Inquiry*. 19:2: 163-190.

Fullan, M. (1982). *The meaning of educational change*. Toronto: OISE.

Haas, Toni. (1991). Why reform doesn't apply: Creating a new story about education in rural America. In A. J. DeYoung (Ed.), *Rural education: Issues and practice*. New York: Garland Publishing.

Handy, C. (1989). *The age of unreason*. Boston: Harvard Business School.

Hathaway, W. E. (1990). *Rural education: Challenges and opportunities*. A paper presented to the Prairie Forum on Rural Education. Brandon, Manitoba. November.

House, E. R. (1981). Three perspectives on innovation. In Lehming, R. and Kane, M. (Eds.), *Improving schools: Using what we know*. Beverly Hills: Sage.

Knight, D. (1991). Implementing teacher evaluation policy. In O'Reilly, R. and Lautar, C. J. (Eds.), *Policy research and development in Canadian education*. Calgary: University of Calgary.

Nachtigal, P. (1982). *Rural education: In search of a better way.* Boulder, Colo.: Westview Press.

Newton, E. and Newton, P. (1992). *Voices, vision, and vitality.* Calgary: Detselig.

Pressman, J. L & Wildavsky, A. (1984). *Implementation* (3rd. ed.) Berkeley, CA: University of California Press.

Senge, P. (1990). *The fifth discipline: The art and practice of the learning organization.* New York: Doubleday.

Schon, D. A. (1983). *The reflective practitioner.* New York: Basic Books.

Schon, D. A. (1987). *Educating the reflective practitioner.* San Francisco: Jossey-Bass.

Staples, B. (1990). *A community education jurisdiction.* Unpublished paper.

Tichy, N. M. (1980). Problem cycles in organizations and the management of change. In T. Kimberly and Miles, R. (Eds.), *The organizational life cycle.* San Francisco: Jossey-Bass.

PRINTED IN CANADA